# Arabic Grammar

## A Revision Guide

# Arabic Grammar

## A Revision Guide

### John Mace

EDINBURGH UNIVERSITY PRESS

Edinburgh University Press
22 George Square, Edinburgh EH8 9LF

Typeset by the author in Times,
Baghdad and Giza, and printed and
bound in Great Britain by
The Cromwell Press, Trowbridge, Wilts

Reprinted 2000, 2002, 2004
A CIP record for this book is available from the British Library.

ISBN 0 7486 1079 0

# Contents

| Chapter | Paragraph | Page |
|---|---|---|
| **Preface** | | xi |
| **1 . Introduction** | | |
| References | 1 | 1 |
| Abbreviations and Symbols | 2 | 1 |
| Transliteration | 3 | 1 |
| Pointing | 4 | 1 |
| *hamza* | 5 | 1 |
| Measures (الأوزان) | 6 | 2 |
| Presentation of Verbs | 7 | 2 |
| Full and Short Pronunciation | 8 | 2 |
| Verbs with Mixed Radicals | 9 | 3 |
| Presentation of Nouns and Adjectives | 10 | 4 |
| **2 . Writing** | | |
| General | 11 | 5 |
| Toothed Letters; Special Forms | 12 | 5 |
| Variants | 13 | 5 |
| Orthographic Signs; Pointing | 14 | 5 |
| Pointing of the Definite Article | 15 | 7 |
| Weak Letters; Vowels; Diphthongs | 16 | 7 |
| Prefixed Words | 17 | 8 |
| Double Letters | 18 | 9 |
| *hamza* | 19 | 9 |
| Handwriting | 20 | 13 |
| Arabic Transliteration | 21 | 15 |
| **3 . Pronunciation** | | |
| General | 22 | 17 |
| Consonants | 23 | 17 |
| Velarised Consonants | 24 | 17 |
| Double Consonants; Assimilation | 25 | 18 |
| Vowels; Diphthongs; Nunation (التنوين) | 26 | 18 |
| Velarised Vowels *a* and *ā* | 27 | 19 |
| *hamzat al-qaṭ'* and *hamzat al-waṣl* | 28 | 19 |
| Stress | 29 | 21 |
| Full, Pause and Short Pronunciation | 30 | 22 |
| **4 . Verbs - General** | | |
| Roots | 31 | 26 |
| Classes | 32 | 26 |
| Government | 33 | 26 |
| Principal Parts | 34 | 27 |
| Agreement | 35 | 27 |
| Voice | 36 | 28 |
| <u>Table I</u>, Verbal Forms: Derivation and Use | 37 | 28 |
| Mood | 38 | 30 |
| <u>Table 2</u>: Perfect (Indicative) Tense, Conjugation | 39 | 30 |

Perfect (Indicative) Tense: Use   40   31
Table 3, Imperfect (Indicative) Tense: Conjugation   41   31
Imperfect (Indicative) Tense: Use   42   32
(Imperfect) Subjunctive Tense: Conjugation   43   33
(Imperfect) Subjunctive Tense: Use   44   33
(Imperfect) Jussive Tense: Conjugation   45   33
(Imperfect) Jussive Tense: Use   46   34
Continuous Perfect Tense   47   34
Pluperfect Tense   48   34
Future Perfect Tense   49   35
Imperative Mood   50   35
Participles (اسم الفاعل واسم المفعول): Derivation   51   36
Participles: Use   52   37
Verbal Noun (المصدر): Derivation   53   38
Verbal Nouns: Use   54   38
Table 4, Passive Voice: Derivation and Use   55   39

**5. Sound Verbs**
General   56   41
Table 5: Active Voice   57   41
Table 6: Passive Voice   58   42
Perfect (Indicative) Tense   59   43
Imperfect (Indicative) Tense   60   43
(Imperfect) Subjunctive Tense   61   44
(Imperfect) Jussive Tense   62   44
Imperative Mood   63   44
Participles   64   45
Verbal Nouns   65   45

**6. Hamzated Verbs**
General   66   47
Table 7: Verbs with Initial-radical *hamza*, Active Voice   67   47
Table 8: Verbs with Initial-radical *hamza*, Passive Voice   68   48
Verbs with Initial-radical *hamza*: Tenses   69   48
Verbs with Initial-radical *hamza*: Imperative   70   50
Verbs with Initial-radical *hamza*: Participles   71   50
Verbs with Initial-radical *hamza*: Verbal Nouns   72   50
Table 9: Verbs with Middle-radical *hamza*, Active Voice   73   50
Table 10: Verbs with Middle-radical *hamza*, Passive Voice   74   51
Verbs with Middle-radical *hamza*: Tenses   75   51
Verbs with Middle-radical *hamza*: Imperative   76   53
Verbs with Middle-radical *hamza*: Participles   77   53
Verbs with Middle-radical *hamza*: Verbal Nouns   78   53
Table 11: Verbs with Final-radical *hamza*, Active Voice   79   53
Table 12: Verbs with Final-radical *hamza*, Passive Voice   80   54
Verbs with Final-radical *hamza*: Tenses   81   55
Verbs with Final-radical *hamza*: Imperative   82   56
Verbs with Final-radical *hamza*: Participles   83   56

Verbs with Final-radical *hamza*: Verbal Nouns 84 56

**7. Doubled Verbs**

General 85 58

Table 13: Active Voice 86 58

Table 14: Passive Voice 87 59

Tenses 88 60

Imperative 89 62

Participles 90 62

Verbal Nouns 91 63

**8. Assimilated Verbs**

General 92 65

Table 15: Verbs with Initial-radical *wāw*, Active Voice 93 65

Table 16: Verbs with Initial-radical *yā'*, Active Voice 94 66

Table 17: Verbs with Initial-radical *wāw* and *yā'*,
 Passive Voice 95 67

Tenses 96 68

Imperative 97 69

Participles 98 70

Verbal Nouns 99 70

**9. Hollow Verbs**

General 100 72

Table 18: Active Voice 101 72

Table 19: Passive Voice 102 74

Tenses 103 75

Imperative 104 79

Participles 105 79

Verbal Nouns 106 80

**10. Defective Verbs**

General 107 81

Table 20: Active Voice 108 81

Table 21: Passive Voice 109 82

Table 22: Perfect (Indicative) Tense, Active Voice 110 83

Perfect Tense, Passive Voice 111 86

Table 23: Imperfect (Indicative) Tense, Active Voice 112 86

Imperfect (Indicative) Tense, Passive Voice 113 89

(Imperfect) Subjunctive Tense 114 89

(Imperfect) Jussive Tense 115 90

Imperative 116 90

Table 24: Participles 117 91

Verbal Nouns 118 92

**11. Doubly Weak Verbs**

General 119 94

Table 25: Active Voice 120 94

Table 26: Passive Voice 121 96

Tenses 122 97

Perfect (Indicative) Tense 123 98

Imperfect (Indicative) Tense                              124      99
(Imperfect) Subjunctive Tense                             125     101
(Imperfect) Jussive Tense                                 126     101
Imperative                                                127     102
Participles                                               128     102
Verbal Nouns                                              129     103

## 12. Nouns and Adjectives

Gender of Nouns                                           130     104
Case                                                      131     105
Definition                                                132     105
Number                                                    133     106
Animate and Inanimate                                     134     106
Relative Adjectives (النسبة)                              135     107
Abstract Nouns                                            136     107
Table 27, Regular Nouns and Adjectives: Indefinite
    Singular and Broken Plural                            137     108
Table 28, Regular Nouns and Adjectives: Definite
    Singular and Broken Plural                            138     110
Definite Article                                          139     112
Table 29: Dual of Nouns and Adjectives, Indefinite
    and Definite                                          140     113
Table 30: Sound Plurals of Nouns and Adjectives,
    Indefinite and Definite                               141     114
Agreement of Adjectives                                   142     117
Broken Plurals of Nouns and Adjectives                    143     118
Table 31: Diptotes                                        144     120
Indeclinable Nouns and Adjectives                         145     122
Table 32: Demonstrative Adjectives                        146     123
Table 33: Possessive Adjective Suffixes                   147     124
Construct (الإضافة)                                       148     128
Collective nouns                                          149     130
Negation of nouns and Adjectives                          150     131
Quasi-, Semi-                                             151     132
All, Some, Same, Other, Both, Any                         152     132
Comparative Degree of Adjectives                          153     135
Superlative Degree of Adjectives                          154     136
First, Last, Other                                        155     138
Better and Worse                                          156     138
Nouns of Place, Activity, Instrument                      157     139
Diminutive Nouns and Adjectives                           158     140
'ab etc.                                                  159     140
Table 34: dhū etc.                                        160     141
Adjectives of Colour and Defect                           161     142
Anomalous Plurals                                         162     142
Improper Annexation (الإضافة غير الحقيقية)                163     143
Apposition                                                164     143

## 13. Pronouns

Table 35: Subject Pronouns 165 145
Table 36: Direct Object Pronoun Suffixes 166 146
Table 37: Independent Direct Object Pronouns 167 148
Table 38: Relative Pronouns 168 148
Interrogative Pronouns 169 151
Relative Interrogative 170 153
Indefinite Pronouns 171 153

## 14. Prepositions

General 172 155
Prepositional Object Pronoun Suffixes 173 156
To Have 174 157

## 15. Adverbs

Derivation 175 158
Negation 176 159
Interrogative Adverbs 177 159
Comparative and Superlative Degrees of Adverbs 178 160

## 16. Syntax

General 179 161
Equations 180 161
Statements 181 162
Nominal Sentences 182 162
Verbal Sentences 183 163
Direct Questions 184 164
Indirect Speech: Statement 185 165
Indirect Speech: Questions 186 167
Indirect Speech: Command and Request 187 167
Conjunction and Particle *fa* 188 168
Complemented Verbs 189 168
Expressions of Purpose, Potential, Obligation,
Uncertainty etc. 190 170
Verbs used as Auxiliaries 191 172
Participial Verb 192 173
Simultaneous Verbs 193 173
Conditional Sentences 194 174
Concessive Sentences 195 176
Expressions of Circumstance (الحال) 196 177
Clauses of Time 197 178
Clauses of Reason 198 180
Topic and Comment (الجملة ذات الوجهين) 199 180
Categorical Negation (تفي الجنس) 200 181
Exceptive Sentences (المستثنى): Only 201 181
Expressions with the Verbal Noun 202 182
Expressions with Indefinite Nouns 203 182
Absolute Object (المفعول المطلق) 204 183
Table 39: Uses of the Accusative 205 183

Table 40: Uses of *mā*                               206    185
Table 41: Alternative Structures                     207    185


**17. Numbers**

Numerals                                             208    189
Cardinal Numbers - General                           209    189
Table 42: Cardinal Numbers 0 to 10                   210    190
Table 43: Cardinal Numbers 11 to 19                  211    191
Table 44: Cardinal Numbers 20 to 99                  212    192
Table 45: Cardinal Numbers above 99                  213    193
Colloquial Pronunciation of Cardinal Numbers         214    194
Ordinal Numbers - General                            215    196
Ordinal Numbers 1st to 10th                          216    196
Ordinal Numbers 11th to 19th                         217    197
Ordinal Numbers above 19th                           218    198
Adverbial Ordinals                                   219    199
Alphabetical Numbering (الأبجد)                       220    199
Fractions                                            221    199
Percentage                                           222    200
Nil                                                  223    200
Time: Complete Hours                                 224    200
Time: Incomplete Hours                               225    201
The Year                                             226    202
Months and Days                                      227    202
Age                                                  228    203

**18. Wishes and Exclamations**

Wishes                                               229    204
Exclamations                                         230    204


**Arabic Index**                                            207
**Grammatical Index**                                       209
**Glossary of Grammatical Terms**                           215

# Preface

The purpose of this grammar book is to act as support for any course of modern written Arabic, and to help students of the language at any point in their studies. With this object in view, each chapter makes the fewest possible assumptions about the student's knowledge. The book does not claim to examine every point in the language, merely to cover the most practical ones.

With brevity in mind, no hard line has been drawn between morphology and syntax; wherever it is convenient to treat matters of syntax in the discussion of the most relevant part of speech, this has been done.

The terminology has been chosen for maximum intelligibility and familiarity; terms of art used only by phoneticians or grammarians are avoided. Similarly, wherever a point can be clearly described in European fashion or by comparison with grammar nearer home, this has unhesitatingly been done. The commoner Arabic terms (e.g. إضافة) are given in parallel with the English equivalent, but there is no deliberate quest for the exotic. There is a glossary explaining those grammatical terms not fully explored in the text.

In this book the Arabic script is pointed, to show pronunciation and to illustrate the working of the rules. The student should, however, never forget that in the outside world pointed text is hardly ever encountered.

The Arabic used in the book is not 'literary' in the sense of belles-lettres; rather it is drawn from professional practice; from the office, the public institute, the departmental meeting, the worksite and so on. Nothing of solely academic or historic interest is included.

Where useful, transliteration is used, showing both the full formal pronunciation and the corresponding short pronunciation more commonly used in professional life. In the same spirit, the spoken form of the numbers, preferred by almost all Arabs, is offered together with the more complex official system (which many people use wrongly anyway).

The indexes supplement the references found in the text, and should, like them, be used fully in the search for the right form or structure.

I take this opportunity to express my great thanks to Viviane Kafrouni for her valuable help in checking the text, and to Marilyn Moore for her tireless support in proof-reading. Any remaining errors are my responsibility.

# 1. Introduction

**1. References.** Numbers in references indicate paragraphs unless shown otherwise.

**2. Abbreviations and Symbols.** The following abbreviations and symbols are used in the text and tables:

| | | | |
|---|---|---|---|
| acc. | accusative | nom. | nominative |
| act. | active | obj. | object |
| adj. | adjective | part. | participle |
| adv. | adverb | pass. | passive |
| an. | animate | pers. | person(al) |
| def. | definite | prep. | preposition(al) |
| dir. | direct | pl. | plural |
| f., fem. | feminine | Q | quadriliteral |
| gen. | genitive | s., sing. | singular |
| inan. | inanimate | tr. | transitive |
| indef. | indefinite | vb. | verb(al) |
| indir. | indirect | I ... X | Form I ... X of verb |
| intr. | intransitive | + | and |
| m., masc. | masculine | /, \ | or |

**3. Transliteration.** The transliteration of Arabic script used here is based on that of the Encyclopedia of Islam, with certain modifications to assist study. The transliteration in this book follows the pronunciation and not the spelling, e.g.:

الدُّنْيَا   ad-dunyā (not al-dunyā) the world

عَرَبِيَّة   ʿarabīya*tun* (not ʿarabiyya*tun*) Arab, Arabian, Arabic

**4. Pointing.** Arabic in daily use is not pointed (i.e. marked with short vowels and other pronunciation guides, see 14); in Arabic language course books it is nowadays only partially pointed. To help reference and revision, the text is fully pointed in this book, except that the definite article (الـ) is pointed with ... (waṣla) or with ... (fatḥa) only in passages where the article or the pointing is explained (14, 15, 28 and 139); otherwise the article is left unpointed.

**5. hamza.** In this book, ء indicates hamzat al-qaṭ'. No hamza is written for hamzat al-waṣl. See 19.

**6. Measures (الأَوْزَانُ).** The structure of words based on a root is represented in this book, as is usual, with 'measures' or patterns of the model root فعل . Thus the word كَتَبَ is constructed on the measure فَعَلَ and مَفَاتِيحُ on the measure مَفَاعِيلُ.

**7. Presentation of Verbs.** Verbs are presented as follows:

'Principal parts' (see 34):

- 1st principal part: 3rd person masculine singular, perfect tense, full pronunciation (see 30).
- 2nd principal part: 3rd person masculine singular, imperfect indicative tense, full pronunciation.

Following usual practice, principal parts are translated in this book as English infinitives. Forms I to X are indicated with the appropriate Roman letter.

Thus كَتَبَ يَكْتُبُ I (either principal part, or both together) is translated as 'to write', the verb being in Form I.

Verbs with a prepositional object (see 33) are often quoted with the preposition, thus:

أَخْبَرَ ب IV to inform of

Tenses:

|  | Singular | Dual | Plural |
|---|---|---|---|
| 1st pers. m./f. | (I) |  | (we) |
| 2nd pers. m. | (you) | (both of you) | (you) |
| 2nd pers. f. | (you) | (both of you) | (you) |
| 3rd pers. m. | (he/it) | (both of them*) | (they**) |
| 3rd pers. f. | (she/it/they***) | (both of them*) | (they**) |

\* animate and inanimate; ** animate plural; *** inanimate plural. (134)

Imperative: masculine singular, affirmative.

Participles: indefinite masculine singular, nominative case.

Verbal Noun: indefinite singular, nominative case.

All reference to verbs implies triliteral, active voice, unless otherwise specified.

**8. Full and Short Pronunciation.** See 30. Certain syllables, words and expressions are transliterated in this book, for clarity. Transliteration in Roman type represents the short pronunciation. Endings in italic are those added in full pronunciation. Where possible, both forms of pronunciation are shown in one mixed transliteration:

يَكْتُبُ رِسَالتَيْنِ.    yaktub*u* risālatayn*i*.

i.e. full: *yaktubu risālatayni*; short: yaktub risālatayn.

Where one transliteration cannot accommodate both, each appears separately:

يَكْتُبُ الرّسَالَتَيْنِ.    *yaktubu r-risālatayni*/yaktub ar-risālatayn. (full/short)

Where full and short forms are identical, no italics appear:

كَتَبَتْ رِسَالتَهَا.    katabat risālatahā.

Pausal form is not shown in the fully pointed text, but is easily inferred.

**9.**   **Verbs with Mixed Radicals.** Verb roots with radicals of mixed kinds are found in the following verb chapters:

| Radical Pattern | | | Typical | Verb |
|---|---|---|---|---|
| Initial | Middle | Final | Root | Chapter |
| *Two sound radicals, one weak radical:* | | | | |
| weak | sound | sound | وجد | 8, Assimilated |
| weak | sound | ≠ sound* | ودّ | 7, Doubled |
| sound | weak | sound | كون | 9, Hollow |
| sound | sound | weak | رمي | 10, Defective |
| *Two sound radicals, one radical* hamza: | | | | |
| hamza | sound | sound | أمر | 6, Hamzated |
| hamza | sound | ≠ sound* | أسّ | 6, Hamzated |
| sound | hamza | sound | سأل | 6, Hamzated |
| sound | sound | hamza | قرأ | 6, Hamzated |
| *One sound radical, two weak radicals:* | | | | |
| sound | weak | weak | نوي | 11, Doubly Weak |
| weak | sound | weak | ولي | 11, Doubly Weak |
| *Three different radicals (one sound, one* hamza, *one weak):* | | | | |
| hamza | weak | sound | أيد | 9, Hollow |
| weak | hamza | sound | يأس | 8, Assimilated |
| hamza | sound | weak | أتي | 11, Doubly Weak |

| sound | hamza | weak  | رَأْي | 11, Doubly Weak |
|-------|-------|-------|------|-----------------|
| sound | weak  | hamza | جيْء  | 11, Doubly Weak |

* roots with identical sound middle and final radicals.

**10. Presentation of Nouns and Adjectives.** Nouns are presented in the indefinite form, singular, nominative case, unless otherwise specified. Adjectives are presented in the positive degree, indefinite form, masculine singular, nominative case, unless otherwise specified.

# 2. Writing

**11. General.** This book assumes that the student already knows the alphabet. This chapter is therefore not a systematic study of the whole writing system. Only aspects of the system requiring special care are examined below. See 3 for the transliteration of Arabic script, and 208 for the numerals.

**12. Toothed Letters; Special Forms.** Certain letters are known as 'toothed' letters. A 'tooth' is the form ـ , found in (for example) the group ب . The toothed forms are:

ـئ ـي ـن ـث ـت ـب

The initial and medial forms of ـص and ـض also have a tooth after the loop.

Isolated ي is often printed and typed without its dots: ى . In this book the dots are retained; the form ى is to be read as 'alif maqṣūra (see 13).

Isolated ه often appears at the head of an alphabetical list (e.g. in directories and indexes) as ﻫ .

In Morocco, Algeria and Tunisia, the letters fā' and qāf are often written so:

ب ﯨ ﭪ fā'      ڧ ﯽ qāf

In this book we follow the commoner Eastern norm, ف ـف fā', ق ـق qāf.

**13. Variants.** Three important variants of alphabetical letters need care:
- آ , pronounced 'ā (for the velarised pronunciation, see 27). See also 19 below.
- ة , occurring only at the end of a word and pronounced -a or -at (the t is not always sounded, see 30). This modified letter changes to ت when any suffix is added.
- ى 'alif maqṣūra, pronounced ā (for the velarised pronunciation, see 27). This modified letter changes to ا when any suffix is added. See also 16 below.

**14. Orthographic Signs; Pointing.** In addition to the alphabetical letters, orthographic signs exist, most of them optional in use:
- ء . See 19 below. In initial position it can be omitted; in medial and final position it must be written.
- Short vowels. These are written over (or, in one case, under) the preceding letter. The names are shown in parentheses:

  ´... (fatḥa) a: كَمْ kam 'how much'

(for the velarised pronunciation of ´..., see 27).

´... (ḍamma) u: هُوَ huwa 'he'

... (kasra) i: بِ bi 'with/in'

- Nunation, in Arabic التَّنْوِينُ . The indefinite cases of many nouns and adjectives (see 137) have the endings -un, -an and -in. This phenomenon is called nunation. It occurs only as a grammatical ending:

´... or ´... -un: كُتُبٌ kutubun 'books'

´... , ´... or ـًى... (varying with the word) -an, -an:

رِسَالَةٌ risālatan 'a letter'; كتبًا kutuban 'books';

مُسْتَشْفًى mustashfan 'a hospital'

... -in: كُتُبٍ kutubin 'books'

The letter nūn is not used here.

- Short-vowel signs followed by weak letters (see 16) giving long vowels:

ٱ... ā: كَانَتْ kānat 'she was' (for velarised pronunciation of ٱ..., see 27).

...ُو ū: يَكُونُونَ yakūnūna 'they will be'

...ِي ī: صِينِيٌّ ṣīnīyun 'Chinese'

- Other signs, with their names:

  - ´... (shadda), written over a letter to double it: مَدَّ maddā 'he stretched'. kasra and kasra-tanwīn, when written with shadda, may be written over the preceding letter: ´... , ´... ; in this book the kasra and kasra-tanwīn are always written below:

    صِينِيٍّ, صِينِيٌّ ṣīnīyi, ṣīnīyin 'Chinese'

  - ˚... (sukūn), written over a letter to indicate that it has no vowel after it: تَدْرِيسٌ tadrīsun 'tuition'

    The two diphthongs ay and aw can be distinguished from long vowels by putting ´... before the letter of the long vowel and ˚... after it:

    ˚...َو, aw: مَوْتٌ mawtun 'death'

    ˚...َي, ay: لَيْلٌ laylun 'night'

    (for the velarised pronunciation of both diphthongs, see 27).

  - ... (waṣla). This sign is put only over an initial 'alif, to show that it has hamzat al-waṣl, see 28: فِي ٱلْمَدْرَسَةِ fi lmadrasati 'in the school'. It is shown in this book only here and in paras. 15, 28 and 139 (i.e. where the definite article is explained).

- ... ('small 'alif'), can be written over the preceding letter in words in which long ā is not expressed with ١: هٰذَا hādhā 'this'

A word or text carrying such orthographic signs is said to be 'pointed'. Text can be unpointed, partially pointed, or fully pointed.

Full pointing is found only in a few books such as language manuals and religious texts. Most printed texts and all typescript are either unpointed or at most partially pointed. The only signs which are compulsory, and are therefore not regarded as pointing, are madda, medial hamza and final hamza.

**15. Pointing of the Definite Article.** The (optional) pointing of the definite article ...اَل (see 139) can be summarised thus:

- Beginning the phrase, the 'alif of the article is pointed with fatḥa: ...اَ .
- When preceded by a final vowel on the preceding word in the same phrase, the 'alif of the article is pointed with waṣla: ...ٱ .
- When the article is attached to a word beginning with a moon letter, the ل of the article is pointed with sukūn: ...اَلْ , ...ٱلْ .
- When the article is attached to a word beginning with a sun letter, the ل of the article is unpointed, and the sun letter is pointed with shadda plus the next vowel, e.g.: ...اَلسّـ , ...ٱلسّـ .

See 17 for the spelling of an article preceded by a one-letter word.

Examples:

اَلْمَكْتَبُ the office    فِي ٱلْمَكْتَبِ in the office    لِلْمَكْتَبِ to the office

اَلطَّالِبُ the student    مَعَ ٱلطَّالِبِ with the student    لِلطَّالِبِ for the student

See 28 for the definite article preceded by a final ...ْ .

In this book the article is pointed only here and in paras. 14, 28 and 139.

**16. Weak Letters; Vowels; Diphthongs.** The three letters ١ , و and ي are so-called 'weak letters'.

١ deserves special attention. It is weak in that it is unstable; it is silent in some situations; in others it serves as a prop for other letters or signs, and in yet others it may be dropped in writing.

Initial ...١ . When a word begins in sound with a vowel* (long or short) or with a glottal stop ( ء , see 23), the first written letter is always ١ . The word cannot begin in writing with a vowel or with ء alone:

Initial long vowel: أُومُل ūmul    hope!      اِيسِرْ īsir    capture!

Initial short vowel: اُكْتُبْ   uktub   write!      اسْمٌ   ism*un*   name

Initial ء:      أَمَلٌ   'amal*un*   hope      آكُلُ   'ākul*u*   I eat

         أُخْرِجُ   'ukhriju   I expel      أُولَئِكَ   'ūlā'ika   those

         إِخْرَاجٌ   'ikhrāj*un*   expulsion      إِيجَابٌ   'ījāb*un*   compulsion

For آ and initial إ\أ\أ , see also 19.

\* In Arabic grammar, such a word is said to begin with hamzat al-waṣl (see 28).

<u>Medial and final ا</u>. Medial or final ا not carrying ء represents ā except in two circumstances:

- in the masculine plural verb-ending ...وا ū, when it is silent:

كَتَبُوا katabū they wrote

(It is dropped from such words in writing as well when a suffix is added, see 39 and 166)

- in the noun and adjective case-ending, and adverbial ending ...ًا -an, where the vowel is always short:

كَتَبَ تَقْرِيرًا طَوِيلاً. katab*a* taqrīr*an* ṭawīl*an*. He wrote a long report.

تَكْتُبُ وَاضِحًا جِدّاً. taktub*u* wāḍiḥ*an* jiddan. She writes very clearly.

ى represents ā except in the ending ...ًى -an, where the vowel is always short:

مُسْتَشْفًى mustashf*an* a hospital

Since ى is written only as final letter, it is replaced by ا when a suffix is added to the word:

رَمَى ramā he threw; *but:* رَمَاهُ ramāhu he threw it

ى occurs often in the defective verbs (Chapter 10) and the doubly weak verbs (Chapter 11); see also 145 and 154.

See 14 above for ...ٰ (small 'alif).

For the velarised pronunciation of a and ā, see 27.

و and ى vary in value; they can appear respectively as the consonants w and y, or as long vowels ū, ī, or as ā, or as diphthongs aw or ay (see 14 above):

Consonant:   وَصَلَ   waṣal*a*   he arrived   يَكْتُبُ   yaktub*u*   he writes

Long vowel:   مُومٌ   mūm*un*   wax      طِينٌ   ṭīn*un*   mud

Diphthong:   صَوْتٌ   ṣawt*un*   noise      كَيْفَ   kayfa   how

و and ى can also change to ا in some circumstances, or be dropped in others.

**17. Prefixed Words.** Words consisting of one letter are written as one with the following word. The spelling of the word is, with one exception, unchanged; the transliteration shows a hyphen:

| بِ | bi | in | مِصْرُ | miṣru Egypt | بِمِصْرَ | bi-miṣra | in Egypt |
| لِ | li | to/for | اِبْنِي | ibnī my son | لِابْنِي | li-bnī | to/for my son |
| فَ | fa | so/then | هُوَ | huwa he | فَهُوَ | fa-huwa | so he/then he |

When the one-letter word is attached to the definite article, the spelling of the article remains unchanged, except that it drops its ا after لِ li 'to/for'. The transliteration shows a hyphen:

| الْكُوَيْتُ | al-kūwaytu Kuwait | بِالْكُوَيْتِ | bi-l-kūwayti | in Kuwait |
| الْمَدْرَسَةُ | al-madrasatu the school | لِلْمَدْرَسَةِ | li-l-madrasati | to (the) school |
| الْبَيْتُ | al-baytu | the house | وَالْبَيْتُ | wa-l-baytu | and the house |

See 15 for the pointing of the definite article.

**18. Double Letters.** Two identical consonants with no intervening vowel are written single. They can be pointed with ّ... :

مُعَلِّمٌ mu'allimun    teacher

Similarly, the combinations -īy-* and -ūw- are written with one letter, which can be pointed with ّ... :

صُحُفِيَّةٌ ṣuḥufīyatun    journalist    مَرْجُوٌّ marjūwun    expected

Exceptions occur with the letter ل , the commonest one being that when the definite article is attached to a word beginning with ل, both letters ل are written:

لُغَةٌ lughatun    a language    اللُّغَةُ al-lughatu    the language

No more than two identical letters may be written together:

مَعَ الْمِصْرِيِّينَ ma' a l-miṣrīyīna        with the Egyptians

See 25 for the pronunciation of double letters.

* Strictly speaking, this is -iyy-; but it is more convenient (and closer to the everyday pronunciation) to show it as -īy-.

**19. hamza.** In this book, the term <u>hamza</u> refers to hamzat al-qaṭ' (see 28) unless otherwise specified.

See 23 for the pronunciation of hamza.

Care is needed in writing it correctly. It is written in one of four ways:

- above or below ا: أ , إ ; we write آ instead of (أَأ) or (اأ)
- above و : ؤ

- above undotted ي : ئ ـئ
- standing alone: ء

The letter over or under which hamza is written is known as its 'seat'.

The following lists show all possible combinations of hamza, some of them rare. In these lists, note:

- The vowels a and ā, and the diphthongs aw and ay, are velarised (see 27) where appropriate.
- The spellings for ū and ī are valid also for the diphthongs aw and ay respectively; only the pointing (see 14) will be different (ـُو... instead of ـُو... , ـَي... instead of ـِي...).

<u>Initial hamza.</u> hamza occurring at the beginning of a word is always followed by a vowel, short or long. Its seat is ا :

| 'a- | أ... | أَكَّدُوا | 'akkadū | they confirmed |
|---|---|---|---|---|
| 'u- | أُ... | أُرِيدُ | 'urīdu | I want |
| 'i- | إِ... | إِرْسَالٌ | 'irsālun | despatch |
| 'ā- | آ... | (for (أأ); no pointing): آكُلُ | 'ākulu | I eat |
| 'ū- | أُو... | أُوخِذَ | 'ūkhidha | he was blamed |
| 'ī- | إِيـ... | إِيمَانٌ | 'īmānun | belief |

With initial hamza, it is not compulsory to write the hamza itself. Since it is optional, it counts as pointing.

Some texts still show ٱ and ٱ for hamzat al-waṣl, not so shown in this book.

A one-letter word or a definite article (see 17 above) prefixed to a word beginning with hamza does not alter the spelling of that word:

| إِيمَانُهُ | 'īmānuhu | his belief | لِإِيمَانِه | li-'īmānihi | for his belief |
|---|---|---|---|---|---|
| آبَارٌ | 'ābārun | wells | الآبَارُ | al-'ābāru | the wells |

In such combinations the hamza is however no longer initial and must be written.

<u>Medial hamza.</u> hamza occurring neither at the beginning of the word nor as last letter in the word is written as follows:

- consonant-hamza-vowel (x represents any consonant):

| - x ' a | ...ـأَ... | يَسْأَلُ | yas'alu | he asks |
|---|---|---|---|---|
| - x ' u | | (no common examples exist) | | |
| - x ' i | ...ـئِـ... | أَسْئِلَةٌ | as'ilatun | questions |
| - x ' ā | ...ـآ... | قُرْآنِيٌّ | qur'ānīyun | Koranic |

- x ' ū    ...نُو...\...ئُو...    سْنْو...    مَسْؤُولْ\مَسْؤُولْ    mas'ūl*un*    responsible

- x ' ī    ...ئِيـ...    تَرْئِيسٌ    tar'īs*un*    appointment as head

• vowel-hamza-consonant (x represents any consonant):

- a ' x    ...أْ...    رَأْسٌ    ra's*un*    head

- u ' x    ...ؤْ...    مُؤْمِنٌ    mu'min*un*    believer

- i ' x    ...ئْـ...    بِئْرٌ    bi'r*un*    a well

- ā ' x, ū ' x, ī ' x    (no common examples exist)

• vowel-hamza-vowel:

- a ' a    ...أَ...    بَدَأَتْ    bada'at    she began

- a ' u    ...ؤُ...    رَؤُفَتْ    ra'ufat    she pitied

- a ' i    ...ئِـ...    رَئِمَتْ    ra'imat    she caressed

- a ' ā    ...آ...    يَقْرَآنِ    yaqra'āni    they both read

- a ' ū    ...أُوا...\...ؤُوا...    قَرَأُوا\قَرَؤُوا    qara'ū    they (have) read

- a ' ī    ...ئِيـ...\...إِيـ...    تَبْدَئِينَ\تَبْدَإِينَ    tabda'īna    you begin

- ā ' a    ...ءَا...    جَاءَتْ    jā'at    she came

- ā ' u    ...اؤُ...\...ءُ...    زُمَلاؤُهُ    zumalā'uhu    his colleagues

- ā ' i    ...ائِـ...    مَعَ زُمَلائِهِ    ma' a zumalā'ihi    with his colleagues

- ā ' ā    ...ءَا...    اسْتِثْنَاءَاتٌ    istithnā'āt*un*    exceptions

- ā ' ū    ...اؤُوا...\...ءُو...    جَاؤُوا\جَاءُوا    jā'ū    they came

- ā ' ī    ...ائِـ...    ابْتِدَائِيَّةٌ    ibtidā'īyat*un*    primary

- u ' a    ...ؤَ...    يُؤَكِّدُ    yu'akkid*u*    he confirms

- u ' u    (no common examples exist)

- u ' i    ...ئِـ...    سُئِلْنَا    su'ilnā    we were asked

- u ' ā    ...ؤَا...    يُؤَامِرُ    yu'āmir*u*    he consults

- u ' ū    ...ؤُو...    رُؤُوسٌ    ru'ūs*un*    heads

- u ' ī    ...ئِيـ...    تُبْطِئِينَ    tubṭu'īna    you are slow

- ū ' a, ū ' u    (no common examples exist)

- ū ' i    ...ؤِئـ...    سُوئِلَ    sū'il*a*    he was questioned

- ū ' ā    ...وءَا...    يَسُوءَانِ    yasū'āni    they both offend

| - ū ' ū | ...وُعُوۡ | يَسُوۡءُوۡنَ | yasū'ūna | they offend |
| - ū ' ī | ...سُوۡئِيۡ | تَسُوۡئِيۡنَ | tasū'īna | you offend |
| - i ' a | ...ـئَ... | بُدِئَتۡ | budi'at | it was begun |
| - i ' u, i ' i | (no common examples exist) | | | |
| - i ' ā | ...ئَا... | تُهَنِّئَانِ | tuhanni'āni | you both congratulate |
| - i ' ū | ...ـئُوۡ... | يُهَنِّئُوۡنَ | yuhanni'ūna | they congratulate |
| - i ' ī | ...ـئِيۡ... | تُنۡشِئِيۡنَ | tunshi'īna | you create |
| - ī ' a | ...ـيئَ... | بِيئَةٌ | bī'atun | environment |
| - ī ' u, ī ' i | (no common examples exist) | | | |
| - ī ' ā | ...يئَا... | يَجِيئَانِ | yajī'āni | they both come |
| - ī ' ū | ...يئُوۡ...\...ـيُوۡ... | يَجِيئُوۡنَ\يَجِيۡوُنَ | yajī'ūna | they come |
| - ī ' ī | ...ـيئِيۡ... | تَجِيئِيۡنَ | tajī'īna | you come |

Alternative Arabic spellings are shown with \; the first one shown is the commoner. Other spellings also exist for some of the combinations.

Medial hamza must always be written. It does not count as pointing.

The complexities of medial hamza can be reduced to a few generally valid rules:

- When medial hamza follows a consonant, its seat is generally the letter most appropriate to the next vowel, thus: 'a أ, 'u ؤ, 'i ئـ .
- When medial hamza follows a vowel, its seat is often the letter most appropriate to that vowel, thus: a' أ, u' ؤ, i' ئـ . However, ي + hamza is always written يى or ـيئـ , as in the last four examples shown above, also in words like هَيئَةٌ hay'atun 'association, society'.
- Two 'alifs cannot appear together. Hence:
  - 'ā is written آ (instead of (أا) or (أأ)). آ is never accompanied by written hamza, and is never pointed.
  - after long ا... the combination 'a is written ء (pointed, ءَ) with no seat (instead of (أا)).

Final hamza. Final hamza (i.e. hamza as last letter in the word) is written:

- After a short vowel, over the letter most appropriate to that vowel:

| - a ' | أ... | بَدَأَ | bada'a | he began |
| - u ' | ؤ... | تَنَبُّؤٌ | tanabbu'un | forecast |
| - i ' | ـئِ... | جِئۡ | ji' | come |

• After a long vowel or a consonant (shown as x), alone, i.e. with no seat:

| | | | | |
|---|---|---|---|---|
| - ā ' | ...ﺍﺀ | ﺟَﺎﺀَ | jā'a | he came |
| - ū ' | ...ﻮُﺀ | ﺳُﻮﺀٌ | sū'un | evil |
| - ī ' | ...ﻲِﺀ | ﻳَﺠِﻲﺀُ | yajī'u | he comes |
| - x ' | ...ﺀ | ﺟُﺰْﺀٌ | juz'un | part |

Final hamza must always be written. It does not count as pointing.

**20. Handwriting.** Certain handwritten forms need care, and many differ from the printed forms. Such handwritten forms are shown below, unpointed.

<u>Dots.</u> Two dots usually assume the form of a hyphen or dash **-**, three dots that of a circumflex accent ᴧ, thus:

ﺩﺕ ﺩَﺕ ﺕ    ﺙﺙ ﺙ ﺙ    ﻳﻲ ﺭِ ﻯ

ﺥ ﺡ ﺝ are joined in handwriting not from the top right corner, as is often the case in print, but from the top left corner (i.e. the beginning of the outline). An initial single tooth (see 12) looks reversed. Examples (for ﺝ only):

| | | | |
|---|---|---|---|
| tooth + jīm: | ﺍ ﻨﺠﺰ | ﺃَﻧْﺠَﺰَ | he implemented |
| | ﻨﺘﺎﺋﺞ | ﻧَﺘَﺎﺋِﺞُ | results |
| teeth + jīm: | ﻴﻨﺠﺰ | ﻳُﻨْﺠِﺰُ | he implements |
| | ﺍ ﻨﺘﺞ | ﺃَﻧْﺘَﺞَ | he produced |
| lām-jīm: | ﺍﻟﺠﺎﺭ | ﺍﻟْﺠَﺎﺭُ | the neighbour |
| | ﺛﻠﺞ | ﺛَﻠْﺞٌ | ice |
| mīm-jīm: | ﺟﺎﻭﺭ | ﻣُﺠَﺎﻭِﺭٌ | adjacent |
| | ﺑﺮ ﻧﺎ ﺟﺞ | ﺑَﺮْﻧَﺎﻣَﺞٌ | programme |

ﺭ ﺯ have a special ligature when following a medial tooth: Examples (for ﺭ only):

| | | | |
|---|---|---|---|
| | initial tooth + rā': | ﺗﺮﺩ ﺩ | ﺗَﺮَﺩُّﺩَ | he hesitated |
| | other letter + rā: | ﺣﺮﺏ | ﺣَﺮْﺏٌ | war |
| *but:* | medial tooth + rā': | ﻳﺘﺮﺩ ﺩ | ﻳَﺘَﺮَﺩُّﺩُ | he hesitates |
| | | ﺻﺮﺕ | ﺻِﺮْﺕُ | I became |
| | | ﻳﺼﻴﺮ | ﻳَﺼِﻴﺮُ | he becomes |
| | | ﻣﺘﺮ | ﻣِﺘْﺮٌ | metre |

س ش : the points of these letters can be flattened into a shallow curve. Initial and isolated س\ـس begin with a small hook. Examples:

ليـس لَيْسَ   he is not              شَابٌّ شـاب   young man

See also below for ش.

ص ض : The initial and medial forms of these letters have a tooth after the loop. Care is needed not to omit the tooth in handwriting:

ضـد ضِدٌّ   against             مصـدر مَصْدَرٌ   source

See also below for ضَ.

ط ظ : The loop of these letters is written first, then the upright. These letters do not have the tooth of initial/medial ص\ـض :

ظلـم ظُلْمٌ   oppression         مطـار مَطَارٌ   airport

ك : Initial and medial kāf before any letter other than ا or ل are written upright; the 'headstroke' is added afterwards, thus:

كتـب كَتَبَ   he wrote            تـكتـب تَكْتُبُ   she writes

In final kāf the ʿ becomes an extension of the flourish, thus:

ملك مَلِكٌ   king               ترك تَرَكَ   he left

The handwritten combinations lām-'alif, kāf-'alif, kāf-lām and kāf-lām-'alif need care. The headstroke of kāf is written last:

| | | | | | |
|---|---|---|---|---|---|
| لا: | لا | لا | not | سلا م سَلَامٌ | peace |
| كا: | كانت كَانَتْ | she was | مكاتـب مَكَاتِبُ | offices |
| كل: | كلـب كَلْبٌ | dog | الكلـب الكَلْبُ | the dog |
| كل: | كل كُلٌّ | all | بكل بِكُلِّ | to every |
| كلا: | كلا م كَلَامٌ | speech | الكلا م الكَلَامُ | the speech |

م : Initial ـم should be written anticlockwise:

مـا مَا   not; what

Medial and final م ـم should be joined to the preceding letter from the top wherever possible, and the bead written anticlockwise. When preceded by a tooth or teeth, the ligature is similar to that for ج or ر (see above):

لم لَمْ   not               لماذا لِمَاذَا   why

كم كَمْ   how much          كما كَمَا   as

رسم رَسْمٌ   drawing         اسمـه اسْمُهُ   his name

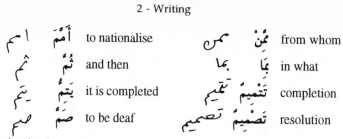

| | | | | | |
|---|---|---|---|---|---|
| أَمَّمَ | to nationalise | | مِمَّنْ | from whom |
| ثُمَّ | and then | | بِمَا | in what |
| يَتِمَّ | it is completed | | تَتْمِيمٌ تَتْمِيم | completion |
| صَمَّ | to be deaf | | تَصْمِيمٌ تَصْمِيم | resolution |

ن : In final ن the dot can become an extension of the curve, thus:

الآنَ    now        ابْنٌ    son

See also below.

ه : The medial form ـهـ is little used in handwriting; the form ـہـ is preferred. For final ـه , an alternative form ـہ can be used, only in handwriting:

لَهَا    to her          لَهُ    to him

ة can be written like final ـہ (ـه). The dots can be omitted when the word is not followed by another word in construct (see 148):

غُرْفَةٌ    room

*but:*    غُرْفَةُ الأَطْفَال    the children's room

أُجْرَةٌ    wages

*but:*    أُجْرَةُ عُمَّالِنَا    our workmen's wages

A common form of educated handwriting is known as الرُّقْعَة . It can be useful to know the following final/isolated forms of certain letters as they appear in الرقعة:

ن = ∿     ق = ـه     ض = صه     ش = ـس

مُفَتِّشٌ   inspector      أَرْضٌ ارضه   land

فَوْقَ   above          مَنْ   who

See 208 for handwritten numerals.

**21. Arabic Transliteration.** Arabic has no standardised transliteration of foreign words. Typical devices used in transliteration are:

- و ي ا may be used both for long and short foreign vowel sounds, especially in stressed syllables:

امستردام   ʾamstirdām     بروكسيل   bruksel   Brussels

روما   rōma           بيرن\برن   birn   Bern

تكنولوجيا   tiknolojīa   technology

- Initial s- plus a consonant other than w or y is transliterated اسْـ...

pronounced is-:

استوكهولم 'istokholm; *but*: سويسرا swisirā Switzerland

- Other sounds not found in Arabic may be represented thus:

ف or ڤ for *v*; چ for *ch* or *g*\*; پ or ب for *p*, چ or ك for *g*\*:

فيزا\ڤيزا vīzā                    فولت vult*un*          volt

بيزا\پيزا pīzā Pisa           چيرنوبيل <u>ch</u>irnobīl Chernobyl

انكلترا\انجلترا 'ingiltirā          England/Britain

\* In Egypt, ج is normally *g*, and چ is used for *j* in foreign words:

جاكارتا jakārta

Most foreign words are indeclinable.

# 3. Pronunciation

**22. General.** Only sounds requiring special care are examined below. The symbol of the International Phonetic Association (IPA) is given in [ ] square brackets after the transliteration in paras. 23 and 24, for those students familiar with the IPA system. The words illustrating the sounds in paras. 23 to 27 below are given in short pronunciation (see 30) for simplicity. See 3 for the transliteration of Arabic script.

**23. Consonants.** Care is needed with the following consonants:

ء   '   [ʔ] (hamza, more precisely hamzat al-qaṭ'), the glottal stop, as in German 'Beamter', or in some English regional speech (no' a lo' o' for *not a lot of*); ألف 'alf 'thousand'. It is pronounced wherever written; care must be taken not to elide it. See 28 below.

ث   <u>th</u>   [θ] (as *th* in 'thought'); ثلث <u>th</u>ul<u>th</u> 'a third'.

ج   j   [dʒ] or [ɟ] as *j* in 'jam'; جديد jadīd 'new'. (In Egypt ج is commonly pronounced as *g* in 'good'.)

ذ   <u>dh</u>   [ð] (as *th* in 'though'); ماذا mā<u>dh</u>ā 'what'.

ر   r   [r] (rolled); never omitted in pronunciation: جار jār 'neighbour'.

ل   l   [l] (front *l*, as in 'leaf'); لنا lanā 'to us'. See also 24 below.

ه   h   [h] (as *h* in 'him'); هم hum 'they'. It is pronounced wherever written; care must be taken not to elide it.

ح   ḥ   [ħ] like h (see above) but produced low in the throat, as if breathing on glass to clean it; نحن naḥnu 'we'.

خ   <u>kh</u>   [x] as *ch* in German 'Buch' or Scots 'loch'; أخ 'a<u>kh</u> 'brother'.

ع   '   [ʕ] a gulp, made by pronouncing a French uvular *r* but with no contact in the throat; عدد 'adad 'number'.

غ   <u>gh</u>   [ɣ] like a French uvular *r*, but with only one contact; غاب <u>gh</u>āb 'he was absent'.

ق   q   [q] like *k* in 'mark', but produced as far back in the throat as possible; قال qāl 'he said'.

ص ṣ, ض ḍ, ط ṭ, ظ ẓ : see 24 below.

**24. Velarised Consonants.** The list below shows velarised consonants, which are pronounced with the tongue as low as possible in the mouth. They are shown with their non-velarised counterparts (which are pronounced much as in English) for comparison. In all cases but one, the velarised consonant has its own letter. It is important to differentiate between the members of each pair; the letter with the more familiar sound is shown first:

س   s   [s]   as *s* in 'see'; سادس sādis 'sixth'.

ص   ṣ   [ṣ]   velarised s; صار ṣār 'he became'.

ت   t   [t]   as *t* in 'ten'; تام tāmm 'perfect'.

ط   ṭ   [ṭ]   velarised t; طار ṭār 'he flew'.

د   d   [d]   as *d* in 'do'; دم dam 'blood'

ض   ḍ   [ḍ]   velarised d; ضرب ḍarab 'he hit'.

ز   z   [z]   as *z* in 'zeal'; زاد zād 'it increased'.

ظ   ẓ   [ẓ]   velarised ẓ; ظل ẓall 'he remained'. ẓ is a common modern
             pronunciation of ظ. The classical pronunciation of ظ, preferred by
             many Arabs, is [ðˠ] or velarised ذ dh.

ل   l   [l]   as *l* in 'leaf': لي 'to me'.

ل   l   [L]   velarised l; , as *ll* in 'wall'. Found only in the word الله
             allāh 'God' in certain contexts.


**25. Double Consonants; Assimilation.** Consonants shown pointed with
ّ must be pronounced double, i.e. held for longer than single consonants:

ذكر dhakar I, 'he mentioned'; *but:* ذكّر dhakkar II 'he recalled'.

See 139 for the assimilation of the l of the definite article to certain initial letters
of nouns and adjectives; this assimilation produces a double letter.


**26. Vowels, Diphthongs, Nunation (التَّنْوِينُ).** It is essential to
distinguish between the three short and and the corresponding three long vowels.
The three pairs are shown below, the short vowel first.

َ   a (fatḥa): [æ] or [a] as *a* in 'man':

       مَن man 'who'. See also 27 below. fatḥa appears only in pointed text.

ا (pointed َا ) ā or ى (pointed ـَى ) ā: [æ:] or [a:] as *a* in 'man', but long:

       كَان kān 'it was'; رَمَى ramā 'he threw'. ى , called 'alif maqṣūra,
       occurs only at the end of a word. See also 27 below.

ُ   u (ḍamma): [u] as *u* in 'push':

       هُم hum 'they'. ḍamma appears only in pointed text.

و (pointed ُو ) ū: [u:] as *u* in 'intrude':

       دُون dūn 'without'.

ِ   i (kasra): [i] or [ɪ] as *i* in 'pin':

       مِن min 'from'. kasra appears only in pointed text.

ي (pointed ـِي ) ī: [i:] as *i* in 'machine':

لِي lī 'to me'.

There are two diphthongs or vowel-combinations:

و (pointed وَ... ) aw: [au] as *ou* in 'house': لُوْن lawn 'colour'. See also 27 below. In modern Arabic often pronounced [ou] like *ou* in 'soul'.

ي (pointed يَ... ) ay: in classical Arabic [aɪ] as *ei* in 'height'; in modern Arabic [eɪ], as *ay* in 'day': كَيْف kayf 'how'. See also 27 below.

See 14 for the phenomenon known as nunation, in Arabic التَّنْوِين. Note that with 'alif-fatha-tanwīn the vowel of اً... and ىً... is pronounced short (-an), despite appearances.

**27. Velarised Vowels a and ā.** See 24 above. When the vowels a and ā occur next to one of the velarised consonants ص, ض, ط, ظ and velarised ل, they too are velarised, i.e. pronounced with the tongue dropped:

velarised a: [ɑ] or [ʌ] as *u* in 'but': ضَرَب ḍarab 'he hit'.

velarised ā: [ɑ:] as *a* in 'calm': صَار ṣār 'he became'.

The vowels are further always velarised when occurring next to ق , and often when occurring next to خ or ر: قَال qāl 'he said', خَارِج khārij 'outside'.

Similarly, the diphthongs aw and ay are velarised in the same circumstances:

velarised aw: [ɑu] as aw (see 26 above) but deeper, as *au* in German 'Haus': ضَوْء ḍaw' 'light'.

velarised ay: [ɑɪ] as *ei* in 'height', but deeper: صَيْف ṣayf 'summer'.

**28. hamzat al-qaṭ' and hamzat al-waṣl.** ء pronounced as a glottal stop (23 above) is called in full hamzat al-qaṭ' 'the hamza of severance'. The other so-called hamza is hamzat al-waṣl 'the hamza of connexion', which is the sign of an initial vowel, pronounced with a glottal stop* except after a word ending in a vowel, when both hamza and vowel are dropped altogether. In full pointing (14), hamzat al-waṣl may be pointed with waṣla ٱ:

|  |  |  |  |
|---|---|---|---|
|  | ب | bi | in, at, with |
|  | الْمَتْحَفُ | al-mathaf*u* | the museum |
| *but:* | بِالْمَتْحَف | bi-l-mathaf*i* | in the museum |
|  | فِي مِلَفِّه | fī milaffihi | in his file |
|  | مَكْتُومُ | maktūm*u* | confidential |

*but:* فِي مِلَفِّه ٱلْمَكْتُوم fī malaffihi l-maktūm*i* in his confidential file

* In theory there is no glottal stop ever with hamzat al-waṣl; but in practice it is almost impossible not to pronounce one when a word with an initial vowel

begins the sentence or phrase. At the beginning of an English sentence, 'I am' is pronounced with a glottal stop before *I*, but none before *am*.

waṣla is marked in this book only here and in paras. 14, 15 and 139.

Initial ا has hamzat al-waṣl when it occurs in the following words and prefixes:

- الـ... al-, as-, at- (etc.) definite article, see 139,
- the following verbal parts:
  - imperative of Form I, e.g.:

    اِفْتَحْ iftaḥ I, open, اُكْتُبْ uktub I, write (sound)

    اِيسِرْ īsir I, capture, اِسْأَلْ is'al I, ask, اِقْرَأْ iqra' I, read (hamzated),

    اُدْلُلْ udlul I, indicate (doubled), اِيجُهْ ījuh I, be eminent (assimilated),

    اِنْسَ insa I, forget (defective)

  - perfect (active and passive), imperative and verbal noun of Forms VII, VIII, IX and X of all classes of verb, e.g.:

    اِنْسَحَبُوا insaḥabū VII they withdrew (perfect active)

    اُتُّخِذَ uttukhida VIII it was taken (perfect passive)

    اِتَّصِلْ ittaṣil VIII get in touch (imperative)

    اِبْيِضَاضٌ ibyiḍāḍun IX turning pale (verbal noun)

    اِسْتِمْرَارٌ istimrārun X continuation (verbal noun)

- اِثْنَانِ ithnāni 'two' and its derivatives (see 210 and 211)
- the singular nouns

  | | | | | | |
  |---|---|---|---|---|---|
  | اِبْنٌ | ibnun | son | اِبْنَةٌ | ibnatun | daughter |
  | اِمْرَأَةٌ | imra'atun | woman | اِسْمٌ | ismun | name |

  and a few others, less common.

Some writers and printers show أ, أ and إ for initial a, u and i carrying either hamzat al-waṣl or hamzat al-qaṭ'. In this book, initial أ, أ and إ indicate exclusively hamzat al-qaṭ'; initial ا, ا, ا and ا indicate exclusively hamzat al-waṣl.

A final written long vowel preceding hamzat al-waṣl is pronounced short. The spelling is unchanged:

         فَهِمُوا    fahimū           they understood

*but:*    فَهِمُوا الخِطَابَ.    fahimu l-khiṭāba.     They understood the speech.

         كَتَبَا    katabā           they both wrote

*but:* كَتَبَا التَّقْرِيرَ. kataba t-taqrīra.  They both wrote the report.

When hamzat al-waṣl is preceded by ْ... , this changes mostly to ِ... :

قَرَأَتْ رِسَالَتَهَا. She read her letter

*but:* قَرَأَتِ الرِّسَالَةَ. She read the letter.

لِكَيْ تَرَيْ أَهَمِّيَّتَهُ so that you see its importance

*but:* لِكَيْ تَرَيِ الأَهَمِّيَّةَ so that you see the importance

Exceptions are:

- the preposition مِنْ 'from', for which see 172,

- final diphthong ـَوْ... or أَوْ... -aw, which becomes ـَوُ... or أَوُ... -awu (the final
  ا being silent):

رَأَوُا التَّظَاهُرَ. They saw the demonstration.

However, the conjunction أَوْ 'or' connects with ِ... :

إِمَّا الْحُكُومَةُ أَوِ الْمُعَارَضَةُ either the government or the opposition

- the possessive and object pronoun suffixes ـكُمْ... , ـهُمْ... and ـهِمْ... , for
  which see 147 and 166.

In this book, all mention of hamza or ء refers to hamzat al-qaṭ' unless hamzat
al-waṣl is specified.


**29. Stress.** In an Arabic word of two or more syllables, one syllable is
stressed, i.e. pronounced more loudly than the rest. The stress is not shown
elsewhere in this book, because it is regular. In the examples accompanying the
following rules the stressed syllable is shown with an acute accent (´) over its
transliterated vowel or diphthong:

- The last 'heavy' syllable is stressed if the word has one. A heavy syllable
  is one consisting of:

  - a long vowel, or a diphthong, plus a consonant:

    بَرْنَامَجٌ barnámaj*un*  programme

    الْبَحْرَيْنُ al-bahráyn*u*  Bahrain

  - a short vowel plus two consonants or a double consonant:

    اُكْتُبْ úktub  write (imperative)

    ذَكَّرْتُهُ <u>dh</u>akkártuhu  I reminded him

    ذَكَّرَنِي <u>dh</u>ákkaranī  he reminded me

But see the last indent below.

- If the word has no heavy syllable, the first syllable is stressed:

$$\text{أَنَا} \qquad \text{'ána} \qquad\qquad \text{I}$$

- The definite article, and the first syllable of verbal Forms VII and VIII are never stressed, and are ignored in situating the stress:

| | | |
|---|---|---|
| الكُتُبُ | al-kútub*u* | the books |
| بالمئَة | bi-l-mí'a*ti* | per cent |
| انسَحَبُوا | insáḥabū | they withdrew |
| نَكتَشِفُ | naktáshif*u* | we discover |
| مُتَّحِدٌ | muttáḥid*un* | united |

**30. Full, Pause and Short Pronunciation.** There are two styles of pronunciation of written Arabic, i.e. full and short pronunciation (see 8 for their transliteration in this book.):

- <u>Full Pronunciation.</u> In full pronunciation, all the sounds which appear or would appear in a fully pointed text are pronounced:

| | | |
|---|---|---|
| حَضَرَ الجَلسَةَ. | ḥaḍara l-jalsata. | He attended the session. |
| مُديرُ البَنْك | mudīru l-banki | the bank manager |

In full pronunciation, the logical end of the phrase or sentence may however be pronounced in so-called pause or pausal form, omitting the pointed ending of the last word; in this situation final ة... , howsoever vowelled, becomes -a:

| | | |
|---|---|---|
| مدير البنك | mudīru l-bank | حَضَرَ الجَلسة. | ḥaḍara l-jalsa. |

Pausal form applies also to the nunated vowels ً... , ٍ... and ٌ... (see 26); the combinations اً... and ىً, however, are pronounced fully (-an):

| | | |
|---|---|---|
| مُديرُ بَنْكٍ | (full throughout:) *mudīru bankin* | |
| | (pause:) *mudīru bank* | a bank manager |
| جَميلٌ جِدًا | (full/pause:) *jamīlun jiddan* | very beautiful |

The ending ءاً... is pronounced fully, -ā'an: مَسَاءً masā'an in the morning. Full pronunciation is mostly used for formal reading of a document.

- <u>Short Pronunciation.</u> In short pronunciation, almost all word-endings not written with a letter of the alphabet (i.e. visible only when pointed) are silent. Note however the following pointed endings which are always pronounced as in full pronunciation (including pausal variants, where applicable):

- those of verbal principal parts (see 34) quoted as such:

  كَتَبَ kataba   to write          يَفْتَتِحُ yaftatiḥu to inaugurate

  (Such words can be pronounced short when used as tenses: كتب
  عنوانه. katab ʿunwānahu. He wrote his address.)
- the verb-endings تِ... (-ti) and نَ... (-na):

  كَتَبْتِ katabti you wrote          تَكْتُبِينَ taktubīna you write

  تَكْتُبُونَ\يَكْتُبُونَ taktubūna/yaktubūna you/they write

  كَتَبْنَ\اُكْتُبْنَ katabna/uktubna      they wrote; write (imperative)
- the ending of the demonstrative: هٰذِه hādhihi 'this',
- the ending نّ... (-nna): أَنَّ\إِنَّ 'anna/'inna 'that'; كُنَّ kunna 'they were'
- the endings of all possessive adjective suffixes and of all personal
  (subject and object) pronouns:

  مُوَظَّفُوهُ muwaẓẓafūhu          his employees

  هِيَ hiya   she      رَمَاهُ ramāhu   he threw it
- the nunated endings اً... , ىً... (-an) and ءً اً... (-āʾan):

  كِتَابًا kitāban    a book          رَسْمِيًّا rasmiyyan official

  مُسْتَشْفًى mustashfan a hospital      إِجْرَاءً 'ijrāʾan   a measure
- the adverbial ending -an, however written:

  كَثِيرًا kathīran    much          عَادَةً ʿādatan usually
- the pointed ending (single or nunated) of certain set phrases:

  لاَ بُدَّ مِنْ lā budda min  it is inevitable

  شَخْصٌ مَا shakhṣun mā somebody or other

The rule that the pointed word-ending is silent in short pronunciation
applies only when no suffix is added to the ending. Once a suffix is
attached, the pointed ending of the verb or the noun is now no longer at
the end of the word, and is pronounced:

  كِتَاب\الكِتَاب kitāb/al-kitāb   a/the book

  *but:*   كِتَابُهَا kitābuhā          her book

  أَشكُر 'ashkur          I thank

  *but:*   أَشْكُرُكُمْ 'ashkurukum  I thank you

The dropping of the pointed ending means that a following hamzat al-
waṣl recovers its original vowel sound; in the definite article this is a-:

  في نص البيان full: *fī naṣṣi l-bayān(i)*

short: fī naṣṣ al-bayān   in the text of the announcement

كان اتصل به.   full: *kāna ttaṣala bihi.*

short: kān ittaṣal bihi       He had contacted him.

The ending ة... in the middle of a construct (see 148) is pronounced -at. Any following hamzat al-waṣl (including that of a definite article) recovers its original vowel sound:

في مسودة البيان   full: *fī musawwadati l-bayān(i)*

short: fī musawwadat al-bayān   in the draft of the announcement

سيارة ابنه   full: *sayyāratu bnihi/sayyārata bnihi/sayyārati bnihi*

short: sayyārat ibnihi       his son's car

The ending ة... not in the middle of a construct is pronounced -a, as in pause (see above):

مدينة قديمة   full: *madīnatun qadīma(tun)*

short: madīna qadīma       an ancient city

ملحق سفارة   full: *mulḥaqun sifāra(tin)*

short: mulḥaq sifāra       an embassy attaché

However, the ending ة... not in construct followed by an adjective carrying the definite article is often pronounced in full in certain set phrases, even when the speaker is pronouncing short otherwise:

الساعة الثانية   as-sā'a*tu* th-thaniya       two o'clock

في العربية السعودية   fi l-'arabīya*ti* s-sa'udīya   in Saudi Arabia

خلال السنة المقبلة   khilāl as-sana*ti* l-muqbila   during next year

Note that in these examples only the first ة (the one on the noun) is pronounced full.

The ending ... of weak nouns and weak participles is pronounced -ī in short pronunciation: قاض 'a judge', full pronunciation *qāḍin*, short qāḍī.

Short pronunciation is very common; it is used for less formal reading of a document - or even, by some, for spontaneous speech instead of colloquial Arabic. With exceptions such as the one shown above, it is almost always used for proper names, even when the speaker is otherwise pronouncing in full.

We can compare short and full/pause pronunciation in a continuous passage, e.g. a news report:

وصل إلى الدوحة صباح أمس وفد تجاري من اليابان بزيارة رسمية تستغرق أسبوعًا كاملاً. وعلم من مصادر حكومية أن الأبحاث ستجري مع سعادة وزير التجارة وكبار المسؤولين في حقلي التجارة والاستثمار وأنها ستبدأ اليوم وأن أهم نقطة على جدول عمل المفاوضين هي تثبيت التبادلات بين الجانبين وحفظ الاستقرار الاقتصادي في المنطقة بصورة عامة ومن المعروف أن مستوى الصادرات اليابانية إلى بلادنا خلال السنة الماضية كان أعلى مما كان في أية مدة من تاريخ علاقاتنا التجارية مع اليابان.

<u>Short</u> (the one optional injection of full pronunciation is italicised):

wasal 'ila d-dauha sabāh 'ams wafd tijārī min al-yābān bi-ziyāra rasmīya tasta<u>ghr</u>iq 'usbū' an kāmilan. wa-' ulim min masādir hukūmīya 'anna l-'ab<u>hāth</u> sa-tajrī ma' sa' ādat wazīr at-tijāra wa-kibār al-mas'ūlīn fī haqlay at-tijāra wa-l-isti<u>thm</u>ār wa-'annahā sa-tabda' al-yawm wa-'anna 'ahamm nuqta ' alā jadwal 'a' māl al-mufāwadīn hiya ta<u>thb</u>īt at-tabādulāt bayn al-jānibayn wa-hifz al-istiqrār al-iqtisādī fi l-mintaqa bi-sūra ' āmma wa-min al-ma' rūf 'anna mustawa s-sādirāt al-yābānīya 'ilā bilādinā <u>kh</u>ilāl as-sana(ti) l-mādiya kān 'a' lā mimmā kān fī 'ayya mudda min tārī<u>kh</u> ' alāqātina t-tijārīya ma' al-yābān.

*Full/pause* (the three injections of short pronunciation for proper names are in non-italic; the six pauses are marked with I ):

*wasala 'ila d-*dauha *sabāha 'amsi wafdun tijārīyun mina l-*yābān *bi-ziyāratin rasmīyatin tasta<u>ghr</u>iqu 'usbū' an kāmilan. wa-' ulima min masādira hukūmīyati 'anna l-' ab<u>hātha</u> sa-tajrī ma' a sa' ādati wazīri t-tijāra*I *wa-kibāri l-mas' ūlīna fī haqlayi t-tijāra*I *wa-l-isti<u>thm</u>ār*I *wa-' annahā sa-tabda'u l-yawm*I *wa-' anna 'ahamma nuqtatin ' alā jadwali 'a' māli l-mufāwadīna hiya ta<u>thb</u>ītu t-tabādulāti bayna l-jānibayni wa-hifzu l-istiqrāri l-iqtisādīyi fi l-mintaqati bi-sūratin ' āmma*I *wa-mina l-ma' rūfi 'anna mustawa s-sādirāti l-yābānīyati 'ilā bilādinā khilāla s-sanati l-mādiya*I *kāna 'a' lā mimmā kāna fī 'ayyati muddatin min tārīkhi ' alāqātina t-tijārīyati ma' a l-*yābān.

This morning a trade delegation arrived in Doha from Japan on an official visit lasting a whole week. It was learned from government sources that the discussions will take place with H.E. the Minister of Trade and senior officials in the fields of trade and investment. These ('and that they') will begin today; ('and that') the most important point on ('of') the negotiators' agenda is the consolidation of exchanges between the two sides and the maintenance of economic stability in the region in general. It will be recalled ('it is known') that the level of Japanese exports to this ('our') country during last year was higher than ('it was') in any period in the history of our trade relations with Japan.

# 4. Verbs - General

**31. Roots.** All mention of roots or verbs in this book refers to triliteral (i.e three-lettered) roots or verbs unless otherwise stated. The letters making up a verb root are known as radicals.

**32. Classes.** There are four classes of verb, grouped as follows:

- Sound roots: Stable (i.e invariable) radicals, ب ت ث ج ح خ د ذ ر ز س
  ش ص ض ط ظ ع غ ف ق ك ل م ن ه . A typical sound root is عمل .
  All quadriliteral (four-lettered) roots conjugate (i.e. form their tenses and other parts) like sound roots. A typical quadriliteral root is ترجم .

- Hamzated roots: ء as one radical, and two sound radicals. Typical hamzated roots are أكل , سأل , بدأ .
  In a dictionary, ء (howsoever written) is usually listed with ا .

- Doubled roots: identical sound middle and final radicals. A typical doubled root is دلّ .
  The initial radical is almost always sound. A few doubled verbs have a weak letter or ء as initial radical.

- Weak roots : و or ي as one radical. The weak class has four sub-classes:
  - Assimilated roots (initial-radical و\ي), e.g. يبس , وجد
  - Hollow roots (middle-radical و\ي), e.g. طير , سوق
  - Defective roots (final-radical و\ي), e.g. بقي , دعو
  - Doubly weak roots, i.e. roots composed in one of the following ways:
    · weak initial and final radicals, e.g. وقي ,
    · weak middle and final radicals, e.g. نوي ,
    · weak letter as final radical and ء as another radical, or vice versa,
      e.g. جيء , رأي , أتي

See 9 for the location in this book of verb roots with mixed radicals.

**33. Government**. Arabic verbs have three possible types of government, i.e. relationship with their object, if any:

- Intransitive. An intransitive verb has no object:
  يَذْهَبُ. He goes.
  Intransitive verbs denoting being, becoming or seeming may have a complement:
  كَانَ مَرِيضًا. He was ill.

- Transitive. A transitive verb has a direct object:

نَسِيَ أَصْدِقَاءَهُ.　He forgot his friends.

كَتَبْنَاهُ.　We wrote it.

A verb may be doubly transitive, i.e. have two direct objects:

عَلَّمُوهَا اللُّغَةَ الْعَرَبِيَّةَ.　They taught her Arabic ('the Arabic language').

- Prepositional. A prepositional verb has an object governed by a preposition ('prepositional object'),:

رَضِيَ بِالِاقْتِرَاحِ.　He approved of the proposal. (preposition ب )

The term 'prepositional object' covers also what we know as an indirect object in English grammar:

قَالُوا لَكَ الْحَقِيقَةَ.　They told ('to') you the truth.

A verb can have both a direct and a prepositional object:

أَخْبَرْنَاهُم بِالتَّفَاصِيلِ.　We informed them of the details.

**34. Principal Parts.** A verb is normally referred to by one or both of its simplest forms which we can call for convenience its 'principal parts':

- first principal part: 3rd person masc. sing. perfect, e.g. عَمِلَ
- second principal part: 3rd person m. s. imperfect indicative, e.g. يَعْمَلُ .

We translate principal parts with the English infinitive: عَمِلَ يَعْمَلُ 'to do'.

**35. Agreement.** In the tenses, the verb agrees with its grammatical subject.

- 1st persons: in person and number,
- 2nd persons: in person, number and gender; feminine plural for an all-female group, masculine plural for an all-male or mixed group,
- 3rd persons: in person, number and gender, as follows:
  - the <u>singular</u> has complete agreement with animate (= people)/inanimate (= other than people) subjects,
  - the <u>dual</u> has complete agreement with animate/inanimate subjects in nominal sentences (182); but see following indents,
  - the <u>plural</u> is used only for animate subjects; feminine plural for an all-female group, masculine plural for an all-male or mixed group; however, in a verbal sentence (183), the verb is singular even for a dual or animate plural subject,
  - the <u>inanimate plural</u> form (identical to the feminine singular) is used for a plural inanimate subject, irrespective of gender.

For the imperative, the provisions given above for the 2nd persons apply.

**36. Voice.** Arabic verbs are found in two voices:

- <u>Active</u>, in which the subject of the verb performs the action or undergoes the state expressed by the verb:

كَتَبَ   he wrote           صَارَتْ   she became

- <u>Passive</u>, in which the subject of the verb suffers the action of the verb:

كُتِبَ التَّقْرِيرُ.   The report was written.

The passive voice is derived from the active voice by changing only the vowels occurring earlier than the final radical. See 55 below for the basic measures, and the beginning of Chapters 5 to 11 for the derivation within each verb class.

**37. Table 1, Verbal Forms: Derivation and Use.** In addition to the basic form of the verb, Arabic has so-called increased forms in which the root is changed by the addition of a consonant or a syllable or the vowel ſ, or by the doubling of a radical, or a combination of these devices. The forms are numbered with Roman letters, the basic form being Form I (IQ for quadriliteral verbs). This book shows ten triliteral forms (I to X) and two quadriliteral forms (IQ and IIQ) of the verb. No verb has all forms; some have no Form I or IQ.

Increased forms XI to XV and IIIQ also exist, but they are little known and extremely rare in modern Arabic, and not covered in this book.

The notation I to X is Western; Arabs refer to the forms by the first principal part of the sound root فعل (for quadriliteral roots the theoretical sound root فعلل ). This root is quoted also for other parts of speech where appropriate.

Table 1a shows the derivation of Forms I to X, active voice. Table 1b shows the use and frequency of the verbal forms.

Table 1a: Derivation of Verbal Forms I to X, Active Voice

| Form | Principal Parts | Imperative | Participle | Verbal Noun |
|------|-----------------|------------|------------|-------------|
| I | فَعَلَ يَفْعَلُ * | أُفْعُلْ\اِفْعَلْ\اِفْعِلْ * | فَاعِلٌ | irregular |
| IQ | فَعْلَلَ يُفَعْلِلُ | فَعْلِلْ | مُفَعْلِلٌ | irregular |
| II | فَعَّلَ يُفَعِّلُ | فَعِّلْ | مُفَعِّلٌ | تَفْعِيلٌ\تَفْعِلَةٌ |
| IIQ | تَفَعْلَلَ يَتَفَعْلَلُ | تَفَعْلَلْ | مُتَفَعْلِلٌ | تَفَعْلُلٌ |
| III | فَاعَلَ يُفَاعِلُ | فَاعِلْ | مُفَاعِلٌ | مُفَاعَلَةٌ\فِعَالٌ |
| IV | أَفْعَلَ يُفْعِلُ | أَفْعِلْ | مُفْعِلٌ | إِفْعَالٌ |
| V | تَفَعَّلَ يَتَفَعَّلُ | تَفَعَّلْ | مُتَفَعِّلٌ | تَفَعُّلٌ |

| | | | | |
|---|---|---|---|---|
| VI | تَفَاعَلَ يَتَفَاعَلُ | تَفَاعُلْ | مُتَفَاعَلٌ | تَفَاعُلٌ |
| VII | انْفَعَلَ يَنْفَعِلُ | انْفَعِلْ | مُنْفَعَلٌ | انفِعَالٌ |
| VIII | ** افْتَعَلَ يَفْتَعِلُ | افْتَعِلْ** | مُفْتَعَلٌ** | افْتِعَالٌ** |
| IX | افْعَلَّ يَفْعَلُّ | افْعَلِلْ\افْعَلَّ | مُفْعَلٌّ | افْعِلَالٌ |
| X | اسْتَفْعَلَ يَسْتَفْعِلُ | اسْتَفْعِلْ | مُسْتَفْعَلٌ | اسْتِفْعَالٌ |

These are measures for sound verbs. Other classes have variants of them.

\* In Form I triliteral, the vowel patterns of the principal parts and the imperative vary.

\*\* In Form VIII the ت of the form changes after certain initial radicals:

- after initial-radical ط ض ص : to ط
- after initial-radical ز : to د
- initial-radical ظ ط د ت + ت become تّ دّ طّ ظّ respectively

Other changes occur in Form VIII in other verb classes: see Chapters 6 and 8.

### Table 1b: Use of Verbal Forms I to X, Active Voice

| Form | Use and Connotation | Frequency |
|---|---|---|
| I | Basic form: intransitive, transitive or prepositional. | High |
| IQ | Basic form: intransitive, transitive or prepositional. | Low |
| II | Usually transitive, often causative of Form I; sometimes intensive in meaning. | High |
| IIQ | Intransitive, no passive. | Low |
| III | Often transitive for the person-object, where the corresponding Form I verb is prepositional. | Middle |
| IV | Transitive, often causative of Form I. | Middle |
| V | Reflexive\* or passive of Form II; passive often impersonal. | High |
| VI | Reciprocal\*\* of Form III; a few passives, used impersonally. | Middle |
| VII | Active voice often has passive meaning of Form I; a few passives, used impersonally. | Low |
| VIII | Often transitive. | High |
| IX | Intransitive, denotes colours or physical defects. Found only in sound and hollow classes. No passive. | Very low |
| X | Intransitive, transitive or prepositional. May express:<br>• ascribing a quality to the object, *or*<br>• seeking fulfilment of the idea implicit in the root. | High |

\* i.e. 'oneself'.   \*\* i.e. 'each other'

**38. Mood.** Arabic verbs are found in four moods:

- <u>Indicative</u>, for statements or questions regarding facts. Two indicative tenses* exist: the perfect and imperfect; see 39 to 42.
- <u>Subjunctive</u>, indicating possibility, probability or purpose. Only the imperfect subjunctive exists; see 43 and 44.
- <u>Jussive</u>, used for certain optative, conditional or negative expressions. Only the imperfect jussive tense exists; see 45 and 46.
- <u>Imperative</u>, expressing direct commands or requests; see 50.

* Arabic tenses are less strictly related to time than are tenses in European languages, and the term *aspects* is preferred by some. In this book the more familiar term *tenses* is used.

**39. Table 2, Perfect (Indicative) Tense: Conjugation.** The personal endings of the perfect tense, active and passive, for all roots with a sound final radical, are given below. See 7 for the arrangement of the persons.

| Singular | Dual | Plural |
|:---:|:---:|:---:|
| ...تُ* | | ...نَا |
| ...بَ* | ...تُمَا | ...تُم |
| ...ت | ...تُمَا | ...تُنَّ |
| ...َ* | ...ا | ...وا |
| ...تَ | ...تَا | ...نَ |

The ending is added to the <u>perfect stem</u> (shown as ... above), for the derivation of which see the appropriate verb chapter. See 35 for the agreement of the verb with its subject.

In the endings marked * the final ´... or ˋ... is sounded in short pronunciation only when a direct object pronoun suffix (see 166) is attached.

These endings are also in principal valid for roots with a weak final radical, but in such roots the stem and the ending are often inextricable, or the final radical may be dropped, and the conjugation is best studied separately. See 110.

Note:

- The 3rd person f. s. ending ...تْ becomes, in full pronunciation, ...تِ before hamzat al-waṣl:

    دَرَسَتِ التَّمْرِينَ.   She studied the exercise.
- The 2nd person m. pl. ending ...تُمْ becomes, in full pronunciation, ...تُمُ before hamzat al-waṣl, and becomes, in full and short pronunciation,

...تُمُو... before a direct object pronoun suffix:

حَضَّرْتُمُ التَّقْرِيرَ. You prepared the report.

هَل حَضَّرْتُمُوهُ؟ Have you prepared it?

- In the 3rd person m. pl. ending ...وا the ا is silent. It is dropped in writing also before a direct object pronoun suffix:

اسْتَعْمَلُوهَا. They used it/them.

**40. Perfect (Indicative) Tense: Use.** The perfect tense denotes a completed action or state, usually situated in the past:

جَاءَ مُتَأَخِّرًا. He came late.

هَل كَتَبَ تَقْرِيرَهُ؟ Has he written his report?

The negative of the perfect tense is made by putting the particle مَا before it:

مَا وَصَلُوا. They did not arrive.

See also the use of the negative particle لَمْ with the jussive tense, with past meaning, in 46 below. لَمْ + the jussive is almost always preferred to مَا + the perfect, and is sometimes compulsory: see 194.

The completeness of an action or state can be emphasised by putting the particle قَدْ or its variant لَقَدْ before the perfect verb:

قَدْ\لَقَدْ بَدَأُوا الْعَمَلَ. They (really) have started the work.

The perfect is also used in conditional sentences, see 194, with any time-reference, not necessarily past.

See 229 for the use of the perfect in expressing a wish.

**41. Table 3, Imperfect (Indicative) Tense: Conjugation.** The personal prefixes and endings of the imperfect indicative tense, active and passive voices, are given below. See 7 for the arrangement of the persons:

| Singular | Dual | Plural |
|----------|------|--------|
| أَ...* | | نَ...* |
| أُ...* | | نُ...* |
| تَ...* | تَ...اَنِ* | تَ...وُنَ |
| تُ...* | تُ...اَنِ* | تُ...وُنَ |
| تَ...ينَ | تَ...اَنِ* | تَ...نَ |
| تُ...ينَ | تُ...اَنِ* | تُ...نَ |

| يَ...ونَ | يَ...انِ* | يَ...* |
|---|---|---|
| يُ...ونَ | يُ...انِ* | يُ...* |
| يَ...نَ | تَ...انِ* | تَ...* |
| يُ...نَ | تُ...انِ* | تُ...* |

The prefixes are valid for all verbs, in Forms I to X. See the note below for the choice of prefix for each person.

The personal endings are valid for all verbs with a sound final radical in Forms I to X, active and passive voice. The endings are only partly valid for roots with a weak final radical; see 112.

The prefix and ending are added to the <u>imperfect stem</u> (shown as ... above); see the appropriate verb chapter for its derivation. See 35 for the agreement of the verb with its subject.

In the endings marked * the final ´... or ˋ... is sounded in short pronunciation only when a direct object pronoun suffix (see 166) is attached.

Note:

- In the active voice of Forms I, IIQ, V, VI, VII, VIII, IX and X the vowel of the prefix is ˋ... ( أَ\تَ\يَ\نَ ). The first prefix of each pair shown in Table 3 above applies.
- In the active voice of Forms IQ, II, III and IV, and in the whole of the passive voice (see 55), the vowel of the prefix is ´... ( أُ\تُ\يُ\نُ ). The second prefix of each pair shown in Table 3 above applies.

**42. Imperfect (Indicative) Tense: Use.** The imperfect tense denotes an incomplete action or situation, usually situated in the present or near future:

يَقْرَأُونَ التَّقْرِيرَ.    They are reading the report.

يَجْتَمِعُونَ الْيَوْمَ.    They (will) meet today.

As in other languages, so in Arabic, in narrative style the imperfect may be used for past events, where the context makes the past time-reference clear.

The negative of the imperfect tense is made by putting the particle لاَ before it:

لاَ نَفْهَمُهُ.    We do not understand it.

A future meaning may be specified by putting the particle سَوْفَ or the prefix ...سَـ before the imperfect verb:

سَوْفَ يَرْجِعُونَ\سَيَرْجِعُونَ.    They will return.

This future construction is especially common in statements or questions relating to intention. For its negative, see the subjunctive tense (44 below).

See 196 for the use of the imperfect in clauses of circumstance, in which it takes its time-reference from the verb on which it depends.

**43. (Imperfect) Subjunctive Tense: Conjugation.** The (imperfect) subjunctive tense is most easily derived from the imperfect (indicative) tense. For verbs with a sound final radical, proceed as follows:

- Change any imperfect personal ending ´... into ¨... (dropped in short pronunciation when no direct object pronoun suffix follows, see 166):

  imperfect يَعْمَلُ I, he does, subjunctive يَعْمَلَ

- Change imperfect personal endings ¨ين... into ي...‚ اُن... into ا...‚ and وُن... into وا... (in which final ا is silent, and is dropped in writing before a direct-object pronoun suffix):

  imperfect تَذْهَبِينَ I, you go, subjunctive تَذْهَبِي

  imperfect تَسْتَفِيدَانِ X you both benefit, subjunctive تَسْتَفِيدَا

  imperfect يُقَرِّرُونَ II they decide, subjunctive يُقَرِّرُوا

- Leave the rest unchanged:
  imperfect indicative and subjunctive يَأْخُذْنَ I they take

See 114 for the formation of the subjunctive of roots with a weak final radical.

**44. (Imperfect) Subjunctive Tense: Use.** The subjunctive tense expresses ideas such as possibility, purpose or will. It is always introduced either by:

- a conjunction indicating purpose, potential, obligation etc. (see 190); *or*
- the particle لَنْ 'shall not/will not', expressing a negative future of intention:

  لَنْ تَذْهَبَ. She will not go.

  See 42 above for the affirmative future.

**45. (Imperfect) Jussive Tense: Conjugation.** The (imperfect) jussive tense is derived from the (imperfect) subjunctive tense. For sound, hamzated and assimilated roots, proceed as follows:

- Drop any subjunctive personal ending ´... :
  subjunctive تَتَكَلَّمَ V you speak, jussive تَتَكَلَّمْ
  The ¨... at the end of such forms becomes, in full pronunciation, ... before hamzat al-waṣl; see 46 below, third indent, for an example.
- Leave the rest unchanged:
  subjunctive and jussive يَسْتَعْمِلُوا X they use

Form IX verbs have an alternative jussive, derived as for doubled verbs; see 62,

88 and 103.

See 88, 103, 115 and 126 respectively for the formation of the jussive of doubled roots, hollow roots, and roots with a weak final radical.

**46. (Imperfect) Jussive Tense: Use.** The jussive tense has four principal uses:

- after the particles لِ 'let ...' and وَلْ\فَلْ 'so let ...' with a verb in the first or third persons:

    لِيَشْرَحُوهُ.  Let them explain it.        فَلْنَسْمَعْ.  So let us listen.

- preceded by the particle لاَ , to form the negative imperative. See 50:

    لاَ تَتَرَدَّدْ.  Do not hesitate.

- after the particles لَمْ 'not' or لَمَّا 'not yet' to negate a past action or state:

    لَمْ يُجِيبُوا.  They did not answer.

    لَمَّا يُقَرِّرُوا.  They have not yet decided.

    لَمْ يُرْسِلِ الرِّسَالَةَ.  He has not sent/did not send the letter.

(See 45 above for the full pronunciation of this last example.)

The negative with لَمْ is mostly preferred to that with مَا plus the perfect tense, see 40 above.

- in certain conditional sentences. See 194.

**47. Continuous Perfect Tense.** The continuous perfect tense is composed of the perfect tense of the hollow verb كَانَ (see 103) and the imperfect (indicative) tense of the operative verb. The compound expresses a repeated or continuous action in the past. Both verbs agree with the subject (see 35):

كُنْتُ أَدْرُسُ فِي الْجَامِعَةِ عِنْدَمَا ...  I was studying at university when ...

كَانَ دَائِمًا يَتَكَلَّمُ عَنْكَ.  He was always talking about you.

The rationale of this compound tense is clear if we interpret these sentences as 'I was (in a current state of) studying ...' and 'He was (in a constant/repeated state of) talking ...', in which the imperfect verbal part acts as a complement of the verb كان exactly as does a noun or adjective, see 189. The imperfect verb takes its time-reference from the verb كان .

Special rules apply regarding agreement in a verbal sentence with a noun subject, see 183.

**48. Pluperfect Tense.** The pluperfect tense is composed of the perfect tense of the hollow verb كَانَ (see 103) and the perfect tense of the operative verb. The compound expresses a past action or state preceding another past action or state. The pluperfect is often reinforced with the particle قَد . Both verbs agree with the subject (see 35):

... كُنْتُ (قَدْ) خَرَجْتُ مِنَ الْجَامِعَةِ عِنْدَمَا    I had left university when ...

The rationale of this compound tense is clear if we interpret this sentence as 'I was in a state of having left ...' , in which the perfect verbal part acts as a complement of the verb كان exactly as does a noun or adjective, see 189.

Special rules apply regarding agreement in a verbal sentence with a noun subject, see 183.

**49. Future Perfect Tense.** The future perfect tense, little used, is composed of the imperfect tense of the hollow verb كَانَ (see 103) and the perfect tense of the operative verb. Often the particle قَد is interposed. The compound expresses an action or state which in the future will be seen as past. Both verbs agree with the subject (see 35):

يَكُونُونَ (قَدْ) وَقَّعُوا الْعَقْدَ قَبْلَ الْعَيْدِ.

They will have signed the contract before the holiday.

The rationale of this compound tense is clear if we interpret this sentence as 'They will be in a state of having signed ...' , in which the perfect verbal part acts as a complement of the verb كان exactly as does a noun or adjective, see 189.

Special rules apply regarding agreement in a verbal sentence with a noun subject, see 183.

**50. Imperative Mood.** The imperative or command mood exists only in the second persons. See 35 for agreement. Derive the imperative from the (imperfect) jussive tense as follows.

For the affirmative imperative ('do'), drop the personal prefix تَـ\ـتُ... of the jussive tense. Then:

- If the remaining form begins with a single consonant followed by a vowel , that form is the the affirmative imperative:

  jussive تُعَلِّمْ II you learn, imperative عَلِّمْ learn

  jussive تَتَعَلَّمُوا V you teach, imperative تَعَلَّمُوا teach

  jussive تَرَ\تَرَوْا I, you see, imperative رَ\رَوْا see

- If the remaining form begins with two consonants with no intervening vowel, or begins with a doubled consonant, then a prefix is required:

- in Form IV, the imperative prefix is ...أَ (with hamzat al-qaṭʿ ):

jussive تُنْشِئُوا IV you construct, أَنْشِئُوا construct

- in Forms I and increased forms other than IV, the imperative prefix is
...أُ if the vowel following the middle radical is ُ..., and ...اِ if that
vowel is anything else. Both ...أُ and ...اِ have hamzat al-waṣl:

jussive تَكْتُبِي I, you write, imperative اُكْتُبِي write

jussive تَنْسَحِبُوا VII you withdraw, imperative اِنْسَحِبُوا withdraw

jussive تَرْمِ I, you throw, imperative اِرْمِ throw

For the negative imperative ('do not'), put the particle لَا before the unaltered
jussive:

jussive تَفْتَحْ I, you open, negative imperative لَا تَفْتَحْ do not open

For verbs with two possible jussive forms (doubled verbs in Forms I, III, IV
and VII-X, Chapter 7; sound and hollow verbs in Form IX, Chapters 5 and 9),
derive the imperatives as shown, from the two alternative jussive forms:

jussive تَسْتَمِرَّ\تَسْتَمْرِرْ X you continue,

imperative اِسْتَمِرَّ\اِسْتَمْرِرْ continue, لَا تَسْتَمِرَّ\لَا تَسْتَمْرِرْ do not continue

jussive تَحْمَرَّ\تَحْمَرِرْ IX you blush,

imperative اِحْمَرَّ\اِحْمَرِرْ blush, لَا تَحْمَرَّ\لَا تَحْمَرِرْ do not blush

In such verbs, the first (i.e, right-hand) form of each pair shown is far
commoner.

See para. 28 for forms ending in ُ... followed by hamzat al-waṣl.

These rules are valid for all classes of root.

All imperatives are active voice. The passive voice has no imperative.

For a form of imperative of the 1st and 3rd persons ('let me/him/her/it/us/them
…'), see 46, first indent.


**51. Participles: Derivation.** Participles are verbal adjectives. Arabic has
active participles (e.g. عَارِف 'knowing') and passive participles (e.g. مَعْرُوف
'known'). Like all adjectives, the participles can also be used as nouns, some of
them with a different or special meaning. For declensions, see 137, 138, 140 and
141 for roots with a sound final radical, and 117 and 145 for roots with a weak
final radical.

Active Participles, Form I. The basic measure, valid for sound, hamzated and
assimilated verbs, is فَاعِل . See 90 (doubled verbs), 105 (hollow), 117
(defective) and 128 (doubly weak) for variants. Certain participles, when used as

nouns, have a broken plural; used adjectivally all have a sound plural.

See 157 for the (rare) 'intensive' active participle of Form I, used as a noun.

<u>Active Participles, Forms IQ, II to IV and VII to X.</u> For roots with a sound final radical, derive the participle from the 2nd principal part (34) as follows:

- Substitute ...مُ for the imperfect personal prefix ...يَـ or ...يُـ .
- Remove the personal ending ... .

For Forms IIQ, V and VI, make the same changes but change also the ... before the fourth or final radical to ... .

This gives us the uninflected masculine singular form, which can be made feminine (142) and is declined regularly; see above for references.

Examples: مَوَّلَ يُمَوِّلُ II to finance: مُمَوِّلٌ financing

اتَّخَذَ يَتَّخِذُ VIII to take: مُتَّخِذٌ taking

A few of these participles have a sound plural when used as nouns; used adjectivally all have a sound plural.

For the defective and doubly weak sub-classes, see 117 and 128.

<u>Passive Participles, Form I.</u> The basic measure, valid for sound verbs, is مَفْعُولٌ .
For variants, see references given above for Form I active participles. A few participles have a sound plural when used as nouns; used adjectivally all have a sound plural.

<u>Passive Participles, Forms IQ and II to X.</u> For roots with a sound final radical, take the active participle and replace the ... before the fourth or final radical with ... .

Example: أَرْسَلَ يُرْسِلُ IV to send: مُرْسَلٌ sent

The participle can be made feminine and is declined regularly. All have a sound plural.

For the defective and doubly weak sub-classes, see references given above.

## 52. Participles: Use.

<u>Active Participles.</u> The active participle used as an adjective follows the rules of adjectival agreement; see 142. The direct object of an active participle used as a noun is expressed with the genitive, either in construct or with the preposition لـ (see 148):

Nom.:        مُؤَلِّفُ التَّقْرِيرِ    the author of the report

الْمُؤَلِّفُ لِلتَّقْرِيرِ السَّنَوِيِّ    the author of the annual report

مُؤَلِّفُو التَّقْرِيرِ الْفَنِّيِّ    the authors of the technical report

Acc:          مُقَدِّمَ هٰذِهِ الْخُطَّةِ          the proponent of this plan

Gen.:         لِمُرْسِلِ الرِّسَالَةِ          for the sender of the letter

See 196 for the active participle used in expressions of circumstance, and 192 for
the active participle replacing a tense.

<u>Passive Participles.</u> The passive participle has gender and number as follows:

- the participle of a transitive verb agrees with its noun or implied noun:

Nom.:         الشُّرُوطُ الْمُقْتَرَحَةُ          the proposed conditions

Acc.:         الزِّيَادَةَ الْمَطْلُوبَةَ          the requested increase

Gen.:         لِلْخُبَرَاءِ الْمُلْحَقِينَ بِالْقِسْمِ          for the experts attached to the department

              لِمُلْحَقِي السِّفَارَةِ          for the attachés of the embassy

- the participle of a prepositional verb, whether used as noun or adjective,
  is always masculine singular. The preposition carries the pronoun suffix
  appropriate to the verb:

Nom.:         السِّيَاسَةُ الْمُوَافَقُ عَلَيْهَا          the policy agreed on/to

Acc.:         الْمُفَاوَضَاتِ الْمَقُومَ بِهَا          the negotiations undertaken

Gen.:         لِلْمَسْمُوحِ لَهُمْ بِالدُّخُولِ          to/for those permitted to enter

See 55 for the same phenomenon with the passive tenses.

See 157 for the use of passive participles of increased forms to denote a place of
activity.


**53. Verbal Noun (الْمَصْدَرُ): Derivation.** Verbal nouns denote the activity of
the verb. They are formed only from active verbs; the passive voice has none.

<u>Form I.</u> Verbal nouns of Forms I and IQ are irregular. Examples:

كَتَبَ يَكْتُبُ   I, to write,        كِتَابَةٌ   writing, script

كَانَ يَكُونُ   I, to be,          كَوْنٌ   existence, being

تَرْجَمَ يُتَرْجِمُ   IQ, to translate, *تَرْجَمَةٌ   translation

Some have a sound plural, some a broken plural, some more than one plural.

\* This measure (فَعْلَلَةٌ) is the commonest for Form IQ verbal nouns, and some
regard it as standard.

<u>Forms II to X.</u> Verbal nouns of the increased forms have a regular pattern, see 65
(sound verbs), 72, 78, 84 (hamzated), 91 (doubled), 99 (assimilated), 106
(hollow), 118 (defective) and 129 (doubly weak). Most such verbal nouns have
a sound plural; a few have a broken plural. Some have alternative plurals with

different meanings.

**54. Verbal Noun: Use.** The direct object of a verbal noun (i.e. where the original verb is transitive, see 33) is expressed with the genitive, either in construct or with the preposition لِ (see 148):

Nom.:     فَهْمُ الْمُشْكِلَة     comprehension of the problem

          فَهْمُهُ لِلْمُشْكِلَة     his comprehension of the problem

Acc.:     تَقْدِيمَ هَذِه الْخُطَّة     the proposal of this plan

Gen.:     لِكِتَابَة الْوَثِيقَة     for the writing of the document

Where both subject and object are nouns, and are mentioned, the subject instead stands in the genitive, the object being shown by the accusative or لِ :

Nom.:فَهْمُ الْخَبِير الْمُشْكِلَة\لِلْمُشْكِلَة     the expert's comprehension of the problem

The prepositional object of a verbal noun (i.e. where the original verb is prepositional), is connected to the verbal noun by its preposition:

Nom.:     الْمُوَافَقَةُ عَلَى الاقْتِرَاح     the agreement to the proposal

Acc.:     مُوَافَقَتَهُمْ عَلَى الاقْتِرَاح     their agreement to the proposal

Gen.:     فِي بَحْثِنَا عَنِ السَّلَام     in our search for peace

**55. Table 4: Passive Voice: Derivation and Use.** This table shows the derivation of Forms I to X of the passive voice:

| Form | Principal Parts | Participle |
|------|-----------------|------------|
| I | فُعِلَ يُفْعَلُ* | مَفْعُولٌ |
| IQ | فُعْلِلَ يُفَعْلَلُ | مُفَعْلَلٌ |
| II | فُعِّلَ يُفَعَّلُ | مُفَعَّلٌ |
| IIQ | no passive | |
| III | فُوعِلَ يُفَاعَلُ | مُفَاعَلٌ |
| IV | أُفْعِلَ يُفْعَلُ | مُفْعَلٌ |
| V | تُفُعِّلَ يُتَفَعَّلُ | مُتَفَعَّلٌ |
| VI | تُفُوعِلَ يُتَفَاعَلُ | مُتَفَاعَلٌ |
| VII | أُنْفُعِلَ يُنْفَعَلُ | مُنْفَعَلٌ |
| VIII | أُفْتُعِلَ يُفْتَعَلُ ** | مُفْتَعَلٌ |

| IX | no passive | |
|---|---|---|
| X | أُسْتُفْعِلَ يُسْتَفْعَلُ | مُسْتَفْعَلٌ |

These are measures for sound verbs. Other classes have variants of them.

\* In Form I passive the vowels are invariable, as for the increased forms.

\*\* See note following Table 1a (para. 37) on Form VIII, valid also here.

A passive verb has gender and number as follows, depending on its government (see 33):

- a transitive verb agrees with its subject, (for rules, see 35):

    (كُتِبَ يُكْتَبُ I, passive 'to be written'):

    كُتِبَتْ رِسَالَتُنَا أَمْسِ.   Our letter was written yesterday.

- an intransitive verb is always masculine singular, and impersonal in meaning:

    (انْسَحَبَ يَنْسَحِبُ VII active 'to withdraw', intransitive);

    passive:       أُنْسُحِبَ.   There was a withdrawal/Somebody withdrew.

                   يُنْسَحَبُ.   There is a withdrawal/Somebody is withdrawing.

- a prepositional verb is always masculine singular, with the preposition followed by its noun or suffixed pronoun:

    (وُوفِقَ يُوَافَقُ عَلَى III passive 'to be agreed on', prepositional):

    وُوفِقَ عَلَى الْوَثِيقَةِ أَمْسِ.   The document was agreed on yesterday.

    وُوفِقَ عَلَيْهَا أَمْسِ.   It was agreed on yesterday.

See 52 for the identical phenomenon with the passive participle.

In practice, the only forms of the passive which are commonly encountered are the 3rd persons of the perfect and imperfect, and the participle, shown in Table 4 above. The passive voice has no imperative and no verbal noun.

Form IX, and the increased forms of quadriliteral verbs (of which only IIQ is shown in this book) have no passive voice.

The agent ('by ...') of a passive verb is normally unstated. However, some reporters use مِنْ قِبَلِ for 'by' with an agent, imitating Western structure:

أُكْتُشِفَ حَقْلُ النَّفْطِ الْجَدِيدُ مِنْ قِبَلِ جِيُولُوجِيِّينَ إِيرَانِيِّينَ.

The new oilfield was discovered by Iranian geologists.

# 5. Sound Verbs

**56. General.** Sound verbs (see 32) have radicals which never vary. The sound class is the only class all of whose roots have radicals all of the same kind.

**57. Table 5: Active Voice.** Examples of sound verbs in the active voice:

| Form, Root, Principal Parts | Imperative | Participle | Verb. Noun | to ... |
|---|---|---|---|---|
| I ذهب ذَهَبَ يَذْهَبُ | اذْهَبْ | ذَاهِبٌ | ذَهَابٌ | go |
| كتب كَتَبَ يَكْتُبُ | أُكْتُبْ | كَاتِبٌ | كِتَابَةٌ | write |
| نزل نَزَلَ يَنْزِلُ | انْزِلْ | نَازِلٌ | نُزُولٌ | descend |
| سمح سَمُحَ يَسْمُحُ | اسْمُحْ | سَامِحٌ | سُمْحٌ | be generous |
| سمع سَمِعَ يَسْمَعُ | اسْمَعْ | سَامِعٌ | سَمَاعٌ | hear |
| IQ ترجم تَرْجَمَ يُتَرْجِمُ | تَرْجِمْ | مُتَرْجِمٌ | تَرْجَمَةٌ | translate |
| II علم عَلَّمَ يُعَلِّمُ | عَلِّمْ | مُعَلِّمٌ | تَعْلِيمٌ | teach |
| جرب جَرَّبَ يُجَرِّبُ | جَرِّبْ | مُجَرِّبٌ | تَجْرِبَةٌ | test |
| IIQ زلزل تَزَلْزَلَ يَتَزَلْزَلُ | تَزَلْزَلْ | مُتَزَلْزِلٌ | تَزَلْزُلٌ | quake |
| III سعد سَاعَدَ يُسَاعِدُ | سَاعِدْ | مُسَاعِدٌ | مُسَاعَدَةٌ | help |
| قتل قَاتَلَ يُقَاتِلُ | قَاتِلْ | مُقَاتِلٌ | قِتَالٌ | battle with |
| IV رسل أَرْسَلَ يُرْسِلُ | أَرْسِلْ | مُرْسِلٌ | إِرْسَالٌ | send |
| V كلم تَكَلَّمَ يَتَكَلَّمُ | تَكَلَّمْ | مُتَكَلِّمٌ | تَكَلُّمٌ | speak |
| VI بدل تَبَادَلَ يَتَبَادَلُ | تَبَادَلْ | مُتَبَادِلٌ | تَبَادُلٌ | exchange |
| VII سحب انْسَحَبَ يَنْسَحِبُ | انْسَحِبْ | مُنْسَحِبٌ | انْسِحَابٌ | withdraw |
| VIII فتح افْتَتَحَ يَفْتَتِحُ | افْتَتِحْ | مُفْتَتِحٌ | افْتِتَاحٌ | inaugurate |
| دحر ادَّحَرَ يَدَّحِرُ | ادَّحِرْ | مُدَّحِرٌ | ادِّحَارٌ | be repelled |
| طلع اطَّلَعَ يَطَّلِعُ | اطَّلِعْ | مُطَّلِعٌ | اطِّلَاعٌ | realise |
| ظلم اظَّلَمَ يَظَّلِمُ | اظَّلِمْ | مُظَّلِمٌ | اظِّلَامٌ | be wronged |
| صنع اصْطَنَعَ يَصْطَنِعُ | اصْطَنِعْ | مُصْطَنِعٌ | اصْطِنَاعٌ | manufacture |
| ضرب اضْطَرَبَ يَضْطَرِبُ | اضْطَرِبْ | مُضْطَرِبٌ | اضْطِرَابٌ | clash |

| | | | | |
|---|---|---|---|---|
| زحم يَزْدَحِمُ اِزْدَحَمَ | اِزْدَحِمْ | مُزْدَحِمٌ | اِزْدِحَامٌ | swarm |
| IX حمر اِحْمَرَّ يَحْمَرُّ اِحْمَرَّ\اِحْمَارَّ | اِحْمَرَّ\اِحْمَارَّ | مُحْمَرٌّ | اِحْمِرَارٌ | turn red |
| X عمل اِسْتَعْمَلَ يَسْتَعْمِلُ اِسْتَعْمَلَ | اِسْتَعْمِلْ | مُسْتَعْمِلٌ | اِسْتِعْمَالٌ | use |

Note:

- In Form I principal parts, the vowel following the middle radical varies.
- Form IX resembles the doubled verbs, see 86.
- For the verbal nouns, Form I and Form IQ are irregular. Forms II and III have two measures, depending on the root.
- All quadriliteral verbs conjugate like sound verbs.

See 37 for Forms I to X.

**58. Table 6: Passive Voice.** Examples of sound verbs in the passive voice:

| Form, Root, Principal Parts | | Participle | to be … |
|---|---|---|---|
| I | كتب | كُتِبَ يُكْتَبُ | مَكْتُوبٌ | written |
| IQ | برهن | بُرْهِنَ يُبَرْهَنُ عَلَى | مُبَرْهَنٌ | proved |
| II | حضر | حُضِّرَ يُحَضَّرُ | مُحَضَّرٌ | prepared |
| III | عمل | عُومِلَ يُعَامَلُ | مُعَامَلٌ | treated |
| IV | خبر | أُخْبِرَ يُخْبَرُ | مُخْبَرٌ | informed |
| V | سلم | تُسُلِّمَ يُتَسَلَّمُ | مُتَسَلَّمٌ | received |
| VI | بدل | تُبُودِلَ يُتَبَادَلُ | مُتَبَادَلٌ | exchanged |
| VII | سحب | أُنْسُحِبَ يُنْسَحَبُ | مُنْسَحَبٌ | withdrawn |
| VIII | عبر | أُعْتُبِرَ يُعْتَبَرُ | مُعْتَبَرٌ | considered |
| | دحر | أُدْحِرَ يُدْحَرُ | مُدْحَرٌ | repelled |
| | طرح | أُطْرِحَ يُطْرَحُ | مُطْرَحٌ | discarded |
| | ظلم | أُظْلِمَ يُظْلَمُ | مُظْلَمٌ | wronged |
| | صحب | أُصْطُحِبَ يُصْطَحَبُ | مُصْطَحَبٌ | escorted |
| | ضهد | أُضْطُهِدَ يُضْطَهَدُ | مُضْطَهَدٌ | persecuted |
| | زرع | أُزْدُرِعَ يُزْدَرَعُ | مُزْدَرَعٌ | sown |

| X | نكر | أُسْتُنْكِرَ يُسْتَنْكَرُ | | مُسْتَنْكَرٌ | rejected |

See 37 for Forms I to X. See 36 and 55 for the passive.

The vowelling of the passive (including Form I) is completely regular. The pattern for sound verbs can be expressed thus (in the 3rd person masc. sing.):

|  | Perfect tense | | | | Imperfect tense | | | |
|---|---|---|---|---|---|---|---|---|
| 2 syllables + pers. ending | u* | i |  | a | u | a | | u |
| 3 syllables + pers. ending | u | u* | i | a | u | a* | a | u |
| 4 syllables + pers. ending | - | | | u | a | a* | a | u |

\* ū for u, ā for a in these positions in Forms III and VI.

**59. Perfect (Indicative) Tense.** The perfect stem of sound verbs is derived by removing the final ´... from the first principal part:

1st principal part, active كَتَبَ I, perfect active stem كَتَبْ...

1st principal part, passive كُتِبَ I, perfect passive stem كُتِبْ...

Add the perfect personal endings (see 39) to produce the perfect tense. Examples:

كَتَبَ يَكْتُبُ I, to write; perfect active tense:

| كَتَبْنَا | | كَتَبْتُ |
|---|---|---|
| كَتَبْتُمْ | كَتَبْتُمَا | كَتَبْتَ |
| كَتَبْتُنَّ | كَتَبْتُمَا | كَتَبْتِ |
| كَتَبُوا | كَتَبَا | كَتَبَ |
| كَتَبْنَ | كَتَبَتَا | كَتَبَتْ |

عُلِّمَ يُعَلَّمُ II to be taught; perfect passive tense:

| عُلِّمْنَا | | عُلِّمْتُ |
|---|---|---|
| عُلِّمْتُمْ | عُلِّمْتُمَا | عُلِّمْتَ |
| عُلِّمْتُنَّ | عُلِّمْتُمَا | عُلِّمْتِ |
| عُلِّمُوا | عُلِّمَا | عُلِّمَ |
| عُلِّمْنَ | عُلِّمَتَا | عُلِّمَتْ |

See 39 also for the modification of some of these personal endings before a direct object pronoun suffix and before hamzat al-waṣl.

**60. Imperfect (Indicative) Tense.** The imperfect stem of sound verbs is derived by removing the initial يَ\يُ and the final ُ... from the second principal part:

2nd principal part, active يَكْتُبُ I, imperfect active stem ...كْتُبـ...

2nd principal part, passive يُكْتَبُ I, imperfect passive stem ...كْتَبـ...

Add the imperfect personal prefixes and endings (see 41) to produce the imperfect (indicative) tense. Examples:

Root فتح : افْتَتَحَ يَفْتَتِحُ VIII to inaugurate; imperfect active tense:

| | | | |
|---|---|---|---|
| | أَفْتَتِحُ | | نَفْتَتِحُ |
| تَفْتَتِحُ | تَفْتَتِحَانِ | تَفْتَتِحُونَ | |
| تَفْتَتِحِينَ | تَفْتَتِحَانِ | تَفْتَتِحْنَ | |
| يَفْتَتِحُ | يَفْتَتِحَانِ | يَفْتَتِحُونَ | |
| تَفْتَتِحُ | تَفْتَتِحَانِ | يَفْتَتِحْنَ | |

Root خبر : أُخْبِرَ يُخْبَرُ ب IV to be informed of; imperfect passive tense:

| | | | |
|---|---|---|---|
| | أُخْبَرُ | | نُخْبَرُ |
| تُخْبَرُ | تُخْبَرَانِ | تُخْبَرُونَ | |
| تُخْبَرِينَ | تُخْبَرَانِ | تُخْبَرْنَ | |
| يُخْبَرُ | يُخْبَرَانِ | يُخْبَرُونَ | |
| تُخْبَرُ | تُخْبَرَانِ | يُخْبَرْنَ | |

## 61. (Imperfect) Subjunctive Tense. See 43. Examples:

imperfect تَذْهَبِينَ I, you go, subjunctive تَذْهَبِي

imperfect يَذْهَبُونَ I, they go, subjunctive يَذْهَبُوا

## 62. (Imperfect) Jussive Tense. See 45. Examples:

subjunctive تَتَكَلَّمَ V you speak, jussive تَتَكَلَّمْ

subjunctive and jussive تَتَكَلَّمْنَ V you speak

Form IX has two jussive tenses, derived as for doubled verbs, see 88:

subjunctive يَصْفَرَّ IX it turns yellow, jussive يَصْفَرِرْ\يَصْفَرَّ

The jussive resembling the subjunctive is much commoner.

## 63. Imperative Mood. See 50. In the sound class, the affirmative imperative has no prefix in Forms II, III, V and VI:

jussive تُكَسَّرْ II you break, كَسِّرْ break, لاَ تُكَسِّرْ do not break

Forms I, IV and VII to X have the appropriate prefix in the affirmative:

jussive تَشْرَبُوا I, you drink, اشْرَبُوا drink, لاَ تَشْرَبُوا do not drink

jussive تَضْرِبْنَ I, you beat, أَضْرِبْنَ beat, لاَ تَضْرِبْنَ do not beat

jussive تُضْرِبُوا IV you (go on) strike, أَضْرِبُوا strike, لاَ تُضْرِبُوا do not strike

jussive تَنْسَحِبْ VII you withdraw,

انْسَحِبْ withdraw, لاَ تَنْسَحِبْ do not withdraw

Form IX imperative is derived from each jussive form, with the appropriate prefix ...ا. The form resembling the subjunctive is much commoner:

jussive تَحْمَرَّ\تَحْمَرِرْ IX you blush,

لاَ تَحْمَرَّ\لاَ تَحْمَرِرْ blush, احْمَرَّ\احْمَرِرْ do not blush

## 64. Participles.
See 51 and 52 for derivation and uses, and 137, 138, 140 and 141 for declension.

Many masculine active participles of Form I sound verbs, when used as animate nouns, have a broken plural:

كُتَّابٌ كَاتِبٌ I, to write, كَتَبَ يَكْتُبُ clerk, pl. كُتَّابٌ

طُلَّابٌ طَالِبٌ I, to seek, طَلَبَ يَطْلُبُ student, pl. طُلَّابٌ

A much smaller number of masculine active and passive participles of Form I of sound verbs used as inanimate nouns also have a broken plural:

عَوَامِلُ * عَامِلٌ I, to do: عَمِلَ يَعْمَلُ factor, pl. * عَوَامِلُ

مَكَاتِيبُ * مَكْتُوبٌ I, to write: كَتَبَ يَكْتُبُ letter, pl. * مَكَاتِيبُ

* Diptote: see 144.

But most other participles have a sound plural:

كَاتِبَاتٌ I, to write: active كَاتِبَةٌ clerk (f.), pl. كَاتِبَاتٌ كَتَبَ يَكْتُبُ

مَعْرُوفُونَ I, to know: passive مَعْرُوفٌ famous, pl. مَعْرُوفُونَ عَرَفَ يَعْرِفُ

مُفَتِّشُونَ II to inspect: active مُفَتِّشٌ inspector, pl. مُفَتِّشُونَ فَتَّشَ يُفَتِّشُ

تَظَاهَرَ يَتَظَاهَرُ VI to demonstrate (politically):

active مُتَظَاهِرٌ demonstrator, pl. مُتَظَاهِرُونَ

## 65. Verbal Nouns.
Form I and IQ verbal nouns are irregular; see 37 and 53. The verbal nouns of Forms II to X have the measures:

| II | | IIQ | III |
|---|---|---|---|
| تَفْعِيلٌ\تَفْعِلَةٌ | | تَفَعْلُلٌ | مُفَاعَلَةٌ\فِعَالٌ |

| | | | | | |
|---|---|---|---|---|---|
| IV | إِفْعَالٌ | V | تَفَعُّلٌ | VI | تَفَاعُلٌ |
| VII | اِنْفِعَالٌ | VIII | اِفْتِعَالٌ | IX | اِفْعِلَالٌ |
| | | X | اِسْتِفْعَالٌ | | |

See 137, 138, 140 and 141 for declension.

Most verbal nouns of sound verbs have a sound plural. A few have a broken plural, either instead or in addition:

عَلِمَ يَعْلَمُ I, to know: عِلْمٌ knowledge, science, pl. عُلُومٌ

فَصَّلَ يُفَصِّلُ II to set forth in detail: تَفْصِيلٌ detail, pl. * تَفَاصِيلُ\تَفْصِيلَاتٌ

* Diptote, see 144.

# 6. Hamzated Verbs

**66. General.** Hamzated verbs (see 32) are verbs with ء as one radical and two sound radicals. With few exceptions, they conjugate like sound verbs, if we substitute ء for one of the sound radicals. See 19 for the writing of ء .

The hamzated class has no verbs in Form IX; further, there are no verbs with initial- or middle-radical ء in Form VII.

Roots with initial-radical ء and identical sound middle and final radicals are also most conveniently included here. Roots with a mixture of ء, one sound and one weak radical are examined in other verb chapters, see 9.

**67. Table 7: Verbs with Initial-radical ء , Active Voice.** Examples of verbs with initial-radical ء, in the active voice:

| Form, Root, Principal Parts | Imperative | Participle | Vb. Noun | to … |
|---|---|---|---|---|
| أمل I  أَمَلَ يَأْمُلُ | أُومُلْ * | آمِلٌ | أَمَلٌ | hope |
| أسر  أَسَرَ يَأْسِرُ | ايسِرْ * | آسِرٌ | أَسْرٌ | capture |
| أمن  أَمِنَ يَأْمَنُ | ايمَنْ * | آمِنٌ | أَمْنٌ | be safe |
| أكل  أَكَلَ يَأْكُلُ | كُلْ * | آكِلٌ | أَكْلٌ | eat |
| أكد II  أَكَّدَ يُؤَكِّدُ | أَكِّدْ | مُؤَكِّدٌ | تَأْكِيدٌ | confirm |
| أم  أَمَّمَ يُؤَمِّمُ | أَمِّمْ | مُؤَمِّمٌ | تَأْمِيمٌ | nationalise |
| أمر III  آمَرَ يُؤَامِرُ | آمِرْ | مؤَامِرٌ | مؤَامَرَةٌ | consult |
| أمن IV  آمَنَ يُؤْمِنُ | آمِنْ | مُؤْمِنٌ | إيمَانٌ | believe |
| أكد V  تَأَكَّدَ يَتَأَكَّدُ | تَأَكَّدْ | مُتَأَكِّدٌ | تَأَكُّدٌ | be sure |
| أسّ  تَأَسَّسَ يَتَأَسَّسُ | تَأَسَّسْ | مُتَأَسِّسٌ | تَأَسُّسٌ | be established |
| ألف VI  تَآلَفَ يَتَآلَفُ | تَآلَفْ | مُتَآلِفٌ | تَآلُفٌ | be compatible |
| أخذ VIII (i)  اتَّخَذَ * يَتَّخِذُ * | اتَّخِذْ * | مُتَّخِذٌ * | اتِّخَاذٌ * | take |
| أمر (ii)  ائْتَمَرَ يَأْتَمِرُ | ائْتَمِرْ | مُؤْتَمِرٌ | ائْتِمَارٌ | deliberate |
| أمر (iii)  ايتَمَرَ * يَأْتَمِرُ | ايتَمِرْ * | مُؤْتَمِرٌ | ايتِمَارٌ * | deliberate |
| أجر X  اسْتَأْجَرَ يَسْتَأْجِرُ | اسْتَأْجِرْ | مُسْتَأْجِرٌ | اسْتِئْجَارٌ | rent |

Note: Only the forms marked * differ from those of the sound verbs, if we substitute ﻋ for the sound initial radical. In particular:

- For the imperative of Form I, see 70 below.
- Form VIII has three patterns:
  - pattern (i) applies only to the root أَخَذ .
  - patterns (ii) (regular) and (iii) apply to all roots except أَخَذ.
  
  The perfect measure beginning ...اِ is used only to begin the sentence.

See 37 for Forms I to X.

## 68. Table 8: Verbs with Initial-radical ﻋ, Passive Voice.

Examples of verbs with initial-radical ﻋ, in the passive voice (not all increased forms·are found):

| Form, Root, Principal Parts | | | Participle | to be ... |
|---|---|---|---|---|
| I | أسر | أُسِرَ يُؤْسَرُ | مَأْسُورٌ | captured |
| II | أكد | أُكِّدَ يُؤَكَّدُ | مُؤَكَّدٌ | confirmed |
| III | أخذ | أُوخِذَ يُوَاخَذُ | مُوَاخَذٌ | blamed |
| IV | أمن | أُومِنَ * يُؤْمَنُ | مُؤْمَنٌ | believed |
| V | أثر | تُؤُثِّرَ يُتَأَثَّرُ | مُتَأَثَّرٌ | emulated |
| VIII | أخذ | اُتُّخِذَ * يُتَّخَذُ * | مُتَّخَذٌ * | taken |
| X | أجر | اُسْتُؤْجِرَ يُسْتَأْجَرُ | مُسْتَأْجَرٌ | rented |

Note:
- Only the forms marked * differ from those of the sound verbs, if we substitute ﻋ for the initial sound radical.
- The theoretical initial combination 'u'- becomes ...أُو 'ū- (Forms III, IV).
- The only common passive of Form VIII is اُتُّخِذَ يُتَّخَذُ , see 67 above.

The diagram showing the vowels of the passive of sound verbs (58) is valid also for initial-radical ﻋ verbs.

See 37 for Forms I to X. See 36 and 55 for the passive

## 69. Verbs with Initial-radical ﻋ: Tenses. Stems are formed on the sound pattern (59 and 60). Prefixes and personal endings are shown in 39, 41, 43 and 45. Examples of tenses:

Perfect tense:

Root أمر ; أَمَرَ يَأْمُرُ I, to order; perfect active tense:

| | | |
|---|---|---|
| أَمَرْتُ | | أَمَرْنَا |
| أَمَرْتَ | أَمَرْتُمَا | أَمَرْتُمْ |
| أَمَرْتِ | أَمَرْتُمَا | أَمَرْتُنَّ |
| أَمَرَ | أَمَرَا | أَمَرُوا |
| أَمَرَتْ | أَمَرَتَا | أَمَرْنَ |

Root أخذ ; أُوخِذَ يُوَاخَذُ III to be blamed; perfect passive tense:

| | | |
|---|---|---|
| أُوخِذْتُ | | أُوخِذْنَا |
| أُوخِذْتَ | أُوخِذْتُمَا | أُوخِذْتُمْ |
| أُوخِذْتِ | أُوخِذْتُمَا | أُوخِذْتُنَّ |
| أُوخِذَ | أُوخِذَا | أُوخِذُوا |
| أُوخِذَتْ | أُوخِذَتَا | أُوخِذْنَ |

Imperfect (Indicative) tense:

Root أكل ; أَكَلَ يَأْكُلُ I, to eat; imperfect active tense:

| | | |
|---|---|---|
| آكُلُ | | نَأْكُلُ |
| تَأْكُلُ | تَأْكُلَانِ | يَأْكُلُونَ |
| تَأْكُلِينَ | تَأْكُلَانِ | تَأْكُلْنَ |
| يَأْكُلُ | يَأْكُلَانِ | يَأْكُلُونَ |
| تَأْكُلُ | تَأْكُلَانِ | يَأْكُلْنَ |

...آ for (أَأ) in the 1st person singular. See 19.

Root أخذ ; أُوخِذَ يُوَاخَذُ III to be blamed; imperfect passive tense:

| | | |
|---|---|---|
| أُوَاخَذُ | | نُوَاخَذُ |
| تُوَاخَذُ | تُوَاخَذَانِ | تُوَاخَذُونَ |
| تُوَاخَذِينَ | تُوَاخَذَانِ | تُوَاخَذْنَ |
| يُوَاخَذُ | يُوَاخَذَانِ | يُوَاخَذُونَ |
| تُوَاخَذُ | تُوَاخَذَانِ | يُوَاخَذْنَ |

(Imperfect) Subjunctive Tense:

imperfect نَتَأَكَّدُ V we are sure, subjunctive نَتَأَكَّدَ

imperfect يُوَاخَذُونَ III they are blamed,  subjunctive يُوَاخَذُوا

(Imperfect) Jussive Tense:

subjunctive يَأْخُذَ I, he takes, jussive يَأْخُذْ

### 70. Verbs with Initial-radical ء: Imperative. See 50. In the affirmative imperative of Form I, initial-radical ء is dropped; two patterns exist:

- In three important roots the initial radical and its syllable are dropped:

Roots أخذ , خُذْ I, take; أكل , كُلْ I, eat; أمر , مُرْ I, order

- In other roots the first syllable is either أُو... or اِـ... as appropriate:

Root أمل , أُومُلْ I, hope;   Root أسر , اِيسِرْ I, capture

All else is derived regularly:

jussive تَأْخُذْ I, you take, لاَ تَأْخُذْ do not take,

jussive تَأْمُلُوا I, you hope, لاَ تَأْمُلُوا do not hope

jussive تَتَّخِذِي VIII you take, اتَّخِذِي take, لاَ تَتَّخِذِي do not take

### 71. Verbs with Initial-radical ء: Participles. See 51:

أَكَلَ يَأْكُلُ I, to eat, active آكِلٌ eating, passive مَأْكُولٌ eaten

أَخَّرَ يُؤَخِّرُ II to delay, active مُؤَخِّرٌ delaying, passive مُؤَخَّرٌ delayed

The plurals are sound. See 137, 138, 140 and 141 for declension.

### 72. Verbs with Initial-radical ء: Verbal Nouns. Verbal nouns of all initial-radical ء verbs except those of the pattern of ايتَمَرَ VIII (see 67 above) are constructed on the sound pattern (65). Most have a sound plural; some (especially in Form I) have a broken plural. The verbal nouns have only one pattern in each of Forms II and III, i.e. تَفعِيلٌ and مُفَاعَلَةٌ respectively:

أَمَرَ يَأْمُرُ I, to order: أَمْرٌ order/affair, pl. * أَوَامِرُ orders, أُمُورٌ affairs

أَكَّدَ يُؤَكِّدُ II to confirm: تَأْكِيدٌ confirmation

آمَرَ يُؤَامِرُ III to consult: مُؤَامَرَةٌ consultation

See 137, 138, 140 and 141 for declension.

* Diptote, see 144

### 73. Table 9: Verbs with Middle-radical ء, Active Voice. Examples of verbs with middle-radical ء, in the active voice:

| Form, Root, Principal Parts | | Imperative | Participle | Vb. Noun | to ... |
|---|---|---|---|---|---|
| I سَأَل | سَأَلَ يَسْأَلُ | اِسْأَلْ\سَلْ* | سَائِلٌ | سُؤَالٌ\مَسْأَلَةٌ | enquire |
| بَأَس | بَئِسَ يَبْأَسُ | اِبْأَسْ | بَائِسٌ | بُؤْسٌ | be miserable |
| بَأَس | بَؤُسَ يَبْؤُسُ | اُبْؤُسْ | بَائِسٌ | بَأْسٌ | be brave |
| II رَأَس | رَأَّسَ يُرَئِّسُ | رَئِّسْ | مُرَئِّسٌ | تَرْئِيسٌ | appoint |
| III سَأَل | سَاءَلَ يُسَائِلُ | سَائِلْ | مُسَائِلٌ | مُسَاءَلَةٌ | question |
| IV سَأَم | أَسْأَمَ يُسْئِمُ | أَسْئِمْ | مُسْئِمٌ | إِسْآمٌ | weary |
| V رَأَس | تَرَأَّسَ يَتَرَأَّسُ | تَرَأَّسْ | مُتَرَئِّسٌ | تَرَأُّسٌ | head |
| VI فَأَل | تَفَاءَلَ يَتَفَاءَلُ | تَفَاءَلْ | مُتَفَائِلٌ | تَفَاؤُلٌ | be optimistic |
| VIII لَأَم | اِلْتَأَمَ يَلْتَئِمُ | اِلْتَئِمْ | مُلْتَئِمٌ | اِلْتِئَامٌ | be convened |
| X رَأَف | اِسْتَرْأَفَ يَسْتَرْئِفُ | اِسْتَرْئِفْ | مُسْتَرْئِفٌ | اِسْتِرْآفٌ | ask for mercy |

Note: Verbal nouns of Forms II and III have only one possible measure each, and one verb ( سَأَلَ يَسْأَلُ I) has an alternative jussive and imperative (the latter marked *); see 75 and 76 below. Otherwise the verbs are of the sound pattern. See 37 for Forms I to X.

**74. Table 10: Verbs with Middle-radical ء, Passive Voice.** No common verbs with middle-radical ء exist in Forms IV to X in the passive. Examples of verbs with middle-radical ء, in the passive voice:

| Form, Root, Principal Parts | | Participle | to be ... |
|---|---|---|---|
| I سَأَل | سُئِل يُسْأَلُ | مَسْؤُولٌ\مَسْئُولٌ | asked |
| II رَأَس | رُئِّسَ يُرَأَّسُ | مُرَأَّسٌ | appointed as head |
| III سَأَل | سُوئِلَ يُسَاءَلُ | مُسَاءَلٌ | questioned |

The diagram showing the vowels of the passive of sound verbs (58) is valid also for middle-radical ء verbs, except that no common middle-radical ء verbs have four syllables + personal ending.

See 37 for Forms I to III. See 36 and 55 for the passive.

**75. Verbs with Middle-radical ء: Tenses.** The perfect stem and tense

follow the sound pattern, see 39 and 59. The imperfect stem and tenses follow
the sound pattern, see 41, 43, 45 and 60, except for the alternative jussive and
imperative of يَسْأَلُ سَأَلَ I (shown below). Examples:

<u>Perfect tense:</u>
Root فأل ; تَفَاءَلَ يَتَفَاءَلُ VI to be optimistic; perfect active tense:

| | | |
|---|---|---|
| تَفَاءَلْتُ | | تَفَاءَلْنَا |
| تَفَاءَلْتَ | تَفَاءَلْتُمَا | تَفَاءَلْتُمْ |
| تَفَاءَلْتِ | تَفَاءَلْتُمَا | تَفَاءَلْتُنَّ |
| تَفَاءَلَ | تَفَاءَلَا | تَفَاءَلُوا |
| تَفَاءَلَتْ | تَفَاءَلَتَا | تَفَاءَلْنَ |

Root رأس ; رُئِّسَ يُرَأَّسُ II to be appointed head; perfect passive tense:

| | | |
|---|---|---|
| رُئِّسْتُ | | رُئِّسْنَا |
| رُئِّسْتَ | رُئِّسْتُمَا | رُئِّسْتُمْ |
| رُئِّسْتِ | رُئِّسْتُمَا | رُئِّسْتُنَّ |
| رُئِّسَ | رُئِّسَا | رُئِّسُوا |
| رُئِّسَتْ | رُئِّسَتَا | رُئِّسْنَ |

<u>Imperfect (Indicative) Tense:</u>
Root لأم ; الْتَأَمَ يَلْتَئِمُ VIII to be convened; imperfect active tense:

| | | |
|---|---|---|
| أَلْتَئِمُ | | نَلْتَئِمُ |
| تَلْتَئِمُ | تَلْتَئِمَانِ | تَلْتَئِمُونَ |
| تَلْتَئِمِينَ | تَلْتَئِمَانِ | تَلْتَئِمْنَ |
| يَلْتَئِمُ | يَلْتَئِمَانِ | يَلْتَئِمُونَ |
| تَلْتَئِمُ | تَلْتَئِمَانِ | يَلْتَئِمْنَ |

Root سأل ; سُئِلَ يُسْأَلُ I, to be asked; imperfect passive tense:

| | | |
|---|---|---|
| أُسْأَلُ | | نُسْأَلُ |
| تُسْأَلُ | تُسْأَلَانِ | تُسْأَلُونَ |
| تُسْأَلِينَ | تُسْأَلَانِ | تُسْأَلْنَ |
| يُسْأَلُ | يُسْأَلَانِ | يُسْأَلُونَ |
| تُسْأَلُ | تُسْأَلَانِ | يُسْأَلْنَ |

(Imperfect) Subjunctive Tense:

imperfect تَتَفَاءَلُونَ VI you are optimistic, subjunctive تَتَفَاءَلُوا

(Imperfect) Jussive Tense:

subjunctive يَسْأَلَ I, he asks/enquires, jussive يَسْأَلْ

This verb ( سَأَلَ يَسْأَلُ I, to ask/enquire) also has an equally common irregular jussive in which the middle radical is dropped: أَسَلْ، تَسَلْ، تَسَلِي (etc.).

**76. Verbs with Middle-radical ء: Imperative.** See 50. Examples:

jussive تُسَائِلْ III you question, سَائِلْ question, لاَ تُسَائِلْ do not question

jussive تَسْأَلْ I, you ask/enquire, اِسْأَلْ ask, لاَ تَسْأَلْ do not ask

jussive تَسَلْ I, you ask, سَلْ ask, لاَ تَسَلْ do not ask

(from the irregular jussive, see 75 above. No imperative prefix.)

تَسْتَرْئِفْ X you beg mercy, اِسْتَرْئِفْ beg mercy, لاَ تَسْتَرْئِفْ do not beg mercy

**77. Verbs with Middle-radical ء: Participles.** See 51. Examples:

سَأَلَ يَسْأَلُ I, to ask/enquire,

active سَائِلٌ enquiring, passive مَسْؤُولٌ\مَسْئُولٌ enquired; responsible

رَأَّسَ يُرَئِّسُ II to appoint as head,

active مُرَئِّسٌ appointing as head, passive مُرَأَّسٌ appointed as head

The plurals are sound. See 137, 138, 140 and 141 for declension.

**78. Verbs with Middle-radical ء: Verbal Nouns.** The sound pattern (65) is valid. Most of these verbal nouns have a sound plural; some (especially in Form I) have a broken plural. There is only one measure in each of Forms II and III, i.e. تَفْعِيلٌ and مُفَاعَلَةٌ respectively:

سَأَلَ يَسْأَلُ I, to enquire:

سُؤَالٌ question, pl. أَسْئِلَةٌ; also مَسْأَلَةٌ matter, pl. * مَسَائِلُ

رَأَّسَ يُرَئِّسُ II to appoint as head: تَرْئِيسٌ appointment as head

سَاءَلَ يُسَائِلُ III to question: مُسَاءَلَةٌ questioning

See 137, 138, 140 and 141 for declension.

* Diptote, see 144.

**79. Table 11: Verbs with Final-radical ء: Active Voice.** Examples of verbs with final-radical ء, in the active voice:

| Form, Root, Principal Parts | | Imperative | Participle | Vb. Noun | to … |
|---|---|---|---|---|---|
| I | قرأ   قَرَأَ يَقْرَأُ | اقْرَأْ | قَارِئٌ | قِرَاءَةٌ | read |
| II | هنأ   هَنَّأَ يُهَنِّئُ | هَنِّئْ | مُهَنِّئٌ | تَهْنِئَةٌ | congratulate |
| III | كفأ   كَافَأَ يُكَافِئُ | كَافِئْ | مُكَافِئٌ | مُكَافَأَةٌ | repay |
| IV | نشأ   أَنْشَأَ يُنْشِئُ | أَنْشِئْ | مُنْشِئٌ | إِنْشَاءٌ | create |
| V | نبأ   تَنَبَّأَ يَتَنَبَّأُ ب | تَنَبَّأْ | مُتَنَبِّئٌ | تَنَبُّؤٌ | forecast |
| VI | كفأ   تَكَافَأَ يَتَكَافَأُ | تَكَافَأْ | مُتَكَافِئٌ | تَكَافُؤٌ | equal |
| VII | كفأ   انْكَفَأَ يَنْكَفِئُ | انْكَفِئْ | مُنْكَفِئٌ | انْكِفَاءٌ | be overturned |
| VIII | بدأ   ابْتَدَأَ يَبْتَدِئُ ب | ابْتَدِئْ | مُبْتَدِئٌ | ابْتِدَاءٌ | begin |
| X | قرأ   اسْتَقْرَأَ يَسْتَقْرِئُ | اسْتَقْرِئْ | مُسْتَقْرِئٌ | اسْتِقْرَاءٌ | investigate |

Note: The patterns are identical to those of the sound verbs, if we substitute ء for the final radical, except that:

- Form I has only one vowel pattern in all common verbs,
- the verbal nouns of Forms II and III have only one possible pattern each.

See 37 for Forms I to X.

**80. Table 12: Verbs with Final-radical ء: Passive Voice.** Examples of verbs with final-radical ء, in the passive voice:

| Form, Root, Principal Parts | | Participle | to be… |
|---|---|---|---|
| I | بدأ   بُدِئَ يُبْدَأُ | مَبْدُوءٌ | begun |
| II | هنأ   هُنِّئَ يُهَنَّأُ | مُهَنَّأٌ | congratulated |
| III | كفأ   كُوفِئَ يُكَافَأُ | مُكَافَأٌ | repaid |
| IV | نشأ   أُنْشِئَ يُنْشَأُ | مُنْشَأٌ | created |
| V | نبأ   تُنُبِّئَ يُتَنَبَّأُ ب | مُتَنَبَّأٌ | forecast |
| VIII | بدأ   أُبْتُدِئَ يُبْتَدَأُ ب | مُبْتَدَأٌ | begun |
| X | نبأ   أُسْتُنْبِئَ يُسْتَنْبَأُ | مُسْتَنْبَأٌ | asked about |

No common passives exist in Forms VI and VII.

The diagram showing the vowels of the passive of sound verbs (58) is valid also for final-radical ء verbs.

See 37 for Forms I to X. See 36 and 55 for the passive.


**81. Verbs with Final-radical ء: Tenses.** The stems are sound. See 39, 41, 43, 45, 59 and 60. Note the writing of final-radical ء before a personal ending beginning with a long vowel; it can present difficulty (see 19):

| | |
|---|---|
| ...a'ā, ...a'āni | ...آن ، ...آ... |
| ...a'ī, ...a'īna: | ...ـَئِين\...ـَين ، ...ـَئِي\...ـَي... |
| ...a'ū, ...a'ūna: | ...ـَؤُون\...ـَون ، ...ـَؤُوا\...ـَأوا... |
| ...i'ā, ...i'āni: | ...ـِئَان ، ...ـِئَا... |
| ...i'ī, ...i'īna: | ...ـِئِين ، ...ـِئِي... |
| ...i'ū, ...i'ūna: | ...ـِئُون ، ...ـِئُوا... |

Alternative Arabic spellings are shown above with \ .

Examples of final-radical ء verbs:

Perfect tense:

Root بدأ; ٱبْتَدَأَ يَبْتَدِئُ VIII to begin; perfect active tense:

| | | |
|---|---|---|
| ٱبْتَدَأْنَا | | ٱبْتَدَأْتُ |
| ٱبْتَدَأْتُمْ | ٱبْتَدَأْتُمَا | ٱبْتَدَأْتَ |
| ٱبْتَدَأْتُنَّ | ٱبْتَدَأْتُمَا | ٱبْتَدَأْتِ |
| ٱبْتَدَأُوا\ٱبْتَدَؤُوا | ٱبْتَدَآ | ٱبْتَدَأَ |
| ٱبْتَدَأْنَ | ٱبْتَدَأَتَا | ٱبْتَدَأَتْ |

Root نبأ ; أَنْبَأَ يُنْبَأُ IV to be informed; perfect passive tense:

| | | |
|---|---|---|
| أُنْبِئْنَا | | أُنْبِئْتُ |
| أُنْبِئْتُمْ | أُنْبِئْتُمَا | أُنْبِئْتَ |
| أُنْبِئْتُنَّ | أُنْبِئْتُمَا | أُنْبِئْتِ |
| أُنْبِئُوا | أُنْبِئَا | أُنْبِئَ |
| أُنْبِئْنَ | أُنْبِئَتَا | أُنْبِئَتْ |

<u>Imperfect (Indicative) Tense:</u>

Root نشأ ; أَنْشَأَ يُنْشِئُ IV to construct; imperfect active tense:

| | | |
|---|---|---|
| نُنْشِئُ | | أُنْشِئُ |
| تُنْشِئُونَ | تُنْشِئَانِ | تُنْشِئُ |
| تُنْشِئْنَ | تُنْشِئَانِ | تُنْشِئِينَ |
| يُنْشِئُونَ | يُنْشِئَانِ | يُنْشِئُ |
| يُنْشِئْنَ | تُنْشِئَانِ | تُنْشِئُ |

Root هنأ ; هُنِّئَ يُهَنَّأُ II to be congratulated; imperfect passive tense:

| | | |
|---|---|---|
| نُهَنَّأُ | | أُهَنَّأُ |
| تُهَنَّأُونَ\تُهَنَّوْنَ | تُهَنَّآنِ | تُهَنَّأُ |
| تُهَنَّأْنَ | تُهَنَّآنِ | تُهَنَّئِينَ\تُهَنَّايِنَ |
| يُهَنَّأُونَ\يُهَنَّوْنَ | يُهَنَّآنِ | يُهَنَّأُ |
| يُهَنَّأْنَ | تُهَنَّآنِ | يُهَنَّأُ |

<u>(Imperfect) Subjunctive Tense:</u>

imperfect يَسْتَقْرِئُ X he investigates, subjunctive يَسْتَقْرِئَ

<u>(Imperfect) Jussive Tense:</u>

subjunctive يَبْتَدِئَ VIII he begins, jussive يَبْتَدِئْ

**82. Verbs with Final-radical ء: Imperative.** See 50. Examples:

jussive تَقْرَأْ I, you read, اقْرَأْ read, لاَ تَقْرَأْ do not read

jussive تُنَبِّئ II you inform, نَبِّئِي inform, لاَ تُنَبِّئِي do not inform

**83. Verbs with Final-radical ء: Participles.** See 51. Examples:

قَرَأَ يَقْرَأُ I, to read: active قَارِئٌ reading, passive مَقْرُوءٌ read

كَافَأَ يُكَافِئُ III to repay: active مُكَافِئٌ repaying, passive مُكَافَأٌ repaid

The plurals are sound. See 137, 138, 140 and 141 for declension.

**84. Verbs with Final-radical ء: Verbal Nouns.** The sound pattern (65) is valid. Most of these verbal nouns have a sound plural. There is only one measure in each of Forms II and III, i.e. تَفْعِلَةٌ and مُفَاعَلَةٌ respectively:

هَنَّأَ يُهَنِّئُ II to congratulate, تَهْنِئَةٌ congratulation

The patterns for Forms IV, VII, VIII and X are coincidentally identical to those
of the defective verbs (see 118):

أَنْشَأَ يُنْشِئُ IV to construct, إِنْشَاءٌ construction

See 137, 138, 140 and 141 for declension.

# 7. Doubled Verbs

**85. General.** Doubled verbs (also called geminate or geminated verbs, see 32) have identical sound middle and final radicals. Almost all have a sound initial radical.

Their conjugation is identical to that of the sound verbs, except that:

- when the two identical radicals are followed by an inflexion (personal or case ending) beginning with a vowel ('vocalic ending') and are not separated by a long vowel, the radicals are pronounced double but written single and may be pointed with ﹽ... ,

- when the identical radicals are followed by an inflexion (personal or case ending) beginning with a consonant ('consonantal ending'), or when they are followed by ﹾ..., or when they are separated by a long vowel, the radicals are written and pronounced separately,

- the jussive and imperative have an alternative pattern which is commoner than the sound pattern.

In Forms II and V the middle radical itself is doubled (see 37), and the two identical radicals separate. The conjugation is then completely sound.

Forms III and VI have two patterns: a 'contracted' form in which the identical radicals follow the rules given above; and an 'uncontracted' form, far less common, which follows the sound pattern throughout. All such verbs are rare.

The only common example of a verb with initial-radical و and identical middle and final sound radicals is وَدَّ يَوَدُّ I, 'to like', which is best treated as a doubled verb. It is included here.

Verbs with initial-radical ء and identical sound middle and final radicals are studied under the hamzated verbs, see 67.

The doubled class has no Form IX. But the rules for the doubled verbs also apply to Form IX, found in the sound and hollow classes.

**86. Table 13: Active Voice.** Examples of doubled verbs, in the active voice:

| Form,Root,Principal Parts | | Imperative | Participle | Vb. Noun | to ... |
|---|---|---|---|---|---|
| I ظَلَّ | ظَلَّ * يَظَلُّ | اظْلَلْ \ *ظَلَّ | ظَالٌّ * | ظُلُولٌ \ ظَلٌّ | remain |
| وَدَّ | وَدَّ * يَوَدُّ * | ايدَدْ\* وَدَّ * | وَادٌّ * | وَدٌّ | like |
| دَلَّ | دَلَّ * يَدُلُّ * | أُدْلُلْ\* دَلَّ * | دَالٌّ * | دَلَالَةٌ | indicate |
| تَمَّ | تَمَّ * يَتِمُّ * | اتْمِمْ \* تَمَّ * | تَامٌّ * | تَمَامٌ | be completed |

| | | | | | |
|---|---|---|---|---|---|
| II قر | قَرَّرَ يُقَرِّرُ | قَرِّرْ | مُقَرَّرٌ | تَقْرِيرٌ | decide/report |
| كَرَّ | كَرَّرَ يُكَرِّرُ | كَرِّرْ | مُكَرَّرٌ | تَكْرَارٌ\تَكْرِيرٌ | repeat |
| III ضدّ | ضَادَّ* يُضَادّ* | ضَادّ* | مُضَادّ* | مُضَادَّةٌ* | oppose |
| ضدّ | ضَادَدَ يُضَادِدُ | ضَادِدْ | مُضَادِدٌ | مُضَادَدَةً | oppose |
| حجّ | حَاجَّ يُحَاجِجُ | حَاجِجْ | مُحَاجِجٌ | مُحَاجَجَةٌ\حِجَاجٌ | dispute |
| IV عدّ | أَعَدَّ* يُعِدّ* | أَعِدّ*\أَعْدِدْ | مُعِدٌّ* | إِعْدَادٌ | prepare |
| V ردّ | تَرَدَّدَ يَتَرَدَّدُ | تَرَدَّدْ | مُتَرَدِّدٌ | تَرَدُّدٌ | hesitate |
| VI ضدّ | تَضَادَّ* يَتَضَادّ* | تَضَادّ* | مُتَضَادّ* | تَضَادّ* | oppose |
| ضدّ | تَضَادَدَ يَتَضَادَدُ | تَضَادَدْ | مُتَضَادَدٌ | تَضَادُدٌ | each other |
| VII حلّ | انْحَلَّ* يَنْحَلّ* | انْحَلّ*\انْحَلِلْ | مُنْحَلّ* | انْحِلَالٌ | be solved |
| VIII حلّ | احْتَلَّ* يَحْتَلّ* | احْتَلّ*\احْتَلِلْ | مُحْتَلّ* | احْتِلَالٌ | occupy |
| ضرّ | اضْطَرَّ* يَضْطَرّ* | اضْطَرّ*\اضْطَرِرْ | مُضْطَرّ* | اضْطِرَارٌ | compel |
| X مرّ | اسْتَمَرَّ* يَسْتَمِرّ* | اسْتَمِرّ*\اسْتَمْرِرْ | مُسْتَمِرّ* | اسْتِمْرَارٌ | continue |

Note: The forms marked * differ from those of the sound verbs, mainly following the provisions given in 85 above. In particular:

- Forms I, IV, VII, VIII and X show the effect of consonantal and vocalic endings, but they also have an alternative imperative form, far less commonly used, on the sound pattern.
- In one imperative of وَدَّ يَوَدُّ I, 'to like', the weak initial radical follows the assimilated conjugation; see 93.

Form II verbal noun has the measures تَفْعِيلٌ and (less common) تَفْعَالٌ .
See 37 for Forms I to X.

**87. Table 14: Passive Voice.** Examples of doubled verbs, in the passive voice (not all increased forms are found):

| Form, Root, Principal Parts | | Participle | to be ... |
|---|---|---|---|
| I مدّ | مُدَّ* يُمَدّ* | مَمْدُودٌ | extended |
| II قر | قُرِّرَ يُقَرَّرُ | مُقَرَّرٌ | decided/reported |
| III ضدّ | ضُودِدَ يُضَادّ* | مُضَادّ* | opposed |
| ضدّ | ضُودِدَ يُضَادَدُ | مُضَادَدٌ | opposed |

| | | | |
|---|---|---|---|
| IV | حَبَّ　　أُحِبَّ* يُحَبُّ* | مُحَبُّ* | loved |
| V | حَسَّ　　تُحُسِّسَ يُتَحَسَّسُ | مُتَحَسَّسُ | touched |
| VIII | حَلَّ　　أُحْتُلَّ* يُحْتَلُّ* | مُحْتَلُّ* | occupied |
| | ضَرَّ　　أُضْطُرَّ* يُضْطَرُّ* | مُضْطَرُّ* | compelled |
| X | حَقَّ　　أُسْتُحِقَّ* يُسْتَحَقُّ* | مُسْتَحَقُّ* | deserved |

Note:

- The patterns marked * are different from those of the sound verbs, mainly following the provisions given in 85 above.
- Doubled verbs in Form III are very rare. Form III passive perfect has no contracted form; the uncontracted form is used.
- In Form VIII the active and passive participles are identical.

See 37 for Forms I to X. See 36 and 55 for the passive.

The passive vowel pattern of doubled verbs can be expressed thus (in the 3rd person masculine singular; note the differing perfect patterns for 2 syllables + personal ending, depending on the increased form):

|  | Perfect tense | | | Imperfect tense | | | |
|---|---|---|---|---|---|---|---|
| 1 syllable + personal ending | | u | a | - | | | |
| 2 syllables (II/III/IV)+ pers. ending | u* | i | a | u | a* | | u |
| 2 syllables (VIII)+ pers. ending | u | u | a | u | a | | u |
| 3 syllables + pers. ending | u | u | i | a | u | a* a | u |
| 4 syllables + pers. ending | | - | | u | a a a | | u |

\* ū for u, ā for a in these positions in Form III.

**88. Tenses.** Doubled verbs form their perfect and imperfect stems, and conjugate in the tenses, like sound verbs, except that:

- The provisions (and their exceptions) given in 85 above apply.
- Apart from Forms II and V and the uncontracted forms of Forms III and VI, all of which follow completely the sound pattern, the doubled verbs have an alternative jussive (and hence also an alternative imperative) which is identical to the subjunctive. This form is commoner.

Examples:

Perfect tense:

Root مَرَّ; مَرَّ يَمُرُّ I, to pass; perfect active tense:

| | | |
|---|---|---|
| مَرَرْنا | | مَرَرْتُ |
| مَرَرْتُمْ | مَرَرْتُما | مَرَرْتَ |
| مَرَرْتُنَّ | مَرَرْتُما | مَرَرْتِ |
| مَرُّوا | مَرّا | مَرَّ |
| مَرَرْنَ | مَرَّتا | مَرَّتْ |

Root حلّ ; اُحْتُلَّ يُحْتَلُّ VIII to be occupied; perfect passive tense:

| | | |
|---|---|---|
| اُحْتُلْنا | | اُحْتُلِلْتُ |
| اُحْتُلِلْتُمْ | اُحْتُلِلْتُما | اُحْتُلِلْتَ |
| اُحْتُلِلْتُنَّ | اُحْتُلِلْتُما | اُحْتُلِلْتِ |
| اُحْتُلُّوا | اُحْتُلّا | اُحْتُلَّ |
| اُحْتُلِلْنَ | اُحْتُلّتا | اُحْتُلّتْ |

Imperfect (Indicative) tense:

Root قرّ ; قَرَّرَ يُقَرِّرُ II to decide or to report; imperfect active tense:

| | | |
|---|---|---|
| نُقَرِّرُ | | أُقَرِّرُ |
| تُقَرِّرُونَ | تُقَرِّرانِ | تُقَرِّرُ |
| تُقَرِّرْنَ | تُقَرِّرانِ | تُقَرِّرينَ |
| يُقَرِّرُونَ | يُقَرِّرانِ | يُقَرِّرُ |
| يُقَرِّرْنَ | تُقَرِّرانِ | تُقَرِّرُ |

Root حبّ ; أَحَبَّ يُحَبُّ IV to be loved; imperfect passive tense:

| | | |
|---|---|---|
| نُحَبُّ | | أُحَبُّ |
| تُحَبُّونَ | تُحَبّانِ | تُحَبُّ |
| تُحَبَبْنَ | تُحَبّانِ | تُحَبِّينَ |
| يُحَبُّونَ | يُحَبّانِ | يُحَبُّ |
| يُحَبَبْنَ | تُحَبّانِ | تُحَبُّ |

(Imperfect) Subjunctive Tense:

imperfect تَمُدُّ I, it extends, subjunctive تَمُدَّ

imperfect يُسْتَحَقُّ III it is deserved, subjunctive يُسْتَحَقَّ

(Imperfect) Jussive Tense:

subjunctive تَمُدَّ\تَمْدُدْ I, it extends, jussive تَمُدَّ\تَمْدُدْ

subjunctive يُحَاجَّ III (contracted) he disputes, jussive يُحَاجَّ\يُحَاجِجْ

subjunctive يُعِدَّ IV he prepares, jussive يُعِدَّ\يُعْدِدْ

subjunctive تُحْتَلَّ VIII it is occupied, jussive تُحْتَلَّ\تُحْتَلِلْ

subjunctive نَتَرَدَّدَ V we hesitate, jussive نَتَرَدَّدْ

## 89. Imperative. See 50.

Affirmative:

jussive تَدُلَّ\تَدْلُلْ I, you indicate, دُلَّ\أُدْلُلْ indicate

jussive تُعِدِّي\تُعْدِدِي IV you prepare, أَعِدِّي\أَعْدِدِي prepare

jussive تُحَاجِجُوا III (uncontracted) you dispute, حَاجِجُوا dispute

Negatives: لاَ تَدُلَّ\لاَ تَدْلُلْ I, do not indicate

لاَ تُعِدِّي\لاَ تُعْدِدِي IV do not prepare

لاَ تُحَاجِجُوا III (uncontracted) do not dispute

In both the affirmative and negative, the form resembling the subjunctive is commoner.

## 90. Participles. See 51 and 85. In the doubled verbs, the identical middle and final radicals fall together in the active participle of Form I, measure فَاعِلٌ:

شَكَّ يَشُكُّ I, to doubt, active شَاكٌّ doubting

The Form I passive participle has the sound measure, مَفْعُولٌ :

مَدَّ يَمُدُّ I, to extend, passive مَمْدُودٌ extended

All other participles are derived following the rules given in para. 51:

حَدَّدَ يُحَدِّدُ II to define, active مُحَدِّدٌ defining, passive مُحَدَّدٌ defined

حَاجَّ يُحَاجُّ III to dispute, active and passive مُحَاجٌّ disputing, disputed

حَاجَجَ يُحَاجِجُ III to dispute, active مُحَاجِجٌ disputing, passive مُحَاجَجٌ disputed

أَعَدَّ يُعِدُّ IV to prepare, active مُعِدٌّ preparing, passive مُعَدٌّ prepared

تَضَادَّ يَتَضَادُّ VI to oppose each other,

active (no passive) مُتَضَادٌّ opposing each other

انْحَلَّ يَنْحَلُّ VII to be solved, active (with passive meaning) مُنْحَلٌّ being solved

احْتَلَّ يَحْتَلُّ VIII to occupy, active and passive مُحْتَلٌّ occupying, occupied

اِسْتَحَقَّ يَسْتَحِقُّ X to deserve,

active مُسْتَحِقٌّ deserving, passive مُسْتَحَقٌّ deserved

The plurals of all these participles are sound. See 137, 138, 140 and 141 for declension.

**91. Verbal Nouns.** In the doubled verbs, the identical middle and final radicals fall together in the following verbal nouns:

- Form I, some examples: شَكَّ يَشُكُّ I, to doubt, شَكٌّ doubt

  (But Form I verbal nouns are irregular, some having middle and final radicals separated by a long vowel, e.g.:

  دَلَّ يَدُلُّ I, to indicate, دَلَالَةٌ indication)

- Form VI (contracted), measure تَفَاعْلٌ:

  تَضَادَّ يَتَضَادُّ VI (contracted) to oppose each other,

  تَضَادٌّ mutual opposition

In the following, the verbal noun has the sound pattern (see 65):

- Forms II and V:

  حَدَّدَ يُحَدِّدُ II to define, تَحْدِيدٌ definition

  تَرَدَّدَ يَتَرَدَّدُ V to hesitate, تَرَدُّدٌ hesitation

- Forms III (contracted/uncontracted) and VI (uncontracted) :

  حَاجَّ يُحَاجُّ III (contracted) to dispute, مُحَاجَّةٌ\حِجَاجٌ dispute

  تَضَادَدَ يَتَضَادَدُ VI (uncontracted) to oppose each other,

  تَضَادُدٌ mutual opposition

- Forms IV, VII, VIII and X:

  أَصَرَّ يُصِرُّ عَلَى IV to insist on, إِصْرَارٌ insistence

  اِنْضَمَّ يَنْضَمُّ إِلَى VII to enrol in, اِنْضِمَامٌ enrolment

  اِهْتَمَّ يَهْتَمُّ ب VIII to care for, اِهْتِمَامٌ care

  اِسْتَقَلَّ يَسْتَقِلُّ X to be independent, اِسْتِقْلَالٌ independence

Some doubled verbal nouns (especially in Forms I and II) have a broken plural or alternative plurals:

شَكٌّ I, doubt, pl. شُكُوكٌ ; حَدٌّ I, limit, pl. حُدُودٌ .

تَقْرِيرٌ II report/decision, pl. *تَقَارِيرُ reports, تَقْرِيرَاتٌ decisions

* Diptote, see 144.

Some verbal nouns of Forms I and II, and most verbal nouns of Forms III to X, have sound plurals, e.g.:

حَسّ I, feeling; دَلَالَة I, indication; تَمْدِيدٌ II extension; إِعْدَادٌ IV preparation

See 137, 138, 140 and 141 for declension.

# 8. Assimilated Verbs

**92. General.** Assimilated verbs (see 32) are the first sub-class of the weak verbs. They are those whose root has a weak letter, و or ي, as initial radical, and two sound radicals. The pattern with initial-radical و is by far the more common. Roots with more than one weak radical are not assimilated but doubly weak, see Chapter 11.

The assimilated verbs follow the sound conjugation except when the initial radical vocalises, i.e. becomes a vowel; or when it is dropped.

Verbs with an initial weak radical, ء as middle radical, and a sound final radical, are regarded by some as doubly weak; they are treated here with assimilated roots.

The only common verb with initial-radical و and identical middle and final sound radicals is best studied as a doubled verb (وَدَّ يَوَدُّ I, see 86), since its initial radical stabilises as a consonant in almost all forms.

The assimilated sub-class has no Forms VII or IX.

**93. Table 15: Initial-radical و : Active Voice.** Examples of initial-radical و verbs, in the active voice:

| Form, Root, Principal Parts | Imperative | Participle | Verbal Noun | to ... |
|---|---|---|---|---|
| I    وجد    وَجَدَ يَجِدُ * | جِدْ* | وَاجِدٌ | وُجُودٌ | find |
| وضع    وَضَعَ يَضَعُ * | ضَعْ* | وَاضِعٌ | وَضْعٌ | place |
| ورث    وَرِثَ يَرِثُ * | رِثْ* | وَارِثٌ | وِرْثٌ | inherit |
| وجه    وَجُهَ يَوجُهُ | اِيجُهْ* | وَاجِهٌ | وَجَاهَةٌ | be eminent |
| II    وصل    وَصَّلَ يُوَصِّلُ | وَصِّلْ | مُوَصِّلٌ | تَوْصِيلٌ | convey |
| III    وفق    وَافَقَ يُوَافِقُ | وَافِقْ | مُوَافِقٌ | مُوَافَقَةٌ\وِفَاقٌ | agree |
| وأم    وَاءَمَ يُوَائِمُ | وَائِمْ | مُوَائِمٌ | مُوَاءَمَةٌ\وِئَامٌ | agree with |
| IV    وجب    أَوْجَبَ يُوجِبُ | أَوْجِبْ | مُوجِبٌ | إِيجَابٌ* | compel |
| V    وجه    تَوَجَّهَ يَتَوَجَّهُ | تَوَجَّهْ | مُتَوَجِّهٌ | تَوَجُّهٌ | face |
| VI    وجه    تَوَاجَهَ يَتَوَاجَهُ | تَوَاجَهْ | مُتَوَاجِهٌ | تَوَاجُهٌ | face each other |
| VIII    وحد    اتَّحَدَ* يَتَّحِدُ* | اتَّحِدْ* | مُتَّحِدٌ* | اتِّحَادٌ* | (be) unite(d) |
| X    ورد    اِسْتَوْرَدَ يَسْتَوْرِدُ | اِسْتَوْرِدْ | مُسْتَوْرِدٌ | اِسْتِيرَادٌ* | import |

Note: Only forms marked * differ from those of the sound verbs. In particular:

- In almost all verbs in Form I, the initial radical is dropped completely in the second principal part and the whole first syllable is dropped in the imperative. A very small number of little-used verbs has a second principal part on the sound pattern.
- The theoretical combination -*uw*- (short vowel + consonant) becomes ...ﻮُ... (-ū-, long vowel), and the theoretical combination -*iw*- (short vowel + consonant) becomes ...ﻴِ... (-ī-, long vowel). Apart from this, the apparently irregular patterns of Forms IV and X are identical to the sound pattern.
- In Form VIII the initial radical assimilates to the ت of the increased form in all verbs (see the same phenomenon in 67, hamzated verbs).

See 37 for Forms I to X.

**94. Table 16: Initial-radical ي : Active Voice.** Examples of initial-radical ي verbs, in the active voice:

| Form, Root, Principal Parts | Imperative | Participle | Verbal Noun | to ... |
|---|---|---|---|---|
| I يبس يَبِسَ يَيْبَسُ | اِيبَسْ | يَابِسٌ | يَبْسٌ | be dry |
| يأس يَئِسَ يَيْأَسُ | اِيأَسْ | يَائِسٌ | يَأْسٌ | renounce |
| II يسر يَسَّرَ يُيَسِّرُ | يَسِّرْ | مُيَسِّرٌ | تَيْسِيرٌ | ease |
| III يسر يَاسَرَ يُيَاسِرُ | يَاسِرْ | مُيَاسِرٌ | مُيَاسَرَةٌ | indulge |
| IV يقن أَيْقَنَ يُوقِنُ* | أَيْقِنْ | مُوقِنٌ | إِيقَانٌ | ascertain |
| V يقظ تَيَقَّظَ يَتَيَقَّظُ | تَيَقَّظْ | مُتَيَقِّظٌ | تَيَقُّظٌ | be alert |
| X يقظ اِسْتَيْقَظَ يَسْتَيْقِظُ | اِسْتَيْقِظْ | مُسْتَيْقِظٌ | اِسْتِيقَاظٌ | awake |

Note: Only the form marked * differs from the sound pattern. Further:

- Initial-radical ي verbs are few in number and little used.
- The theoretical combination -*uy*- becomes ...ﻮُ... (-ū-, long vowel) and the theoretical combination -*iy*- (short vowel + consonant) becomes ...ﻴِ... (-ī-, long vowel). Apart from this, the apparently irregular patterns in the Form I imperative, and in Forms IV and X, are identical to the sound pattern.
- Both principal parts of Form I are regular. They follow the sound pattern, except that all roots have the same vowelling.

See 37 for Forms I to X.

**95. Table 17: Initial-radical و and Initial-radical ي : Passive Voice.**

Examples of assimilated verbs (initial-radical و and initial-radical ي ), in the passive voice (not all increased forms are found):

| Form, Root, Principal Parts | | | Participle | to be … |
|---|---|---|---|---|
| I | وجد | وُجِدَ يُوجَدُ | مَوْجُودٌ | found |
| | يأس | يُئِسَ يُوأَسُ * | مَيْؤُوسٌ | hopeless |
| II | وصل | وُصِّلَ يُوَصَّلُ | مُوَصَّلٌ | conveyed |
| | يسر | يُسِّرَ يُيَسَّرُ | مُيَسَّرٌ | facilitated |
| III | وفق | وُوفِقَ يُوافَقُ | مُوافَقٌ | agreed |
| | يسر | يُوسِرَ يُياسَرُ | مُياسَرٌ | indulged |
| IV | وفد | أُوفِدَ يُوفَدُ | مُوفَدٌ | delegated |
| | يقظ | أُوقِظَ * يُوقَظُ * | مُوقَظٌ | wakened |
| V | وسم | تُوُسِّمَ يُتَوَسَّمُ | مُتَوَسَّمٌ | scrutinised |
| | يقن | تُيُقِّنَ يُتَيَقَّنُ | مُتَيَقَّنٌ | ascertained |
| VIII | وفق | أُتُّفِقَ * يُتَّفَقُ * | مُتَّفَقٌ * | agreed |
| X | وصف | أُستُوصِفَ يُستَوصَفُ | مُستَوصَفٌ | consulted |
| | يأس | أُستُيئِسَ * يُستَياسُ | مُستَياسٌ | despaired of |

Note:

- The forms marked * differ from the sound pattern. The theoretical combination -uy- (short vowel + consonant), in Forms I, IV and X of initial-radical ي verbs, becomes ...وُ... -ū- (long vowel).
- In Form VIII of initial-radical و verbs the initial radical assimilates to the ت of the increased form in the passive also (see 93 above).
- Form IV initial-radical و verbs and initial-radical ي verbs are identical in the passive.
- The passive voice of initial-radical ي verbs is even rarer than the active.

See 37 for Forms I to V, VIII and X. See 36 and 55 for the passive.

The passive vowel pattern of assimilated verbs can be expressed diagrammatically thus (in the 3rd person masculine singular):

|                                | Perfect tense |     |     | Imperfect tense |      |      |     |
| ------------------------------ | ------------- | --- | --- | --------------- | ---- | ---- | --- |
| 2 syllables + personal ending  | u*            | i   | a   | ū               |      | a    | u   |
| 3 syllables + personal ending  | u u*          | i   | a   | u               | a*   | a    | u   |
| 4 syllables + personal ending  | -             |     |     | u               | a    | a  a | u   |

\* ū for u in these positions in Forms III, IV, and X; ā for a in this position in Form III, and aw or ay for a in this position in Form X.

**96. Tenses.** Assimilated verbs form their perfect and imperfect stems, and conjugate in the tenses, like sound verbs except that:

- the active voice imperfect tenses of Form I of the most common initial-radical و verbs lose the initial radical, leaving nothing between the personal prefix and the middle radical,
- the theoretical combinations -uw- and -uy- (short vowel + consonant) found in Form IV (see 93 above) become ...وُ... (-ū-, long vowel).

Examples:

Perfect tense:

Root وصل ; وَصَلَ يَصِلُ I, to arrive; perfect active tense:

| وَصَلْنَا  |          | وَصَلْتُ  |
| ---------- | -------- | --------- |
| وَصَلْتُمْ | وَصَلْتُمَا | وَصَلْتَ  |
| وَصَلْتُنَّ | وَصَلْتُمَا | وَصَلْتِ  |
| وَصَلُوا   | وَصَلَا   | وَصَلَ    |
| وَصَلْنَ   | وَصَلَتَا  | وَصَلَتْ  |

Root وجب ; أَوْجَبَ يُوجِبُ IV to compel; perfect active tense:

| أَوْجَبْنَا  |            | أَوْجَبْتُ  |
| ------------ | ---------- | ----------- |
| أَوْجَبْتُمْ | أَوْجَبْتُمَا | أَوْجَبْتَ  |
| أَوْجَبْتُنَّ | أَوْجَبْتُمَا | أَوْجَبْتِ  |
| أَوْجَبُوا   | أَوْجَبَا   | أَوْجَبَ    |
| أَوْجَبْنَ   | أَوْجَبَتَا  | أَوْجَبَتْ  |

Root وفد ; أُوفِدَ يُوفَدُ IV to be delegated; perfect passive tense:

| أُوفِدْنَا  |            | أُوفِدْتُ  |
| ----------- | ---------- | ---------- |
| أُوفِدْتُمْ | أُوفِدْتُمَا | أُوفِدْتَ  |
| أُوفِدْتُنَّ | أُوفِدْتُمَا | أُوفِدْتِ  |

أُوفِدُوا    أُوفِدَا    أُوفِدَ

أُوفِدْنَ    أُوفِدَتَا    أُوفِدَتْ

<u>Imperfect (Indicative) tense:</u>

Root وجد ; وَجَدَ يَجِدُ I, to find; imperfect active tense:

نَجِدُ    أَجِدُ

تَجِدُونَ    تَجِدَانِ    تَجِدُ

تَجِدْنَ    تَجِدَانِ    تَجِدِينَ

يَجِدُونَ    يَجِدَانِ    يَجِدُ

يَجِدْنَ    تَجِدَانِ    تَجِدُ

Root يبس ; يَبِسَ يَيْبَسُ I, to be dry; imperfect active tense:

نَيْبَسُ    أَيْبَسُ

تَيْبَسُونَ    تَيْبَسَانِ    تَيْبَسُ

تَيْبَسْنَ    تَيْبَسَانِ    تَيْبَسِينَ

يَيْبَسُونَ    يَيْبَسَانِ    يَيْبَسُ

يَيْبَسْنَ    تَيْبَسَانِ    تَيْبَسُ

Root وصف ; أَسْتُوصِفَ يُسْتَوْصَفُ X to be consulted; imperfect passive tense:

نُسْتَوْصَفُ    أُسْتَوْصَفُ

تُسْتَوْصَفُونَ    تُسْتَوْصَفَانِ    تُسْتَوْصَفُ

تُسْتَوْصَفْنَ    تُسْتَوْصَفَانِ    تُسْتَوْصَفِينَ

يُسْتَوْصَفُونَ    يُسْتَوْصَفَانِ    يُسْتَوْصَفُ

يُسْتَوْصَفْنَ    تُسْتَوْصَفَانِ    تُسْتَوْصَفُ

<u>(Imperfect) Subjunctive Tense:</u>

imperfect نُوَصِّلُ II we convey, subjunctive نُوَصِّلَ

imperfect يُوجَدُ I, it is found, subjunctive يُوجَدَ

<u>(Imperfect) Jussive Tense:</u>

subjunctive تَتَّفِقَ VIII she agrees, jussive تَتَّفِقْ

subjunctive يَرِثَ I, he inherits, jussive يَرِثْ

**97. Imperative.** The affirmative imperative of assimilated verbs is regularly derived from the jussive (see 50), except that:

- in the imperative of Form I of the less common of the initial-radical و verbs, and of the even rarer initial-radical ي verbs, the theoretical combinations *iw-* and *iy-* become اِيـ... (ī-, long vowel):

     jussive تُوْجَلْ I, you are afraid, اِيجَلْ be afraid

     jussive تَيْأَسْ I, you renounce, اِيأَسْ renounce

- in the imperative of Form IV of initial-radical ي verbs, the first syllable is ...أَيـ... :

     jussive تُوقِنِي IV you ascertain, *but*: أَيقِنِي ascertain

The affirmative imperative of all remaining increased forms, and the negative imperative of all assimilated verbs without exception, are regular:

     jussive تُوجِبُوا IV you compel, أَوْجِبُوا compel, لاَ تُوجِبُوا do not compel

     jussive تَضَعْ I, you place, ضَعْ place, لاَ تَضَعْ do not place

     jussive تَتَوَسَّعُوا V you expand, تَوَسَّعُوا expand, لاَ تَتَوَسَّعُوا do not expand

**98. Participles.** Participles are regularly derived as shown in 51:

وَرَثَ يَرِثُ I, to inherit, active وَارِثٌ inheriting, passive مَوْرُوثٌ inherited

وَصَّلَ يُوَصِّلُ II to convey, active مُوَصِّلٌ conveying, passive مُوَصَّلٌ conveyed

أَوْفَدَ يُوفِدُ IV to delegate, active مُوفِدٌ delegating, passive مُوفَدٌ delegated

أَيْقَنَ يُوقِنُ IV to ascertain, active مُوقِنٌ ascertaining, passive مُوقَنٌ ascertained

اِتَّفَقَ يَتَّفِقُ عَلَى VIII to agree on/to, active مُتَّفِقٌ agreeing, passive مُتَّفَقٌ agreed

اِسْتَيْقَظَ يَسْتَيْقِظُ X to awake: active (no passive) مُسْتَيْقِظٌ awake

The plurals are sound. See 137, 138, 140 and 141 for declension.

**99. Verbal Nouns.** Assimilated verbal nouns follow the sound pattern (65) except that:

- in Form IV, the theoretical combination '*iw-* becomes إِيـ... (see 93):

     أَوْجَبَ يُوجِبُ IV to compel, إِيجَابٌ compulsion

- in Form VIII, initial-radical و assimilates to the ت of the increased form (see 93):

     اِتَّصَلَ يَتَّصِلُ ب VIII to get in touch with, اِتِّصَالٌ contact

There are no initial-radical ي verbs in Form VIII.

The other assimilated verbal nouns follow the sound pattern, including the irregularity of Form I (see 65):

وَجَدَ يَجِدُ I, to find: وُجُودٌ existence

وَافَقَ يُوَافِقُ III to conform to: مُوَافَقَةٌ، وِفَاقٌ conformity

The plurals of all these verbal nouns are sound. See 137, 138, 140 and 141 for declension.

# 9. Hollow Verbs

**100.  General.** Hollow verbs (see 32) are the second sub-class of the weak verbs. They are those whose root has a weak letter, و or ي, as middle radical, and two sound radicals. The weak middle radical can take different guises:

- it can stabilise, i.e. assume its corresponding consonantal form و or ي;
- it can vocalise, i.e. assume vocalic form, either long or short;
- between two vowels, it can appear as ء.

The effect of a consonantal or a vocalic ending in full pronunciation (see 85, doubled verbs) is felt in hollow verbs when the middle radical is vocalised (in Forms I, IV, VII, VIII and X):

- the middle radical becomes a long vowel when the final radical is followed by a vocalic (personal or case) ending or before ة...,
- the middle radical becomes a short vowel when the final radical is followed by a consonantal ending or ْ... .

Details are given in the notes following Table 18 below.

The middle radical has its consonantal form in Forms II, III, V, VI and IX, whereupon the conjugation is sound.

Roots with more than one weak radical are not hollow but doubly weak, see 119.

Roots with initial-radical ء, a weak middle radical and sound final radical are regarded by some as doubly weak; they are treated here with hollow roots.

**101.  Table 18: Active Voice.** Examples of middle-radical و and middle-radical ي verbs, in the active voice:

| Form, Root, Principal Parts | | Imperative | Participle | Verbal Noun | to ... |
|---|---|---|---|---|---|
| I | قول   قَالَ* يَقُولُ* | قُلْ* | قَائِلٌ * | قَوْلٌ | say |
| | أوب   آبَ* يَأُوبُ*\يَؤُوبُ* | أُبْ* | آئِبٌ * | إِيَابٌ | return |
| | نوم   نَامَ* يَنَامُ* | نَمْ* | نَائِمٌ* | نَوْمٌ | sleep |
| | صير   صَارَ* يَصِيرُ* | صِرْ* | صَائِرٌ * | مَصِيرٌ | become |
| II | مول   مَوَّلَ يُمَوِّلُ | مَوِّلْ | مُمَوِّلٌ | تَمْوِيلٌ | finance |
| | ميز   مَيَّزَ يُمَيِّزُ | مَيِّزْ | مُمَيِّزٌ | تَمْيِيزٌ | distinguish |
| | إيد   أَيَّدَ يُؤَيِّدُ | أَيِّدْ | مُؤَيِّدٌ | تَأْيِيدٌ | support |
| III | حور   حَاوَرَ يُحَاوِرُ | حَاوِرْ | مُحَاوِرٌ | مُحَاوَرَةٌ\حِوَارٌ | converse |
| | حيد   حَايَدَ يُحَايِدُ | حَايِدْ | مُحَايِدٌ | مُحَايَدَةٌ\حِيَادٌ | abstain |

| | | | | | |
|---|---|---|---|---|---|
| قوم IV | أَقامَ* يُقيمُ* | أَقِمْ* | مُقيمٌ* | إِقامَةٌ* | organise |
| حوج | أَحْوَجَ يُحْوِجُ إلى | أَحْوِجْ | مُحْوِجٌ | إِحْوَاجٌ | need |
| فيد | أَفادَ* يُفيدُ* | أَفِدْ* | مُفيدٌ* | إِفادَةٌ* | benefit |
| صور V | تَصَوَّرَ يَتَصَوَّرُ | تَصَوَّرْ | مُتَصَوِّرٌ | تَصَوُّرٌ | imagine |
| غير | تَغَيَّرَ يَتَغَيَّرُ | تَغَيَّرْ | مُتَغَيِّرٌ | تَغَيُّرٌ | change |
| عون VI | تَعاوَنَ يَتَعاوَنُ | تَعاوَنْ | مُتَعاوِنٌ | تَعاوُنٌ | cooperate |
| زيد | تَزايَدَ يَتَزايَدُ | تَزايَدْ | مُتَزايِدٌ | تَزايُدٌ | increase |
| حوز VII | انْحازَ* يَنْحازُ* | انْحَزْ* | مُنْحازٌ* | انْحِيازٌ | be secluded |
| بيع | انْباعَ* يَنْباعُ* | انْبَعْ* | مُنْباعٌ* | انْبِياعٌ | be sold |
| حوج VIII | احْتاجَ* يَحْتاجُ* إلى | احْتَجْ* | مُحْتاجٌ* | احْتِياجٌ | need |
| زوج | ازْدَوَجَ يَزْدَوِجُ | ازْدَوِجْ | مُزْدَوِجٌ | ازْدِواجٌ | be paired |
| ميز | امْتازَ* يَمْتازُ* | امْتَزْ* | مُمْتازٌ* | امْتِيازٌ | be distinguished |
| سود IX | اسْوَدَّ يَسْوَدُّ | اسْوَدَّ \ اسْوَدِدْ | مُسْوَدٌّ | اسْوِدادٌ | be/turn black |
| بيض | ابْيَضَّ يَبْيَضُّ | ابْيَضَّ \ ابْيَضِضْ | مُبْيَضٌّ | ابْيِضاضٌ | be/turn white |
| روح X | اسْتَراحَ* يَسْتَريحُ* | اسْتَرِحْ* | مُسْتَريحٌ* | اسْتِراحَةٌ* | rest |
| جوب | اسْتَجْوَبَ يَسْتَجْوِبُ | اسْتَجْوِبْ | مُسْتَجْوِبٌ | اسْتِجْوابٌ | interrogate |
| فيد | اسْتَفادَ* يَسْتَفيدُ* مِنْ | اسْتَفِدْ* | مُسْتَفيدٌ* | اسْتِفادَةٌ* | benefit from |

See 37 for Forms I to X.

In the active voice the vocalised weak middle radical takes the following forms:

| | middle و and ي | | middle ي Form I | middle و Form I |
|---|---|---|---|---|
| | Forms VII + VIII | Forms IV + X | | |
| perfect | ...َا\... | ...َا\... | ...َا\... | ...َا\...ُ |
| imperfect + imperative | ...َا\... | ...يا\... | ...يا\... | ...و\...ُ |
| participle | ا... | ...ي | ...ئ | ...ئ |
| verbal noun | يَا... | ا... | *(irregular)* | |

The forms marked * in Table 18 above differ from the sound pattern, mainly because of the vocalisation of the middle radical. Note:

- In a small but important group of anomalous middle-radical و verbs (e.g. root نوم above) the middle radical becomes in Form I ...\ا... in the perfect and ...\ا... in the imperfect and imperative.

- In Forms IV, VII, VIII and X, middle-radical و and middle-radical ي verbs conjugate identically.

- In Forms IV, VIII and X, a few anomalous middle-radical و verbs have the sound measure, with a stable (i.e. consonantal) middle radical.

**102. Table 19: Passive Voice.** Examples of hollow verbs in the passive voice (not all increased forms are found):

| | Form, Root, Principal Parts | Participle | to be … |
|---|---|---|---|
| I | سوق    سِيقَ* يُسَاقُ* | مَسُوقٌ * | driven |
| | بيع    بِيعَ* يُبَاعُ* | مَبِيعٌ * | sold |
| II | صور    صُوِّرَ يُصَوَّرُ | مُصَوَّرٌ | depicted |
| | غير    غُيِّرَ يُغَيَّرُ | مُغَيَّرٌ | changed |
| | أيد    أُيِّدَ يُؤَيَّدُ | مُؤَيَّدٌ | supported |
| III | حول    حُووِلَ يُحَاوَلُ | مُحَاوَلٌ | attempted |
| | بين    بُويِنَ يُبَايَنُ | مُبَايَنٌ | opposed |
| IV | رود    أُرِيدَ* يُرَادُ* | مُرَادٌ * | wanted |
| | فيد    أُفِيدَ يُفَادُ* | مُفَادٌ * | benefited |
| V | عود    تُعُوِّدَ يَتَعَوَّدُ عَلَى | not used | accustomed |
| | غير    تُغُيِّرَ يَتَغَيَّرُ | not used | altered |
| VI | نول    تُنُووِلَ يُتَنَاوَلُ | not used | reached |
| | بيع    تُبُويِعَ يُتَبَايَعُ | not used | contracted |
| VIII | حوج    أُحْتِيجَ* يُحْتَاجُ* إِلَى | مُحْتَاجٌ * | needed |
| | خير    أُخْتِيرَ* يُخْتَارُ* | مُخْتَارٌ* | selected |
| X | ثور    أُسْتُثِيرَ * يُسْتَثَارُ* | مُسْتَثَارٌ * | incited |
| | جوب    أُسْتُجْوِبَ يُسْتَجْوَبُ | مُسْتَجْوَبٌ | interrogated |
| | ضيف    أُسْتُضِيفَ * يُسْتَضَافُ* | مُسْتَضَافٌ* | invited |

See 37 for Forms I to X. See 36 and 55 for the passive.

Forms marked * differ from the sound pattern.

Note:

- In Form I, middle-radical و verbs and middle-radical ي verbs conjugate identically in the passive tenses but not in the participle.
- In Forms IV, VII, VIII and X, middle-radical و verbs and middle-radical ي verbs conjugate identically in the whole of the passive.

The passive vowel pattern of hollow verbs, Forms I, IV, VIII and X, can be expressed thus (in the 3rd person masculine singular):

|  | Perfect tense | | | | Imperfect tense | | | |
|---|---|---|---|---|---|---|---|---|
| 1 syllable + pers. ending | | | ī* | a | | - | | |
| 2 syllables + pers. ending | u | | ī* | a | u | ā* | | u |
| 3 syllables + pers. ending | u | u | ī* | a | u | a | ā* | u |

* i for ī, a for ā before a consonantal ending in other persons, or before ... .

For those increased forms in which the middle radical stabilises to a consonant (Forms II, III, V, VI and certain anomalous verbs in other increased forms) the diagram showing the sound passive pattern (58) is valid.

**103. Tenses.** Paras. 39 and 41 (prefixes and personal endings) and 59 and 60 (perfect and imperfect stems) are valid also here, subject to the provisions of para. 100 and the notes following Table 18 (para. 101) above.

Examples of tenses:

Perfect tense, Active:

Root كون ; كَانَ يَكُونُ I, to be; perfect active tense:

| | | |
|---|---|---|
| كُنَّا | | كُنْتُ |
| كُنْتُمْ | كُنْتُمَا | كُنْتَ |
| كُنْتُنَّ | كُنْتُمَا | كُنْتِ |
| كَانُوا | كَانَا | كَانَ |
| كُنَّ | كَانَتَا | كَانَتْ |

See 189 for this important verb.

Root طير ; طَارَ يَطِيرُ I, to fly; perfect active tense:

| | | |
|---|---|---|
| طِرْنَا | | طِرْتُ |
| طِرْتُمْ | طِرْتُمَا | طِرْتَ |
| طِرْتُنَّ | طِرْتُمَا | طِرْتِ |

| طَارَ | طَارَا | طَارُوا |
|---|---|---|
| طَارَتْ | طَارَتَا | طِرْنَ |

Anomalous root خوف ; خَافَ يَخَافُ (مِنْ) I, to fear; perfect active tense:

| | خِفْنَا |
|---|---|
| خِفْتُ | |

| خِفْتَ | خِفْتُمَا | خِفْتُمْ |
|---|---|---|
| خِفْتِ | خِفْتُمَا | خِفْتُنَّ |
| خَافَ | خَافَا | خَافُوا |
| خَافَتْ | خَافَتَا | خِفْنَ |

Important verbs also conjugated so:

• root نوم , نَامَ يَنَامُ I, to sleep

• root زول\زيل , زَالَ يَزَالُ I, to cease (see 189)

Anomalous verb لَيْسَ I, not to be; see 189. Its full personal endings are always pronounced, even in short pronunciation. Perfect active tense:

| | لَسْنَا |
|---|---|
| لَسْتُ | |

| لَسْتَ | لَسْتُمَا | لَسْتُمْ |
|---|---|---|
| لَسْتِ | لَسْتُمَا | لَسْتُنَّ |
| لَيْسَ | لَيْسَا | لَيْسُوا |
| لَيْسَتْ | لَيْسَتَا | لَسْنَ |

Root فيد ; أَفَادَ يُفِيدُ IV to benefit; perfect active tense:

| | أَفَدْنَا |
|---|---|
| أَفَدْتُ | |

| أَفَدْتَ | أَفَدْتُمَا | أَفَدْتُمْ |
|---|---|---|
| أَفَدْتِ | أَفَدْتُمَا | أَفَدْتُنَّ |
| أَفَادَ | أَفَادَا | أَفَادُوا |
| أَفَادَتْ | أَفَادَتَا | أَفَدْنَ |

Root كون ; كَوَّنَ يُكَوِّنُ II to constitute; perfect active tense:

| | كَوَّنَّا |
|---|---|
| كَوَّنْتُ | |

| كَوَّنْتَ | كَوَّنْتُمَا | كَوَّنْتُمْ |
|---|---|---|
| كَوَّنْتِ | كَوَّنْتُمَا | كَوَّنْتُنَّ |
| كَوَّنَ | كَوَّنَا | كَوَّنُوا |

كُوِّنْتَ    كُوِّنْتَا    كُوِّنْ

## Imperfect (Indicative) tense, Active:

Root كون ; كَانَ يَكُونُ I, to be; imperfect active tense:

نَكُونُ    أَكُونُ

تَكُونُونَ    تَكُونَانِ    تَكُونُ

تَكُنَّ    تَكُونَانِ    تَكُونِينَ

يَكُونُونَ    يَكُونَانِ    يَكُونُ

يَكُنَّ    تَكُونَانِ    تَكُونُ

Root صير ; صَارَ يَصِيرُ I, to become; imperfect active tense:

نَصِيرُ    أَصِيرُ

تَصِيرُونَ    تَصِيرَانِ    تَصِيرُ

تَصِرْنَ    تَصِيرَانِ    تَصِيرِينَ

يَصِيرُونَ    يَصِيرَانِ    يَصِيرُ

يَصِرْنَ    تَصِيرَانِ    تَصِيرُ

Anomalous root خوف ; خَافَ يَخَافُ (مِنْ) I, to fear; imperfect active tense:

نَخَافُ    أَخَافُ

تَخَافُون    تَخَافَانِ    تَخَافُ

تَخَفْنَ    تَخَافَانِ    تَخَافِينَ

يَخَافُون    يَخَافَانِ    يَخَافُ

يَخَفْنَ    تَخَافَانِ    تَخَافُ

See earlier in this paragraph for other important verbs with the same pattern.

Root أيد ; أَيَّدَ يُؤَيِّد II to support; imperfect active tense:

نُؤَيِّدُ    أُؤَيِّدُ

تُؤَيِّدُونَ    تُؤَيِّدَانِ    تُؤَيِّدُ

تُؤَيِّدْنَ    تُؤَيِّدَانِ    تُؤَيِّدِينَ

يُؤَيِّدُونَ    يُؤَيِّدَانِ    يُؤَيِّدُ

يُؤَيِّدْنَ    تُؤَيِّدَانِ    تُؤَيَّدُ

## Perfect Tense, Passive:

Root زور ; زِيرَ يُزَارُ I, to be visited; perfect passive tense:

زُرْتُ                          زُرْنَا

زُرْتَ            زُرْتُمَا        زُرْتُمْ

زُرْتِ            زُرْتُمَا        زُرْتُنَّ

زِيرَ             زِيرَا          زِيرُوا

زِيرَتْ           زِيرَتَا         زِرْنَ

Root خير ؛ أُخْتِيرَ يُخْتَارُ VIII to be selected; perfect passive tense:

أُخْتِرْتُ                        أُخْتِرْنَا

أُخْتِرْتَ          أُخْتِرْتُمَا      أُخْتِرْتُمْ

أُخْتِرْتِ          أُخْتِرْتُمَا      أُخْتِرْتُنَّ

أُخْتِيرَ          أُخْتِيرَا        أُخْتِيرُوا

أُخْتِيرَتْ         أُخْتِيرَتَا       أُخْتِرْنَ

Imperfect (Indicative) Tense, Passive:

Root زور ؛ زِيرَ يُزَارُ I, to be visited; imperfect passive tense:

أُزَارُ                           نُزَارُ

تُزَارُ            تُزَارَانِ        تُزَارُونَ

تُزَارِينَ         تُزَارَانِ        تُزَرْنَ

يُزَارُ            يُزَارَانِ        يُزَارُونَ

تُزَارُ            تُزَارَانِ        يُزَرْنَ

Root زيد ؛ زُيِّدَ يُزَيَّدُ II to be increased; imperfect passive tense:

أُزَيَّدُ                          نُزَيَّدُ

تُزَيَّدُ           تُزَيَّدَانِ        تُزَيَّدُونَ

تُزَيَّدِينَ        تُزَيَّدَانِ        تُزَيَّدْنَ

يُزَيَّدُ           يُزَيَّدَانِ        يُزَيَّدُونَ

تُزَيَّدُ           تُزَيَّدَانِ        يُزَيَّدْنَ

(Imperfect) Subjunctive Tense:

imperfect نُفِيدُ IV we benefit, subjunctive نُفِيدَ

imperfect يُخْتَارُ VIII it is selected, subjunctive يُخْتَارَ

The anomalous verb كَانَ يَكُونُ I, 'to be' has present meaning in the subjunctive:

imperfect نَكُونُ I, we shall be, subjunctive نَكُونَ we are

(Imperfect) Jussive Tense:

subjunctive تَقُولَ I, she says, jussive تَقُلْ

subjunctive and jussive تَقُولِي I, you say

subjunctive يُسْتَشَارَ X he is consulted, jussive يُسْتَشَرْ

The anomalous verb كَانَ يَكُونُ I, 'to be' has present meaning in the jussive:

subjunctive نَكُونَ I, we are, jussive نَكُنْ

Form IX has two jussive tenses. Derive them as for doubled verbs, see 88:

subjunctive يَسْوَدَّ IX it turns black, jussive يَسْوَدَّ\يَسْوَدِدْ

**104. Imperative.** See 50 :

jussive تَكُنْ I, you are, كُنْ be, لاَ تَكُنْ do not be

jussive تُمَيِّزْ II you distinguish, مَيِّزْ distinguish, لاَ تُمَيِّزْ do not distinguish

jussive تَسْتَرِيحُوا X you rest, اِسْتَرِيحُوا rest, لاَ تَسْتَرِيحُوا do not rest

**105. Participles.** In Form I participles the sound measures (51) apply except for the middle radical:

- in the active participle the middle radical is replaced by ء :

قَالَ يَقُولُ I, to say, active قَائِلٌ saying; طَارَ يَطِيرُ I, to fly, active طَائِرٌ flying

- In the passive participle the theoretical combinations -wū- and -yū- (i.e. the middle radical and its vowel) become ...ُو... and ...ِي... respectively:

قَالَ يَقُولُ I, to say, passive مَقُولٌ said

زَادَ يَزِيدُ I, to increase, passive مَزِيدٌ increased

The participles of the increased forms are regularly derived as shown in 51:

مَوَّلَ يُمَوِّلُ II to finance, active مُمَوِّلٌ financing, passive مُمَوَّلٌ financed

أَفَادَ يُفِيدُ IV to benefit, active مُفِيدٌ beneficial, passive مُفَادٌ benefited

اِنْبَاعَ يَنْبَاعُ VII to be sold, active مُنْبَاعٌ being sold

اِحْتَاجَ يَحْتَاجُ إِلَى VIII to need, active and passive مُحْتَاجٌ needing, needed

اِبْيَضَّ يَبْيَضُّ IX to turn white, active مُبْيَضٌّ turning white

اِسْتَرَاحَ يَسْتَرِيحُ X to rest, active مُسْتَرِيحٌ resting, passive مُسْتَرَاحٌ rested

The plurals of all these participles are sound; see 137, 138, 140 and 141 for declension.

**106. Verbal Nouns.** The hollow verbal nouns follow the pattern of the sound verbal nouns (see 65) in Forms II, III and V to IX:

مَوَّلَ يُمَوِّلُ II to finance, تَمْوِيلٌ financing

تَعَاوَنَ يَتَعَاوَنُ VI to cooperate, تَعَاوُنٌ cooperation

انْحَازَ يَنْحَازُ VII to be secluded, انْحِيَازٌ seclusion

امْتَازَ يَمْتَازُ VIII to be distinguished, امْتِيَازٌ distinction

ابْيَضَّ يَبْيَضُّ IX to turn white, ابْيِضَاضٌ turning white

In Forms IV and X the middle radical and its vowel become ...ا... , and ة is added after the final radical:

أَرَادَ يُرِيدُ IV to want, إِرَادَةٌ wish

اسْتَقَالَ يَسْتَقِيلُ X to resign, اسْتِقَالَةٌ resignation

The plurals of all these verbal nouns are sound. See 137, 138, 140 and 141 for declension.

# 10. Defective Verbs

**107. General.** Defective verbs (see 32) are the third sub-class of the weak verbs. They are those whose root has a weak letter, و or ي , as final radical, and two sound radicals. The weak final radical can take different guises:

- it can stabilise, i.e. assume its corresponding consonantal form;
- it can vocalise, i.e. assume vocalic form:
  - as the corresponding long or short vowel ُ...و , ي... , ... ٰ or ... ,
  - as ى... or ا...,
  - as ...ْ, combining with و to form the diphthong ...َوْ or with ي to form the diphthong ...َيْ ;
- it can appear as ء at the end of some verbal nouns;
- it can be dropped altogether, leaving nothing between the middle radical and the personal ending.

Roots with more than one weak radical, or with a weak letter as final radical and ء as another radical, or vice versa, are classed as doubly weak, see 119.

The defective sub-class has no Form IX.

**108. Table 20: Active Voice.** Examples of defective verbs, active voice:

| Form, Root, Principal Parts | Imperat. | Participle | Verbal Noun | to ... |
|---|---|---|---|---|
| I/1 رجو رَجَا يَرْجُو | اُرْجُ | رَاجٍ\الرَّاجِي | رَجَاءٌ | expect |
| /2 رضي\رضو ب رَضِيَ يَرْضَى | اِرْضَ | رَاضٍ\الرَّاضِي | رِضًى\الرِّضَى | approve |
| /2 نسي نَسِيَ يَنْسَى | اِنْسَ | نَاسٍ\النَّاسِي | نِسْيَانٌ | forget |
| /3 رمي رَمَى يَرْمِي | اِرْمِ | رَامٍ\الرَّامِي | رَمْيٌ | throw |
| /4 سعي سَعَى يَسْعَى إِلَى | اِسْعَ | سَاعٍ\السَّاعِي | سَعْيٌ | strive for |
| II ربو رَبَّى يُرَبِّي | رَبِّ | مُرَبٍّ\الْمُرَبِّي | تَرْبِيَةٌ | educate |
| III ندو نَادَى يُنَادِي | نَادِ | مُنَادٍ\الْمُنَادِي | مُنَادَاةٌ\نِدَاءٌ | call |
| IV عطو أَعْطَى يُعْطِي | أَعْطِ | مُعْطٍ\الْمُعْطِي | إِعْطَاءٌ | give to |
| V لقي تَلَقَّى يَتَلَقَّى | تَلَقَّ | مُتَلَقٍّ\الْمُتَلَقِّي | تَلَقٍّ\التَّلَقِّي | receive |
| VI عفو تَعَافَى يَتَعَافَى | تَعَافَ | مُتَعَافٍ\الْمُتَعَافِي | تَعَافٍ\التَّعَافِي | recover |
| VII قضي اِنْقَضَى يَنْقَضِي | اِنْقَضِ | مُنْقَضٍ\الْمُنْقَضِي | اِنْقِضَاءٌ | end |
| VIII شري اِشْتَرَى يَشْتَرِي | اِشْتَرِ | مُشْتَرٍ\الْمُشْتَرِي | اِشْتِرَاءٌ | buy |

| | | | | | |
|---|---|---|---|---|---|
| دعو | ادَّعَى يَدَّعِي | ادَّعِ | مُدَّعٍ\الْمُدَّعِي | ادِّعَاءُ | allege |
| X غني اسْتَغْنَى يَسْتَغْنِي عَنْ | | اسْتَغْنِ | مُسْتَغْنٍ\الْمُسْتَغْنِي | اسْتِغْنَاءُ | forgo |

See 37 for Forms I to X.

Note: The measures resemble those of the sound verbs only as far as the middle radical, sometimes the middle radical plus its vowel. Roots with final-radical ي are the most numerous. In particular, for the active voice:

- Form I has four groups:
  - Group 1 has only final-radical و verbs;
  - Group 2 has roots with either final-radical و or ي, sometimes both in the same root, all conjugating on the pattern of ي;
  - Groups 3 and 4 have only final-radical ي verbs.
- A small number of verbs has one root with final-radical و and another with final-radical ي, Form I being conjugated in Group 1 or Group 3 as appropriate. The root with final-radical ي is in each case the commoner.
- The masc. sing. participle has different indefinite and definite forms. See 117 below for the declension.
- In each of the increased forms, all the root patterns conjugate identically.

See Tables 22 (para. 110) and 23 (para. 112) for the conjugation of the tenses.

**109. Table 21: Passive Voice.** Examples of defective verbs in the passive voice (not all increased forms are found):

| Form, Root, Principal Parts | | | Participle | to be ... |
|---|---|---|---|---|
| I/1 | دعو | دُعِيَ يُدْعَى | مَدْعُوٌّ | summoned |
| /2 | رضو\رضي | رُضِيَ يُرْضَى ب | مَرْضِيٌّ | approved |
| /2 | نسي | نُسِيَ يُنْسَى | مَنْسِيٌّ | forgotten |
| /3 | رمي | رُمِيَ يُرْمَى | مَرْمِيٌّ | thrown |
| /4 | سعي | سُعِيَ يُسْعَى إِلَى | مَسْعِيٌّ | striven for |
| II | ربو | رُبِّيَ يُرَبَّى | مُرَبًّى\الْمُرَبَّى | educated |
| III | ندو | نُودِيَ يُنَادَى | مُنَادًى\الْمُنَادَى | called |

| IV | عفو | أُعْفِيَ يُعْفَى لِ | مُعْفًى\الْمُعْفَى | excused |
|---|---|---|---|---|
| V | لقي | تُلُقِّيَ يُتَلَقَّى | مُتَلَقًّى\الْمُتَلَقَّى | received |
| VI | ندو | تُنُودِيَ يُتَنَادَى | مُتَنَادًى\الْمُتَنَادَى | assembled |
| VIII | شري | أُشْتُرِيَ يُشْتَرَى | مُشْتَرًى\الْمُشْتَرَى | bought |
| X | ثني | أُسْتُثْنِيَ يُسْتَثْنَى | مُسْتَثْنًى\الْمُسْتَثْنَى | excepted |

See 37 for Forms I to X. See 36 and 55 for the passive.

Note: The measures resemble those of the sound verbs only as far as the middle radical, sometimes the middle radical plus its vowel. In particular, for the passive voice:

- Throughout the table, the 1st principal part ends in ـِيَ... and the 2nd principal parts ends in ـَى... .
- In Form I, Groups 1, 2, 3 and 4 all have the same measures for the principal parts. In addition, Groups 2, 3 and 4 all have the same measure for the participle.
- In all the increased forms, final-radical و verbs and final-radical ي verbs conjugate identically.
- In the increased forms, the masc. sing. participle has different indefinite and definite forms. See 117.
- The 2nd principal part has the same pattern in both Forms I and IV.

See 111 and 113 for the conjugation of the tenses.

**110. Table 22: Perfect (Indicative) Tense, Active Voice.** The personal endings of the perfect tense, active voice, of defective verbs are given below. The symbols (و) and (ي) in the first column indicate the final radical of the root. See 7 for the arrangement of persons:

| Form, (ي\و) | Singular | Dual | Plural |
|---|---|---|---|
| I/1 (و) | ...َوْتُ | | ...َوْنَا |
| | ...َوْتَ | ...َوْتُمَا | ...َوْتُم |
| | ...َوْتِ | ...َوْتُمَا | ...َوْتُنَّ |
| | ...َا | ...َوَا | ...َوْا |
| | ...َتْ | ...َتَا | ...َوْنَ |

| (و\ي) I/2 | ...يتُ | | ...ينَا |
|---|---|---|---|
| | ...يتَ | ...يتُمَا | ...يتُمْ |
| | ...يت | ...يتُمَا | ...يتُنَّ |
| | ...ي | ...يَا | ...وا |
| | ...يَتْ | ...يتَا | ...ينَ |
| I/3, I/4 (ي), II to X (و\ي) | ...يْتُ | | ...يْنَا |
| | ...يْتَ | ...يْتُمَا | ...يْتُمْ |
| | ...يْت | ...يْتُمَا | ...يْتُنَّ |
| | ...ى | ...يَا | ...وْا |
| | ...تْ | ...تَا | ...ينَ |

These endings, which are a combination of weak final radical and personal ending, are added to the perfect stem, which in defective verbs is derived from the 1st principal part by removing everything following the middle radical (the doubled middle radical in Forms II and V). In addition, note:

- Wherever the 1st principal part ends in ـَى... or ـا..., then the perfect tense will have ـَ... after the middle radical throughout the tense; otherwise it will not. Contrast the endings of Form I Group 2 with those of all the other verbs.

- Final -ā is written with ا :
  - always before a pronoun suffix, with all verbs (since ى only ever appears as last letter of the word):

    رَمَى I, he threw; *but*: رَمَاهُ. He threw it.

    تَلَقَّى V he received; *but*: تَلَقَّاهَا. He received them.

  - in Form I of final-radical و verbs, with or without a pronoun suffix:

    رَجَا I, he expected; رَجَاهُ. He expected it.

- Final -ā is written with ى :
  - in Form I of final-radical ي verbs when no suffix follows:

    مَشَى بِسُرْعَة. He walked fast.

  - in Forms II to X of all verbs when no suffix follows:

    اسْتَغْنَى عَنْ تَعَاوُنِ زُمَلَائَه. He did without the cooperation of his colleagues.

- See 28 and 166 for the modification of the personal endings with a final long vowel or final ˙... before hamzat al-waṣl and before object pronoun suffixes.

Examples of tenses:

<u>Perfect tense, Active:</u>

Root دعو ; دَعَا يَدْعُو I, to summon; perfect active tense:

| | | |
|---|---|---|
| دَعَوْتُ | | دَعَوْنَا |
| دَعَوْتَ | دَعَوْتُمَا | دَعَوْتُمْ |
| دَعَوْتِ | دَعَوْتُمَا | دَعَوْتُنَّ |
| دَعَا | دَعَوَا | دَعَوْا |
| دَعَتْ | دَعَتَا | دَعَوْنَ |

Root بقي ; بَقِيَ يَبْقَى I, to remain; perfect active tense:

| | | |
|---|---|---|
| بَقِيتُ | | بَقِينَا |
| بَقِيتَ | بَقِيتُمَا | بَقِيتُمْ |
| بَقِيتِ | بَقِيتُمَا | بَقِيتُنَّ |
| بَقِيَ | بَقِيَا | بَقُوا |
| بَقِيَتْ | بَقِيَتَا | بَقِينَ |

Root جري ; جَرَى يَجْرِي I, to flow; perfect active tense:

| | | |
|---|---|---|
| جَرَيْتُ | | جَرَيْنَا |
| جَرَيْتَ | جَرَيْتُمَا | جَرَيْتُمْ |
| جَرَيْتِ | جَرَيْتُمَا | جَرَيْتُنَّ |
| جَرَى | جَرَا | جَرَوْا |
| جَرَتْ | جَرَتَا | جَرَيْنَ |

Root عطو ; أَعْطَى يُعْطِي IV to give to; perfect active tense:

| | | |
|---|---|---|
| أَعْطَيْتُ | | أَعْطَيْنَا |
| أَعْطَيْتَ | أَعْطَيْتُمَا | أَعْطَيْتُمْ |
| أَعْطَيْتِ | أَعْطَيْتُمَا | أَعْطَيْتُنَّ |
| أَعْطَى | أَعْطَيَا | أَعْطَوْا |
| أَعْطَتْ | أَعْطَتَا | أَعْطَيْنَ |

Root دعو ; ادَّعَى يَدَّعِي VIII to allege; perfect active tense:

$$\begin{array}{cccc}
\text{ادَّعَيْتُ} & & & \text{ادَّعَيْنَا} \\
\text{ادَّعَيْتَ} & \text{ادَّعَيْتُمَا} & & \text{ادَّعَيْتُمْ} \\
\text{ادَّعَيْتِ} & \text{ادَّعَيْتُمَا} & & \text{ادَّعَيْتُنَّ} \\
\text{ادَّعَى} & \text{ادَّعَيَا} & & \text{ادَّعَوْا} \\
\text{ادَّعَتْ} & \text{ادَّعَتَا} & & \text{ادَّعَيْنَ}
\end{array}$$

**111. Perfect Tense, Passive Voice.** All defective verbs, whatever their root, have in the perfect passive, in Forms I to X, the same personal endings as Form I, Group 2 (رضو\رضي) active verbs, i.e. the middle group shown in Table 22 (para. 110) above. Examples:

Root نفو\نفي ; نُفِيَ يُنْفَى I, to be denied; perfect passive tense:

$$\begin{array}{cccc}
\text{نُفِيتُ} & & & \text{نُفِينَا} \\
\text{نُفِيتَ} & \text{نُفِيتُمَا} & & \text{نُفِيتُمْ} \\
\text{نُفِيتِ} & \text{نُفِيتُمَا} & & \text{نُفِيتُنَّ} \\
\text{نُفِيَ} & \text{نُفِيَا} & & \text{نُفُوا} \\
\text{نُفِيَتْ} & \text{نُفِيَتَا} & & \text{نُفِينَ}
\end{array}$$

Root لقي ; تُلُقِّيَ يُتَلَقَّى V to be received; perfect passive tense:

$$\begin{array}{cccc}
\text{تُلُقِّيتُ} & & & \text{تُلُقِّينَا} \\
\text{تُلُقِّيتَ} & \text{تُلُقِّيتُمَا} & & \text{تُلُقِّيتُمْ} \\
\text{تُلُقِّيتِ} & \text{تُلُقِّيتُمَا} & & \text{تُلُقِّيتُنَّ} \\
\text{تُلُقِّيَ} & \text{تُلُقِّيَا} & & \text{تُلُقُّوا} \\
\text{تُلُقِّيَتْ} & \text{تُلُقِّيَتَا} & & \text{تُلُقِّينَ}
\end{array}$$

**112. Table 23: Imperfect (Indicative) Tense, Active Voice.** The personal endings of the imperfect tense, active voice, of defective verbs are given below. The symbols (و) and (ي) in the first column indicate the final radical of the root. See 7 for the arrangement of persons:

| Form, (و\ي) | Singular | Dual | Plural |
|---|---|---|---|
| I/1 (و) | ...وُ | | ...وُ |
| | ...وُ | ...وُانِ | ...وُنَ |
| | ...ينَ | ...وُانِ | ...وُنَ |
| | ...وُ | ...وُانِ | ...وُنَ |
| | ...وُ | ...وُانِ | ...وُنَ |
| I/2 (و\ي), I/4 (ي), V and VI (و\ي) | ...ىَ | | ...ىَ |
| | ...ىَ | ...يَانِ | ...وْنَ |
| | ...يْنَ | ...يَانِ | ...يْنَ |
| | ...ىَ | ...يَانِ | ...وْنَ |
| | ...ىَ | ...يَانِ | ...يْنَ |
| I/3 (ي), II to IV (و\ي), VII to X (و\ي) | ...ي | | ...ي |
| | ...ي | ...يَانِ | ...وُنَ |
| | ...ينَ | ...يَانِ | ...ينَ |
| | ...ي | ...يَانِ | ...وُنَ |
| | ...ي | ...يَانِ | ...ينَ |

These endings, which are a combination of weak final radical and personal ending, are added to the imperfect stem, which in defective verbs is derived from the 2nd principal part by removing the personal prefix يَ\يُ , and everything following the middle radical (the doubled middle radical in Forms II and V). In addition, note:

- The imperfect personal prefixes are those of the sound verbs (see 41):

  نَرْجُو I/1, we expect      تُرَبِّي II you educate

  يُعْطُونَ IV they give      تَسْتَثْنِي X she excepts

- The only full-form endings curtailed in short pronunciation are those of the dual (-āni).
- Wherever the 2nd principal part ends in ...ىَ, then the imperfect tense will have ...ـ after the middle radical throughout the tense; otherwise it will not. Contrast the endings of Form I Groups 2 and 4, and Forms V and VI, with those of all the other verbs.
- Final -ā is written with ى when no pronoun object suffix is attached, and

with ﺍ before a pronoun suffix, with all verbs (since ﻯ only ever appears as last letter of the word):

يَنْسَى I, he forgets; *but*: يَنْسَاهُ. He forgets it.

يَتَلَقَّى V he receives; *but*: يَتَلَقَّاهَا He receives them.

لاَ يَرْضَى بِالإِجْرَاءِ الْمُقْتَرَحِ. He does not approve of the proposed measure.

- See 28 and 166 for the modification of the personal endings with a final long vowel or final ٔ... before hamzat al-waṣl and before object pronoun suffixes, and the modification of some third-person object pronoun suffixes after the ending ي... .

Examples:

Imperfect (Indicative) tense, Active:

Root عفو ؛ ل عَفَا يَعْفُو I, to excuse; imperfect active tense:

| | | | |
|---|---|---|---|
| | أَعْفُو | | نَعْفُو |
| تَعْفُو | تَعْفُوَانِ | | تَعْفُونَ |
| تَعْفِينَ | تَعْفُوَانِ | | يَعْفُونَ |
| يَعْفُو | يَعْفُوَانِ | | تَعْفُونَ |
| تَعْفُو | تَعْفُوَانِ | | يَعْفُونَ |

Root سعي ؛ ل سَعَى يَسْعَى I, to strive for; imperfect active tense:

| | | | |
|---|---|---|---|
| | أَسْعَى | | نَسْعَى |
| تَسْعَى | تَسْعَيَانِ | | تَسْعَوْنَ |
| تَسْعَيْنَ | تَسْعَيَانِ | | تَسْعَيْنَ |
| يَسْعَى | يَسْعَيَانِ | | يَسْعَوْنَ |
| تَسْعَى | تَسْعَيَانِ | | يَسْعَيْنَ |

Root سوي ؛ سَوَّى يُسَوِّي II to level; imperfect active tense:

| | | | |
|---|---|---|---|
| | أُسَوِّي | | نُسَوِّي |
| تُسَوِّي | تُسَوِّيَانِ | | تُسَوُّونَ |
| تُسَوِّينَ | تُسَوِّيَانِ | | تُسَوِّينَ |
| يُسَوِّي | يُسَوِّيَانِ | | يُسَوُّونَ |
| تُسَوِّي | تُسَوِّيَانِ | | يُسَوِّينَ |

Root ندو ; نَادَى يُنَادِي III to call; imperfect active tense:

| | | | |
|---|---|---|---|
| | أُنَادِي | | نُنَادِي |
| تُنَادِي | تُنَادِيَانِ | تُنَادُونَ | |
| تُنَادِينَ | تُنَادِيَانِ | تُنَادِينَ | |
| يُنَادِي | يُنَادِيَانِ | يُنَادُونَ | |
| تُنَادِي | تُنَادِيَانِ | يُنَادِينَ | |

**113. Imperfect (Indicative) Tense, Passive Voice.** All defective verbs, whatever their root, have in the perfect passive, in Forms I to X, the same personal endings as Form I, Group 2 (رضو\رضي) active verbs, i.e. the middle group shown in 112 above. The personal prefixes are those of the sound verbs (see 41). Example:

Root دعو ; دُعِيَ يُدْعَى I, to be summoned; imperfect passive tense:

| | | | |
|---|---|---|---|
| | أُدْعَى | | نُدْعَى |
| تُدْعَى | تُدْعَيَانِ | تُدْعَوْنَ | |
| تُدْعَيْنَ | تُدْعَيَانِ | تُدْعَيْنَ | |
| يُدْعَى | يُدْعَيَانِ | يُدْعَوْنَ | |
| تُدْعَى | تُدْعَيَانِ | يُدْعَيْنَ | |

**114. (Imperfect) Subjunctive Tense.** Derive the (imperfect) subjunctive tense of defective verbs from the imperfect (indicative) tense, as follows:

- Imperfect (indicative) endings ...وُ and ...ي : add ...َ (dropped in short pronunciation when no object pronoun suffix is attached):

  imperfect يَرْجُو I, he expects, subjunctive يَرْجُوَ

  imperfect يُنَادِي III he calls, subjunctive يُنَادِيَ

- Imperfect personal endings ...ن\...نَ , other than the feminine plurals: drop ...ن\...نَ and add silent ا (dropped in writing before an object pronoun suffix) after any resultant final و :

  imperfect يَنْسَوْنَ I, they forget, subjunctive يَنْسَوْا

  imperfect تُرَبِّيَانِ II you educate, subjunctive تُرَبِّيَا

  imperfect تُنَادَيْنَ III you (f. sing.) are called, subjunctive تُنَادَيْ

- Leave the rest unchanged:

imperfect and subjunctive تُنَادَيْنَ III you (f. pl.) are called

These rules are different from those valid for verbs with a sound final radical.
See 28 and 166 for the modification of the personal endings with a final long
vowel or final ـً ... before hamzat al-waṣl and before object pronoun suffixes, and
the modification of some third-person object pronoun suffixes after the endings
ـِي ... and ـَيْ ... :

يَجُوزُ أَنْ يَنْسُوا القَضِيَّةَ.   Perhaps they will forget the matter.

**115.  (Imperfect) Jussive Tense.** Derive the (imperfect) jussive tense of
defective verbs from the (imperfect) subjunctive tense, as follows:

- For subjunctive endings ـُو ... , ـَى ... \ ـَا ... , and ـِي ... : substitute the
  corresponding short vowel, ـُ ... , ـَ ... , ـِ ... respectively:

  subjunctive نَرْجُوَ I, we expect, jussive نَرْجُ

  subjunctive تُشْتَرَى VIII it is bought, jussive تُشْتَرَ

  subjunctive يَجْرِيَ I, it flows, jussive يَجْرِ

- Leave the rest unchanged:

  subjunctive and jussive يُسَوَّيَا II they are both levelled

These rules are different from those valid for verbs with a sound final radical.

See 28 and 166 for the modification of the personal endings with a final long
vowel or final ـً ... before hamzat al-waṣl and before object pronoun suffixes, and
the modification of some third-person object pronoun suffixes after the endings
ـِي ... and ـَيْ ... :

لِيَبْقَوُا الآنَ.   Let them stay now.

**116.  Imperative.** The affirmative imperative of defective verbs is regularly
derived from the jussive (see 50); the negative imperative is also regularly formed
by putting لاَ before the unchanged jussive.

  jussive تَعْفُ I, you forgive, أُعْفُ forgive, لاَ تَعْفُ do not forgive

  jussive تَلْقِ I, you meet, الْقِ meet, لاَ تَلْقِ do not meet

  jussive تَنْسَوُا I, you forget, انْسَوُا forget, لاَ تَنْسَوُا do not forget

  jussive تَشْتَرِ VIII you buy, اشْتَرِ buy, لاَ تَشْتَرِ do not buy

See 28 and 166 for the modification of the personal endings with a final long
vowel or final ـً ... before hamzat al-waṣl and before object pronoun suffixes, and
the modification of some third-person object pronoun suffixes after the endings

ي...ِ and يَ...ْ :

انْسَوُا التَّعْوِيضَ الْمَطْلُوبَ.   Forget the compensation demanded.

لاَ تَنْسَيِ الْمَبْدَأَ الأَسَاسِيَّ.   Do not forget the basic principle.

**117.  Table 24: Participles.** The patterns of the participles of the sound verbs (see 51) are all valid for the participles of the defective verbs, except for the masculine singular participle which is anomalous. Table 24 below shows the active participles:

| Typical Root and Verb | Nom. + Gen. Indefinite/Definite | Accusative Indefinite/Definite | |
|---|---|---|---|
| رجو    رَجَا  I, to expect | راجٍ\الرَّاجِي | راجِيًا\الرَّاجِيَ | expecting |
| شري   اشْتَرَى  VIII to buy | مُشْتَرٍ\الْمُشْتَرِي | مُشْتَرِيًا\الْمُشْتَرَيَ | buying |

Note:

- The masc. sing. active participle has the endings ٍ... (nominative and genitive) and يًا... (accusative) for the indefinite form; and ي...ِ (nominative and genitive) and يَ... (accusative) for the definite form.
- The stem to which the endings are added is derived as follows:
    - Form I: take the root. Put ا... after the initial radical. Drop the final radical.
    - Forms II to X : take the second principal part. Substitute ...مُ for the prefix ...يَ or ...يُ. Drop everything following the middle radical.

The other forms of these active participles (built on the same stem, but regularly declined, see 137, 138, 140 and 141), are (in the nominative):

Root رمي : رَمَى يَرْمِي I, to throw:

masc.:                      dual  رَامِيَانِ   pl.  رَامُونَ

fem.:  sing. رَامِيَةٌ   dual رَامِيَتَانِ   pl. رَامِيَاتٌ

A few participles of this type are used principally as nouns. Common examples:

Root قضي ; قَضَى يَقْضِي I, to judge:

قَاضٍ\الْقَاضِي judge, pl. قُضَاةٌ , regular declension

Root حمي ; حَامَى يُحَامِي III to defend:

مُحَامٍ\الْمُحَامِي lawyer, pl. مُحَامُونَ (sound)

Root ندو , نَادَى يُنَادِي III to call:

نَاد\النَّادِي club, pl. أَنْدِيَةٌ, regular declension

See also 162 for non-participial nouns following this ...ي\... pattern in the plural.
See 147 for the modification of some third-person possessive suffixes after the
ending ...ي : nom./gen. مُحَامِيهِ his lawyer

The passive participles of Form I (all roots) are formed as follows. Declension is
regular:

Final-radical و : رَجَا يَرْجُو I, to expect: مَرْجُوٌّ

Final-radical ي : نَسِيَ يَنْسَى I, to forget: مَنْسِيٌّ

The passive participles of Forms II to X (all roots) are invariable for case in the
masculine singular. The stem is the same as for the active participle, see above:

اشْتَرَى يَشْتَرِي VIII to buy; all cases: indefinite مُشْتَرًى, definite الْمُشْتَرَى
These are the masculine singular forms. The other forms, regularly declined, are
(in the nominative):

Root رِبو : رَبَّى يُرَبِّي II to educate:

| masc.: | | dual | مُرَبَّيَانِ | pl. | مُرَبَّوْنَ |
| fem.: | sing. مُرَبَّاةٌ | dual | مُرَبَّتَانِ | pl. | مُرَبَّيَاتٌ |

## 118. Verbal Nouns.

The defective verbal nouns are irregular in Form I. Those
of the Forms II to X follow the pattern of the sound verbal nouns (see 65) as far as
the middle radical, sometimes as far as the middle radical plus its vowel. In
particular, note:

- In Form II the noun ends ...يَةٌ :

  رَبَّى يُرَبِّي II to educate: تَرْبِيَةٌ education
- The commoner pattern of Form III ends ...اةٌ :

  لَاقَى يُلَاقِي III to encounter; مُلَاقَاةٌ encounter
- The less common pattern of Form III, and the measures of Forms IV,
  VII, VIII and X end with ء . In Forms IV, VII, VIII and X, this
  produces a pattern often identical to that of final-radical hamza verbs
  (see 84):

  لَاقَى يُلَاقِي III to encounter; لِقَاءٌ encounter

  أَلْقَى يُلْقِي IV to deliver (a speech, recital etc.): إِلْقَاءٌ delivery, recital

  انْقَضَى يَنْقَضِي VIII to be finished: انْقِضَاءٌ expiry

  اشْتَرَى يَشْتَرِي VIII to buy: اشْتِرَاءٌ purchase

اِسْتَثْنَى يَسْتَثْنِي X to except: اِسْتِثْنَاءٌ exception

See 137, 138, 140 and 141 for the full declension of these nouns.

- In Forms V and VI the verbal noun has endings identical to those of the corresponding masculine singular active participle (see 117 above):

تَلَقَّى يَتَلَقَّى V to receive: indefinite تَلَقٍّ, definite التَّلَقِّي reception

تَعَافَى يَتَعَافَى VI to recover in health:

indefinite تَعَافٍ, definite التَّعَافِي recovery

See 147 for the modification of some third-person possessive suffixes after the ending ي... : nom./gen. تَعَافِيهِ his recovery

# 11. Doubly Weak Verbs

**119.** **General.** Doubly weak verbs (see 32) are the fourth sub-class of the weak verbs. They are those whose root has two weak letters, one of them as final radical, in one of the following patterns:

- و as initial radical, a sound middle radical, and ي as final radical,
- a sound initial radical with ء as middle radical (or vice versa); and ي as final radical,
- a sound initial radical, و or ي as middle radical, and ء as final radical.

Other patterns are in theory possible, but those shown cover all common verbs.

In doubly weak verbs, each radical follows its own rules of conjugation, with two important exceptions:

- In roots with middle-radical و or ي and final-radical ي , the middle radical stabilises as a consonant.
- In doubly weak roots with final-radical ء , the Form I active participle follows the weak (i.e defective or doubly weak) pattern; see 117, also 128 below.

**120.** **Table 25: Active Voice.** Although important, the doubly weak verbs are so few that most students find them easiest to learn one by one. Examples of doubly weak verbs in the active voice:

| Form/Root/Principal Parts | Imperat. | Participle | Verbal Noun | to ... |
|---|---|---|---|---|
| I   وقي   وَقَى يَقِي | قِ | وَاقٍ\الْوَاقِي | وِقَايَةٌ | protect |
| ولي   وَلِيَ يَلِي | لِ | وَالٍ\الْوَالِي | وِلاَيَةٌ | administer |
| رأي   رَأَى يَرَى* | رَ* | رَاءٍ\الرَّائِي | رَأْيٌ | see |
| أتي   أَتَى يَأْتِي | ت\ائتِ | آتٍ\الآتِي | إِتْيَانٌ | come |
| أبي   أَبَى يَأْبَى | ائبَ | آبٍ\الآبِي | إِبَاءٌ | reject |
| سوء   سَاءَ يَسُوءُ | سُؤْ | سَاءٍ\السَّائِي | سُوءٌ | be evil |
| شيء   شَاءَ يَشَاءُ | شَأْ | شَاءٍ\الشَّائِي | مَشِيئَةٌ | wish |
| جيء   جَاءَ يَجِيءُ | جِئْ | جَاءٍ\الْجَائِي | مَجِيءٌ | come |
| نوي   نَوَى يَنْوِي | انْوِ | نَاوٍ\النَّاوِي | نِيَّةٌ | intend |
| حيّ\حيي   حَيَّ\حَيِيَ يَحْيَا حيّ\احيي | احْيَ | not used | حَيَاةٌ | live |

| | | | | | |
|---|---|---|---|---|---|
| سوي | سَوِيَ يَسْوَى | اِسْوَ | سَاوٍ\السَّاوِي | سُوًى\السَّوَى | equal |
| II    ولي | وَلَّى يُوَلِّي | وَلِّ | مُوَلٍّ\المُوَلِّي | تَوْلِيَةٌ | appoint |
| سوي | سَوَّى يُسَوِّي | سَوِّ | مُسَوٍّ\المُسَوِّي | تَسْوِيَةٌ | level |
| III    ولي | وَالَى يُوَالِي | وَالِ | مُوَالٍ\المُوَالِي | مُوَالَاةٌ | sponsor |
| سوي | سَاوَى يَسَاوِي | سَاوِ | مُسَاوٍ\المُسَاوِي | مَسَاوَاةٌ | equalise |
| IV    أتي | آتَى يُؤْتِي | آتِ | مُؤْتٍ\المُؤْتِي | إِيتَاءٌ | bring |
| رأي | أَرَى* يُرِي* | أَرِ* | مُرٍ*\المُرِي* | إِرَاءَةٌ | show |
| V    ولي | تَوَلَّى يَتَوَلَّى | تَوَلَّ | مُتَوَلٍّ\المُتَوَلِّي | تَوَلٍّ\التَّوَلِّي | assume |
| VI    ولي | تَوَالَى يَتَوَالَى | تَوَالَ | مُتَوَالٍ\المُتَوَالِي | تَوَالٍ\التَّوَالِي | follow on |
| VII    زوي | انْزَوَى يَنْزَوِي | انْزَوِ | مُنْزَوٍ\المُنْزَوِي | انْزِوَاءٌ | be isolated |
| VIII    وقي | اتَّقَى يَتَّقِي | اتَّقِ | مُتَّقٍ\المُتَّقِي | اتِّقَاءٌ | be wary |
| سوء | اسْتَاءَ يَسْتَاءُ مِنْ | اسْتَأْ | مُسْتَاءٌ | اسْتِيَاءٌ | be offended |
| حوي | احْتَوَى يَحْتَوِي | احْتَوِ | مُحْتَوٍ\المُحْتَوِي | احْتِوَاءٌ | enclose |
| X    ولي    اسْتَوْلَى يَسْتَوْلِي | اسْتَوْلِ | مُسْتَوْلٍ\المُسْتَوْلِي | اسْتِيلَاءٌ | appropriate |

See 37 for Forms I to VIII and X.

Note:

- There is only one common verb with middle-radical ء and final-radical ي in Form I: رَأَى يَرَى 'to see'; it drops its middle radical in the imperfect tenses and imperative. The same root drops its middle radical in Form IV, in everything except the verbal noun: أَرَى يُرِي 'to show'. The anomalous patterns are marked * in the table.

- In Form I, active voice, of doubly weak verbs, final-radical ء is stable (i.e. follows the conjugation of sound and of hamzated verbs, see 79) in the tenses, imperative and verbal noun, but behaves like a weak radical in the participle. In the increased forms, final-radical ء is stable throughout the verb.

- The theoretical combination 'a'- becomes آ... , the theoretical combination 'ī'- becomes إِيـ... , and the theoretical combinations i'i- and -iw- become اِيـ...\...ـيـ... .

- In Form VIII, initial-radical و assimilates to the ت of the increased form, as in the assimilated verbs. See 93.

- The writing of final-radical ء before a personal ending beginning with a long vowel can present difficulty (see 18):

| | |
|---|---|
| ...ā'ā, ...ā'āni | ...ءَاءَ، ...ءَاءَان |
| ...ā'ū, ...ā'ūna | ...ءَاؤُوا \ ...ءَاءُوا، ...ءَاؤُونَ \ ...ءَاءُونَ |
| ...ī'ū, ...ī'ūna | ...يِؤُوا \ ...يِئُوا، ...يِؤُونَ \ ...يِئُونَ |
| ...ī'ā, ...ī'āni | ...يِئَا، ...يِئَان |

Alternative Arabic spellings are shown with \.

- For the verb حَيُّ\حَيِيَ يَحْيَا I, 'to live': in the 2nd principal part, and with it many persons in the imperfect tenses, the ending when sounded -ā is written with ا because ى cannot follow ي .

**121. Table 26: Passive Voice.** Examples of doubly weak verbs in the passive voice (not all increased forms are found):

| Form, Root, Principal Parts | | | Participle | to be ... |
|---|---|---|---|---|
| I | وقي | وُقِيَ يُوقَى | مَوْقِيٌّ | protected |
| | رأي | رُئِيَ يُرَى* | مَرْئِيٌّ | seen |
| | أبي | أُبِيَ يُؤْبَى | مَأْبِيٌّ | rejected |
| | شيء | شِيءَ يُشَاءُ | مَشِيءٌ | wished |
| | نوي | نُوِيَ يُنْوَى | مَنْوِيٌّ | intended |
| II | ولي | وُلِّيَ يُوَلَّى | مُوَلًّى\المُوَلَّى | appointed |
| | سوي | سُوِّيَ يُسَوَّى | مُسَوًّى\المُسَوَّى | levelled |
| III | ولي | وُولِيَ يُوَالَى | مُوَالًى\المُوَالَى | sponsored |
| IV | رأي | أُرِيَ* يُرَى* | مُرًى*\المُرَى* | shown |
| | أتي | أُوتِيَ يُؤْتَى | مُؤْتًى\المُؤْتَى | brought |
| V | وخي | تُوُخِّيَ يُتَوَخَّى | مُتَوَخًّى\المُتَوَخَّى | intended |
| VIII | وقي | أُتُّقِيَ يُتَّقَى | مُتَّقًى\المُتَّقَى | guarded against |
| X | ولي | أُسْتُولِيَ يُسْتَوْلَى | مُسْتَوْلًى\المُسْتَوْلَى | appropriated |

See 37 for Forms I to X. See 36 and 55 for the passive.

Note:

- Throughout the passive, in the roots with final-radical ي, the 1st principal part ends in ـِيَ... and the 2nd principal parts ends in ـِيَ... .
- Forms I and IV of verbs with initial-radical ء and final-radical ي have identical 2nd principal parts.
- See 120, first indent, above, for Forms I and IV of the root رأي . The anomalous forms are marked *.
- In the passive of doubly weak verbs, final-radical ء is stable (i.e. follows the conjugation of hamzated verbs, see 80, 81 and 83) throughout the verb.
- The patterns of Forms II, III, V and VI are identical to those of the defective verbs, see 109.
- The theoretical combination 'u'- (root أتي, Form IV, 1st principal part) becomes ...أُو... , and the theoretical combination -ui- (root وقي, Form I, 2nd principal part; root ولي, Form X , 1st principal part) becomes ...وُ... .
- In Form VIII, initial-radical و assimilates to the ت of the increased form, as in the assimilated verbs. See 95.
- The writing of final-radical ء before a personal ending beginning with ...ا... or ...وُ... can present difficulty:

...ā'ā, ...ā'āni    ...ءَا ، ...ءَاَنِ

...ā'ū, ...ā'ūna    ...ءُونَ \ ...ءُوا ، ...ءُوُنَ \ ...ءُوُوا...

Alternative Arabic spellings are shown with \.

**122.** **Tenses.** In doubly weak verbs, each radical (with one exception, see weak middle radicals below) follows the rules of its own conjugation in the tenses:

- sound radicals: sound pattern (59 to 62),
- initial- or final-radical ء : hamzated pattern (69 and 81); the only common root with middle-radical ء is anomalous, see 120 and 121,
- weak radicals:
    - initial و or ي (the latter is very rare): assimilated pattern (96),
    - middle و or ي before a sound final radical or final-radical ء : hollow pattern (103)
    - middle و or ي before a final-radical ي (final و does not occur) stabilises to a consonant: defective pattern (110 to 115),
    - final ي ( و is very rare): defective pattern (110 to 115),

In addition, the imperfect prefixes are those appropriate to the initial radical (sound/hamzated 39, assimilated 96) in the appropriate form (I to X).

See 28 and 166 for the modification of the personal endings with a final long vowel or final ْ... before hamzat al-waṣl and before object pronoun suffixes, and the modification of some third-person object pronoun suffixes after the endings ي...ْ and ـيَ...ْ .

**123. Perfect (Indicative) Tense.** For the personal endings of the perfect tense of doubly weak verbs, see 81 for roots with final-radical ء , and Table 22, para. 110 for roots with final-radical ي .

Examples of doubly weak verbs, perfect tense:

Root وقي ; وَقَى يَقِي I, to protect; perfect active tense:

| | | |
|---|---|---|
| | | وَقَيْتُ |
| وَقَيْنَا | | |
| وَقَيْتَ | وَقَيْتُمَا | وَقَيْتُمْ |
| وَقَيْتِ | وَقَيْتُمَا | وَقَيْتُنَّ |
| وَقَى | وَقَيَا | وَقَوْا |
| وَقَتْ | وَقَتَا | وَقَيْنَ |

Root ولي ; وَلِيَ يَلِي I, to be next; perfect active tense:

| | | |
|---|---|---|
| وَلِيتُ | | |
| وَلِينَا | | |
| وَلِيتَ | وَلِيتُمَا | وَلِيتُمْ |
| وَلِيتِ | وَلِيتُمَا | وَلِيتُنَّ |
| وَلِيَ | وَلِيَا | وَلُوا |
| وَلِيَتْ | وَلِيَتَا | وَلِينَ |

Root جيئ ; جَاءَ يَجِيءُ I, to come; perfect active tense:

| | | |
|---|---|---|
| جِئْتُ | | |
| جِئْنَا | | |
| جِئْتَ | جِئْتُمَا | جِئْتُمْ |
| جِئْتِ | جِئْتُمَا | جِئْتُنَّ |
| جَاءَ | جَاءَا | جَاؤُوا\جَاءُوا |
| جَاءَتْ | جَاءَتَا | جِئْنَ |

Anomalous root رأي ; أَرَى يُرِي IV to show; perfect active tense:

| | |
|---|---|
| أَرَيْتُ | أَرَيْنَا |

| | | |
|---|---|---|
| أَرَيْتَ | أَرَيْتُمَا | أَرَيْتُمْ |
| أَرَيْتِ | أَرَيْتُمَا | أَرَيْتُنَّ |
| أَرَى | أَرَيَا | أَرَوْا |
| أَرَتْ | أَرَتَا | أَرَيْنَ |

Root حيي\حيّ ; حَيَّ\حَيِيَ يَحْيَا I, to live; perfect active tense:

| | | |
|---|---|---|
| حَيِيتُ | | حَيِينَا |
| حَيِيتَ | حَيِيتُمَا | حَيِيتُمْ |
| حَيِيتِ | حَيِيتُمَا | حَيِيتُنَّ |
| حَيَّ\حَيِيَ | حَيَّا | حَيُّوا |
| حَيَّتْ\حَيِيَتْ | حَيَّتَا | حَيِينَ |

Root أبي ; أُبِيَ يُؤْبَى I, to be rejected; perfect passive tense:

| | | |
|---|---|---|
| أُبِيتُ | | أُبِينَا |
| أُبِيتَ | أُبِيتُمَا | أُبِيتُمْ |
| أُبِيتِ | أُبِيتُمَا | أُبِيتُنَّ |
| أُبِيَ | أُبِيَا | أُبُوا |
| أُبِيَتْ | أُبِيَتَا | أُبِينَ |

Root ولي ; أُسْتُولِيَ يُسْتَوْلَى X to be appropriated; perfect passive tense:

| | | |
|---|---|---|
| أُسْتُولِيتُ | | أُسْتُولِينَا |
| أُسْتُولِيتَ | أُسْتُولِيتُمَا | أُسْتُولِيتُمْ |
| أُسْتُولِيتِ | أُسْتُولِيتُمَا | أُسْتُولِيتُنَّ |
| أُسْتُولِيَ | أُسْتُولِيَا | أُسْتُولُوا |
| أُسْتُولِيَتْ | أُسْتُولِيَتَا | أُسْتُولِينَ |

**124. Imperfect (Indicative) Tense.** For the personal endings of the imperfect tense of doubly weak verbs, see 81 for roots with final-radical ء , and Table 23, para. 112 for roots with final-radical ي . The personal prefix is that appropriate to the initial radical (sound/hamzated 41, assimilated 96) in the appropriate form (I to X).

See 122 above, last sentence.

Examples of doubly weak verbs, imperfect (indicative) tense:

Anomalous root رأي ; رَأَى يَرَى I, to see; imperfect active tense:

| | | | |
|---|---|---|---|
| | أَرَى | | نَرَى |
| تَرَى | تَرَيَانِ | تَرَوْنَ | |
| تَرَيْنَ | تَرَيَانِ | تَرَيْنَ | |
| يَرَى | يَرَيَانِ | يَرَوْنَ | |
| تَرَى | تَرَيَانِ | يَرَيْنَ | |

Root جيء ; جَاءَ يَجِيءُ I, to come; imperfect active tense:

| | | | |
|---|---|---|---|
| | أَجِيءُ | | نَجِيءُ |
| تَجِيءُ | تَجِيئَانِ | تَجِيئُونَ\تَجِيئُونَ | |
| تَجِيئِينَ | تَجِيئَانِ | تَجِئْنَ | |
| يَجِيءُ | يَجِيئَانِ | يَجِيئُونَ\يَجِيئُونَ | |
| تَجِيءُ | تَجِيئَانِ | يَجِئْنَ | |

Root حيي\حيّ ; حَيَّ\حَيِيَ يَحْيَا I, to live; imperfect active tense:

| | | | |
|---|---|---|---|
| | أَحْيَا | | نَحْيَا |
| تَحْيَا | تَحْيَانِ | تَحْيَوْنَ | |
| تَحْيَيْنَ | تَحْيَانِ | تَحْيَيْنَ | |
| يَحْيَا | يَحْيَانِ | يَحْيَوْنَ | |
| تَحْيَا | تَحْيَانِ | يَحْيَيْنَ | |

See 120, last indent.

Root وقي ; اتَّقَى يَتَّقِي VIII to protect; imperfect active tense:

| | | | |
|---|---|---|---|
| | أَتَّقِي | | نَتَّقِي |
| تَتَّقِي | تَتَّقِيَانِ | تَتَّقُونَ | |
| تَتَّقِينَ | تَتَّقِيَانِ | تَتَّقِينَ | |
| يَتَّقِي | يَتَّقِيَانِ | يَتَّقُونَ | |
| تَتَّقِي | تَتَّقِيَانِ | يَتَّقِينَ | |

Root سوء ; اسْتَاءَ يَسْتَاءُ مِنْ VIII to be offended at; imperfect active tense:

| | | | |
|---|---|---|---|
| | أَسْتَاءُ | | نَسْتَاءُ |
| تَسْتَاءُ | تَسْتَاءَانِ | تَسْتَاءُونَ\تَسْتَاءُونَ | |

| | | |
|---|---|---|
| تَسْتَائِينَ | تَسْتَاءَانِ | تَسْتَأْنَ |
| يَسْتَاءُ | يَسْتَاءَانِ | يَسْتَاؤُونَ \ يَسْتَاءُونَ |
| تَسْتَاءُ | تَسْتَاءَانِ | يَسْتَأْنَ |

Root وقي ; وُقِيَ يُوقَى I, to be protected; imperfect passive tense:

| | | |
|---|---|---|
| أُوقَى | | نُوقَى |
| تُوقَى | تُوقَيَانِ | تُوقَوْنَ |
| تُوقَيْنَ | تُوقَيَانِ | تُوقَيْنَ |
| يُوقَى | يُوقَيَانِ | يُوقَوْنَ |
| تُوقَى | تُوقَيَانِ | يُوقَيْنَ |

Root وخي ; وُخِيَ يُوخَى II to be guided; imperfect passive tense:

| | | |
|---|---|---|
| أُوخَى | | نُوخَى |
| تُوخَى | تُوخَيَانِ | تُوخَوْنَ |
| تُوخَيْنَ | تُوخَيَانِ | تُوخَيْنَ |
| يُوخَى | يُوخَيَانِ | يُوخَوْنَ |
| تُوخَى | تُوخَيَانِ | يُوخَيْنَ |

**125. (Imperfect) Subjunctive Tense.** Derive the (imperfect) subjunctive tense of doubly weak verbs from the imperfect (indicative) tense, according to the final radical (hamzated 43, defective 114). Examples:

imperfect يَرَوْنَ I, they see, subjunctive يَرَوْا

imperfect تُؤْتِينَ IV you bring, subjunctive تُؤْتِي

imperfect يَسْتَاءُ VIII he is offended, subjunctive يَسْتَاءَ

imperfect and subjunctive يُؤْتَى IV it is brought

See 122 above, last sentence:

يَجُوزُ أَنْ يَرَوُا الْوَزِيرَ.   Perhaps they will see the minister.

**126. (Imperfect) Jussive Tense.** Derive the (imperfect) jussive tense of doubly weak verbs from the (imperfect) subjunctive tense, according to the middle and final radicals (hamzated 45, hollow 103, defective 115). Examples:

subjunctive يَلِيَ I, he is next, jussive يَلِ

subjunctive نَجِيءَ I, we come, jussive: نَجِئْ
See 122 above, last sentence.

**127. Imperative.** The affirmative imperative of doubly weak verbs is regularly derived from the jussive (see 50); the negative imperative is also regularly formed by putting لا before the unchanged jussive. In roots which are both assimilated and defective, or where a radical ء is dropped, the imperative of Form I may be reduced to its only sound radical. Examples:

jussive تَقِ I, you protect, قِ protect, لا تَقِ do not protect

jussive تَرَ I, you see, رَ see, لا تَرَ do not see

jussive تَسْتَوْلُوا X you appropriate,

اِسْتَوْلُوا appropriate, لا تَسْتَوْلُوا do not appropriate
See 122 above, last sentence.

**128. Participles.** The participles of doubly weak verbs with final-radical ي follow completely the rules for defective participles, see 117 and 145.
For the participles of doubly weak verbs with final-radical ء :

- the ء counts as a weak letter (i.e. participle has the defective pattern) in the active participle of Form I,
- the ء is stable (i.e. sound) in all other participles (active, Forms II to X; passive, Forms I to X).

Examples (all nominative masculine singular):

أَتَى يَأْتِي I, to come: active آتٍ\الآتِي coming

جَاءَ يَجِيءُ I, to come: active جَاءٍ\الجَائِي coming

شَاءَ يَشَاءُ I, to wish: active شَاءٍ\الشَّائِي wishing, passive مَشِيءٌ wished

رَأَى يَرَى I, to see: active رَاءٍ\الرَّائِي seeing, passive مَرْئِيٌّ seen

نَوَى يَنْوِي I, to intend: active نَاوٍ\النَّاوِي intending, passive مَنْوِيٌّ intended

وَلَّى يُوَلِّي II to appoint:

active مُوَلٍّ\المُوَلِّي appointing, passive مُوَلًّى\المُوَلَّى appointed

أَرَى يُرِي IV to show: active مُرٍ\المُرِي showing, passive مُرًى\المُرَى shown

اِنْزَوَى يَنْزَوِي VII to live in seclusion:

active (no passive) مُنْزَوٍ\المُنْزَوِي living in seclusion

اِسْتَاءَ يَسْتَاءُ مِنْ VIII to be offended at: active (no passive) مُسْتَاءٌ offended

See 147 for the modification of some third-person possessive suffixes after the ending ي...: nom./gen. وَاقِيهِمْ their guardian

Para. 117 shows the feminine, dual and plural forms, for the declension of which see 137, 138, 140 and 141.

**129. Verbal Nouns.** The doubly weak verbal nouns follow essentially the pattern of the sound and hamzated verbs (see 65), but with modifications dictated by each radical other than sound or hamzated (assimilated 99, hollow 106, defective 118). Final-radical ء hamza is not a weak letter in any of the verbal nouns, as it is in the Form I active participles (see 128 above). Examples:

رَأَى يَرَى I, to see: رَأْيٌ view

وَلَّى يُوَلِّي II to appoint: تَوْلِيَةٌ appointment

آتَى يُؤْتِي IV to bring: إِيتَاءٌ bringing

تَوَلَّى يَتَوَلَّى V to assume office: تَوَلٍّ\التَّوَلِّي assumption of office

اسْتَاءَ يَسْتَاءُ مِنْ VIII to be offended at: اسْتِيَاءٌ indignation

اسْتَوْلَى يَسْتَوْلِي X to appropriate: اسْتِيلاءٌ appropriation

See 147 for the modification of some third-person possessive suffixes after the ending ي...: nom./gen. تَوَلِّيهِمْ their assumption of office

Para. 117 shows the declension of the anomalous verbal nouns of Forms V and VI; for the declension of the other verbal nouns see 137, 138, 140 and 141. Plurals, if any, are sound.

# 12. Nouns and Adjectives

**130. Gender of Nouns.** Nouns are either masculine (m.) or feminine (f.).
Feminine nouns are:

- nouns denoting female persons, e.g.:

    أُمّ mother       بِنْتٌ girl; daughter       صُحُفِيَّةٌ journalist

- nouns ending in ة and not denoting male persons, e.g.:

    بِنَايَةٌ building       وَثِيقَةٌ document       إِدَارَةٌ administration

- nouns denoting a double part of the body, e.g.:

    عَيْنٌ eye                                    يَدٌ hand

- nouns ending in ا or ى when this is not a radical, e.g.:

    الدُّنْيَا the world       ذِكْرَى memory

- nouns ending in ء ا when the ء is not a radical, e.g.:

    صَحْرَاءُ desert

- most names of countries, e.g.:

    مِصْرُ Egypt

- a small number of other nouns, e.g.:

| | | | | | |
|---|---|---|---|---|---|
| أَرْضٌ | land | بِئْرٌ | well | حَرْبٌ | war |
| خَمْرٌ | wine | دَلْوٌ | bucket | دَارٌ | house |
| رِيحٌ | wind | شَمْسٌ | sun | عَصًا | stick |
| فَأْسٌ | axe | كَأْسٌ | cup | نَفْسٌ | soul |
| | | نَارٌ | fire | | |

Masculine nouns are:

- nouns denoting male persons, e.g.:

    رَجُلٌ man       خَلِيفَةٌ successor       صُحُفِيٌّ journalist

- most nouns ending in a consonant (including a radical ء), e.g.:

    كِتَابٌ book       مَسَاءٌ evening       افْتِتَاحٌ inauguration

- participles, used as nouns, of defective and doubly weak verbs, and not
  ending in ة , e.g.:

    قَاضٍ judge       مُسْتَشْفًى hospital

A few nouns are both masculine and feminine, e.g.:

    طَرِيقٌ (m./f.) road       لِسَانٌ (m./f.) tongue

Some words like رَهِينَةٌ 'hostage', which are feminine in form, are treated as
masculine when they refer to a male person.

**131.  Case.** Arabic nouns and adjectives have three grammatical cases:

- Nominative (nom.): denoting the subject of a verb (when the clause does
  not begin with one of the sisters of أَنَّ, see 182); or the subject and
  complement of an equation, i.e. a sentence with no verb (see 180):

  وَصَلَ المُدِيرُ.    The director has arrived.

  الوَزِيرُ مَوْجُودٌ.    The minister is present.

  هِيَ صُحُفِيَّةٌ.    She is a journalist.

  أَنَا المُمَثِّلُ.    I am the representative.

- Accusative (acc.): denoting the direct object or complement of a verb (see
  33 and 189); or the subject of a verb after one of the sisters of أَنَّ :

  كَتَبُوا جَوَابًا.    They wrote an answer.

  إِنَّ الوَثِيقَةَ هَامَّةٌ.    The document is important.

  قَالَ إِنَّ المُشْكِلَةَ عَاجِلَةٌ.    He said that the problem is/was urgent.

  كَانَ مُفِيدًا.    It was useful.

  مَا زَالَ ضَرُورِيًّا.    It was still necessary.

  The accusative is also found in a variety of other uses; the main ones are
  summarised, with paragraph references, in Table 39, para. 205.

- Genitive (gen.): after a preposition; or for the last or middle element of a
  construct (see 148):

  مَعَ المِفْتَاح   with the key        مِفْتَاحُ المَكْتَب   the office key

  مَعَ مِفْتَاحِ المَكْتَب   with the office key

**132.  Definition.** Nouns and adjectives are either indefinite or definite. An
indefinite noun is a common noun (i.e not a proper noun, see below) which is
not specified within its category:

  مُوَظَّفٌ   an employee          مُوَظَّفُونَ   employees

  تَقْرِيرٌ   a report             رِسَالَاتٌ   letters

  مَعَ كَاتِبَيْنِ   with two clerks

A definite noun is either a proper noun (i.e. a name regarded as unique):

لُبْنَانُ Lebanon                    لُطْفِيَّةُ Lutfiya

(NB.: Certain proper nouns carry the definite article (148): الْعِرَاقَ Iraq),
or else a common noun either specified within its category or generalised to cover
its category. A common noun is made definite in one of three ways:

- the noun carries the definite article and is declined accordingly:

الْمُوَظَّفُ the employee                    الْمَأْمُورُونَ the officials

حَسَبَ الْوَثِيقَتَيْنِ according to both documents الْحَيَاةُ وَالْمَوْتُ life and death
Note from the last example that the article is often used with an abstract noun,
when it is deemed to cover its whole category, i.e. *(all)* life, *(all)* death.

- the noun carries a possessive suffix (see 147):

وَاجِبِي my duty                    أَوْلَادُهَا her children

ثَمَنُهُ its price                    مِنْ رِسَالَتَيْهِمْ from their two letters

- the noun is defined by the following noun in a definite construct (see 148):

عُنْوَانُ الْبَنْكِ the bank's address

اسْمُ مُدِيرِ الشَّرِكَةِ the company director's name

مَعَ نِقَابَاتِ الْعُمَّالِ with the trade unions

See 117, 137, 138, 140, 141, 144 and 145 for definite and indefinite declension.
For definite and indefinite adjectives, see 142 and 180.


**133.  Number.** For nouns and adjectives, as for verbs and pronouns, there
are three numbers in Arabic: singular (sing., for one), dual (for two) and plural
(pl., for more than two).


**134.  Animate and Inanimate.** We distinguish between animate (an.)
nouns, which denote a person or persons:

الشَّخْصُ the person                    أَشْخَاصٌ persons

أُمٌّ a mother                    أَسَاتِذَةٌ professors

and inanimate (inan.) nouns, which denote anything else:

حَيَوَانٌ an animal                    الْمَكَاتِبُ the offices

Three other parts of speech which can assume either gender (adjectives,
pronouns and verbs), when referring to an inanimate noun in the plural, have the
same form as their feminine singular:

بِنَايَاتٌ قَدِيمَةٌ ancient buildings

هِيَ ثَقِيلَةٌ. They (e.g. the bags/stones/responsibilities etc.) are heavy.

أَقْلَعَتِ الْقِطَارَاتُ. The trains have left.

A noun denoting a group of people is itself inanimate, e.g.:

أَحْزَابٌ مُخْتَلِفَةٌ various (political) parties

إِنَّ الْوُفُودَ تَرَكَتِ الْمُؤْتَمَرَ. The delegations have left the conference.

The distinction between animate and inanimate is grammatically important only for the plural. It has no grammatical force in the singular or dual.

**135. Relative Adjectives (النَّسْبَةُ).** Many useful adjectives, known as relative adjectives, are formed from nouns by adding the ending ـِي . When the last written letter of the noun is a consonant, the ending is added directly:

| | | | |
|---|---|---|---|
| اقْتِصَادٌ | economy | اقْتِصَادِيٌّ | economic |
| مَالٌ | wealth | مَالِيٌّ | financial |

With most nouns having a final vowel or ـة , this is dropped before ـِي is added:

| | | | |
|---|---|---|---|
| أَمْرِيكَا | America | أَمْرِيكِيٌّ | American |
| نِسْبَةٌ | relationship | نِسْبِيٌّ | relative |
| ضَرُورَةٌ | necessity | ضَرُورِيٌّ | necessary |

With a few such nouns, the final vowel or ـة is either followed or replaced by و before ـِي is added:

| | | | |
|---|---|---|---|
| فَرَأْنْسَا | France | فَرَنْسَاوِيٌّ | French |
| سَنَةٌ | year | سَنَوِيٌّ | annual |

Some relative adjectives are formed from the broken plural of the noun:

| | | | |
|---|---|---|---|
| دُوَلٌ | states | دُوَلِيٌّ | international |

Like other adjectives, relative adjectives can in turn be used as nouns; with some, this may be their commonest use:

| | | | |
|---|---|---|---|
| فَرَنْسَاوِيٌّ | a Frenchman | مِصْرِيٌّ | (an) Egyptian |
| صُحُفِيٌّ | journalist(ic) | لُغَوِيٌّ | linguist(ic) |

All the examples of relative adjectives given here are masculine indefinite nominative singular forms, and are declinable. See 142 for the formation of the feminine; and 146, 147, 149 and 150 for the declension.

**136. Abstract Nouns.** Many useful abstract nouns are formed by adding ـَة

to a relative adjective, giving a form identical to the feminine singular of the adjective (see 142):

| | | | |
|---|---|---|---|
| اشْتِراكِيّ | socialist | اشْتِراكِيّةٌ | socialism |
| جُمْهُورِيّ | republican | جُمْهُورِيّةٌ | republicanism |
| انْسانِيّ | human(e) | انْسانِيّةٌ | humanity, humaneness |

Some such abstract nouns are derived from other sources:

| | | | |
|---|---|---|---|
| إمْكانٌ | capacity | إمْكانِيّةٌ | possibility |
| أَهَمّ | more important | أَهَمِّيّةٌ | importance |
| أَقْدَم | prior | أَقْدَمِيّةٌ | priority |

**137. Table 27, Regular Nouns and Adjectives: Indefinite Singular and Broken Plural.** A noun or adjective which is regular in the indefinite singular or indefinite broken plural (see 143) declines as follows in indefinite form:

| Gender, Number | Nominative | Accusative | Genitive | |
|---|---|---|---|---|
| 1. Uninflected word-ending, consonant: nom. ... -*un*, acc. ... -*an*, gen. ... -*in*: | | | | |
| masc. sing. | كِتابٌ | كِتاباً | كِتابٍ | book |
| inan. pl. | كُتُبٌ | كُتُباً | كُتُبٍ | books |
| masc. sing. | شَكٌّ | شَكّاً | شَكٍّ | doubt |
| masc. sing. | جُزْءٌ | جُزْءاً | جُزْءٍ | part |
| inan. pl. | فُرَصٌ | فُرَصاً | فُرَصٍ | opportunities |
| masc. sing. | زَيْدٌ | زَيْداً | زَيْدٍ | Zayd |
| masc. sing. | كَبِيرٌ | كَبِيراً | كَبِيرٍ | big |
| masc. an. pl. | كِثارٌ | كِثاراً | كِثارٍ | many |
| 2. Uninflected word-ending ء ... : nom. ... -*un*, acc. ... -*an*, gen. ... -*in*: | | | | |
| masc. sing. | ابْتِداءٌ | ابْتِداءً | ابْتِداءٍ | beginning |
| 3. Uninflected word-ending ي : nom. ... -*yun*, acc. ... -*yan*, gen. ... -*yin*: | | | | |
| masc. sing. | صُحُفِيّ | صُحُفِيّاً | صُحُفِيّ | journalist |
| masc. sing. | فَنِّيّ | فَنِّيّاً | فَنِّيّ | technical |

| 4. Uninflected word-ending ة... : nom. ٌ... -*tun*, acc. ً... -*tan*, gen. ... -*tin*: | | | |
|---|---|---|---|
| fem. sing. | رِسَالَةٌ | رِسَالَةً | رِسَالَةٍ | letter |
| masc. sing. | خَلِيفَةٌ | خَلِيفَةً | خَلِيفَةٍ | successor |
| inan. pl. | أَسْئِلَةٌ | أَسْئِلَةً | أَسْئِلَةٍ | questions |
| f. sing./inan. pl. | كَبِيرَةٌ | كَبِيرَةً | كَبِيرَةٍ | big |
| fem. sing. | صُحُفِيَّةٌ | صُحُفِيَّةً | صُحُفِيَّةٍ | journalist |
| f. sing./inan. pl. | فَنِّيَّةٌ | فَنِّيَّةً | فَنِّيَّةٍ | technical |

There are four types of words, grouped according to their last written letter in uninflected form. The indefinite case-endings are added to this letter; ي... becomes ـيّ... -*īy*-*, and ة... is pronounced -at- when the ending is pronounced. After a final consonant and after ي... , the accusative ending is spelt ًا... ; after ء ا... and ة... it is spelt ً... . However spelt, the vowel of the accusative is pronounced short, -a-.

In short pronunciation, the only one of these endings usually sounded is the masculine accusative, ً...\ ـيًّا...\ ًا... . Proper nouns are almost always pronounced short in all cases.

* Strictly speaking the uninflected ending is -iy-, becoming -iyy-, but the transliterations -ī- and -īy- used in this book reflect the everyday pronunciation more closely.

Nouns ending in ء ا... in which neither the ء nor the ا is (or represents) a radical, do not fall under this declension but are diptotes when indefinite. See 144. Some important forms of broken plural are also diptote.

Some important masculine proper nouns (e.g. زَيْدٌ in the table) follow the declension pattern shown here; they are commonly used in indefinite form, despite their inherently definite meaning. However, most masculine, and almost all feminine, proper nouns are diptote.

Other examples:

| | | |
|---|---|---|
| Nom.: | تَقْرِيرٌ طَوِيلٌ | a long report |
| | تَقْرِيرٌ رَسْمِيٌّ | an official report |
| | مُرَاسَلَةٌ مَكْتُومَةٌ | confidential correspondence |
| | مُرَاسَلَةٌ سِرِّيَّةٌ | secret correspondence |
| | ضُبَّاطٌ كِبَارٌ | senior ('big') officers |
| Acc.: | تَقْرِيراً مَكْتُوماً | a confidential report |

|  | |
|---|---|
| تَقْرِيرًا رَسْمِيًّا | an official report |
| أَنْبَاءَ مُفِيدَةً | useful items of news |
| وَثِيقَةً طَوِيلَةً | a long document |
| وَثِيقَةً شَخْصِيَّةً | a personal document |

Gen.:

|  | |
|---|---|
| فِي مِلَفٍّ كَبِيرٍ | in a big file |
| لِبَنْكٍ لُبْنَانِيٍّ | for a Lebanese bank |
| لِبُنُوكٍ لُبْنَانِيَّةٍ | for Lebanese banks |
| لِأَسَاتِذَةٍ جُدُدٍ | for new professors |
| لِصُحُفِيَّةٍ مَشْهُورَةٍ | for a famous journalist |
| مَعَ مُحَمَّدٍ | with Muhammad |
| فِي شَرِكَةٍ عَرَبِيَّةٍ | in an Arab company |

**138. Table 28, Regular Nouns and Adjectives: Definite Singular and Broken Plural.** A noun or adjective which is regular in the definite singular or definite broken plural (see 143) declines as follows in definite form:

| Gender, Number | Nominative | Accusative | Genitive | |
|---|---|---|---|---|
| 1. Uninflected word-ending, consonant: nom. ´... -u, acc. ´... -a, gen. ... -i: | | | | |
| masc. sing. | كِتَابٌ | كِتَابَ | كِتَابِ | book |
| inan. pl. | كُتُبٌ | كُتُبَ | كُتُبِ | books |
| masc. sing. | شَكٌّ | شَكَّ | شَكِّ | doubt |
| masc. sing. | جُزْءٌ | جُزْءَ | جُزْءِ | part |
| masc. sing. | ابْتِدَاءٌ | ابْتِدَاءَ | ابْتِدَاءِ | beginning |
| inan. pl. | فُرَصٌ | فُرَصَ | فُرَصِ | opportunities |
| masc. sing. | كَبِيرٌ | كَبِيرَ | كَبِيرِ | big |
| masc. an. pl. | كِثَارٌ | كِثَارَ | كِثَارِ | many |
| 2. Uninflected word-ending ...ي : nom. ´... -yu, acc. ´... -ya, gen. ´... -yi: | | | | |
| masc. sing. | صُحُفِيٌّ | صُحُفِيَّ | صُحُفِيِّ | journalist |
| masc. sing. | فَنِّيٌّ | فَنِّيَّ | فَنِّيِّ | technical |

| 3. Uninflected word-ending ة... : nom. ...ُ -tu, acc. ...َ -ta, gen. ...ِ -ti: | | | |
|---|---|---|---|
| fem. sing. | رِسَالَةٌ | رِسَالَةَ | رِسَالَةِ | letter |
| masc. sing. | خَلِيفَةٌ | خَلِيفَةَ | خَلِيفَةِ | successor |
| inan. pl. | أَسْئِلَةٌ | أَسْئِلَةَ | أَسْئِلَةِ | questions |
| f. sing./inan. pl. | كَبِيرَةٌ | كَبِيرَةَ | كَبِيرَةِ | big |
| fem. sing. | صُحُفِيَّةٌ | صُحُفِيَّةَ | صُحُفِيَّةِ | journalist |
| f. sing./inan. pl. | فَنِّيَّةٌ | فَنِّيَّةَ | فَنِّيَّةِ | technical |

There are three groups of words, according to their last written letter or letters in uninflected form.

For common nouns, the definite ending alone does not suffice to make the noun definite. See 132 for the three ways in which the noun is fully defined. All three ways demand definite case-endings.

See 137 for proper nouns.

In the definite form, words ending in ...اء and following this declension pattern are declined like those ending in a consonant.

The definite case-ending is added before any possessive suffix. Since ة may stand only at the end of a word, it is replaced by ...ت before a possessive suffix is added.

In short pronunciation these endings are heard only when a possessive suffix (147) is added. Note also the provision described in 30 for feminine nouns with a following adjective (العربية السعودية), and see 148 for the short pronunciation of ة... in a construct.

Further examples (all with the definite article; see 139):

| Nom.: | التَّقْرِيرُ المَكْتُومُ | the confidential report |
|---|---|---|
| | التَّقْرِيرُ الرَّسْمِيُّ | the official report |
| | المُرَاسَلَةُ المَكْتُومَةُ | (the) confidential correspondence |
| | الرُّسُومُ الفَنِّيَّةُ | the technical drawings |
| Acc.: | التَّقْرِيرَ المَكْتُومَ | the confidential report |
| | التَّقْرِيرَ الرَّسْمِيَّ | the official report |
| | الوَثِيقَةَ الطَّوِيلَةَ | the long document |
| | الوَثِيقَةَ الرَّسْمِيَّةَ | the official document |

Gen.:       في المَلَفّ الكَبِير      in the big file

للبَنْكِ اللُّبْنَانِيّ      for the Lebanese bank

للضُّبَّاطِ الصِّغَار      for the junior ('small') officers

في الأَنْبَاءِ المُخْتَلِفَة      in the various items of news

للأَسَاتِذَة الجُدُد      for the new professors

للصُّحُفِيَّة المَشْهُورَة      for the famous journalist

في الشَّرِكَة العَرَبِيَّة      in the Arab company

**139. Definite Article.** The definite article is a prefix, invariable for gender, case or number, written as one word with the defined noun or adjective, which then has a definite ending (see 138, 145, 117). The basic form of the prefixed article is ...الْ, in which the ل is pronounced l:

الكِتَابُ   al-kitābu  the book

The l of the article has hamzat al-waṣl (see 28) and therefore has no sound after a vowel in the same phrase. In this situation it can be pointed آ:

في آلوَثِيقَةِ آلهَامَة   fi l-wathīqati l-hāmmati  in the important document

However, before a so-called 'sun letter', the ل of the article adopts the sound of that letter, forming a doubled letter, which may be pointed with ـّ . The ل then loses its ـْ in pointing. The sun letters are those fourteen consonants formed with the tip or near-tip of the tongue, i.e.: ت ث د ذ ر ز س ش ص ض ط ظ ل ن . The spelling of the article is maintained. Examples:

التَّمْرِينُ   at-tamrīnu   the exercise      الثَّقَافَةُ   ath-thaqāfatu  culture

السَّيَّارَةُ   as-sayyāratu  the car       بِالرَّمْل   bi-r-ramli       with sand

In short pronunciation, when the pointed ending of the preceding word is dropped, the article recovers its original initial vowel a-:

السُّؤَالُ آلصَّعْبُ   as-su'ālu ṣ-ṣa'bu/as-su'āl aṣ-ṣa'b  the difficult question

The letters other than the fourteen sun letters are called 'moon letters'.

See 15 summarising the pointing of the definite article.

See 28 for the shortened pronunciation of any final long vowel preceding a definite article:

في رِسَالة   fī risālatin  in a letter  *but:* في آلرِّسَالة   fi r-risālati  in the letter

The article is fully pointed in this paragraph and in paras 14, 15 and 28, but not elsewhere in this book.

**140. Table 29: Dual of Nouns and Adjectives, Indefinite and Definite.** All nouns and adjectives are regular in the dual. Dual nouns and adjectives decline as follows, both in indefinite and definite forms:

| Gender | Nominative | Accusative and Genitive | |
|---|---|---|---|
| 1. Uninflected word-ending, consonant: nom. ان... -āni, acc./gen. ـَيْن... -ayni: | | | |
| masculine | كِتَابَان | كِتَابَيْن | two books |
| masculine | تِلْمِيذَان | تِلْمِيذَيْن | two pupils |
| masculine | خَطَّان | خَطَّيْن | two lines |
| masculine | جُزْآن | جُزْئَيْن | two parts |
| feminine | يَدَان | يَدَيْن | two hands |
| masculine | فَقِيرَان | فَقِيرَيْن | poor |
| 2. Uninflected word-ending ي... : nom. ـَان... -yāni, acc./gen. ـَيْن... -yayni: | | | |
| masculine | مِصْرِيَّان | مِصْرِيَّيْن | two Egyptians |
| masculine | سِرِّيَّان | سِرِّيَّيْن | secret |
| 3. Uninflected word-ending ة... : nom. تَان... -tāni, acc./gen. تَيْن... -tayni: | | | |
| feminine | نُسْخَتَان | نُسْخَتَيْن | two copies |
| feminine | مُعَلِّمَتَان | مُعَلِّمَتَيْن | two teachers |
| masculine | خَلِيفَتَان | خَلِيفَتَيْن | two successors |
| feminine | فَقِيرَتَان | فَقِيرَتَيْن | poor |
| feminine | رَسْمِيَّتَان | رَسْمِيَّتَيْن | official |

There are three groups of words, according to their last written letter in uninflected form, the same as shown in Table 28, para. 138. Since ة may stand only at the end of a word, it is replaced by ت... before the dual ending is added.

As each word stands in this table, it is undefined. See 132 for the three ways in which the noun or adjective is fully defined.

In short pronunciation, the final ... of the dual is not sounded.

See 147 for the manner in which possessive suffixes are added to dual nouns, and 148 for the manner in which a dual noun is modified in construct.

Further examples:

Nom.:    مُوَظَّفَان طَيِّبَان    two good employees

جُنْدِيَّان تُرْكِيَّان    two Turkish soldiers

|  | | |
|---|---|---|
| | الْمُشْكِلَتَان الْمُعَقَّدَتَان | both complex problems |
| Acc.: | مُوَظَّفَيْن طَيِّبَيْن | two good employees |
| | جُنْدِيَّيْن تُرْكِيَّيْن | two Turkish soldiers |
| | الْمُشْكِلَتَيْن الْمُعَقَّدَتَيْن | both complex problems |
| Gen.: | مَعَ الْمُوَظَّفَيْن الطَّيِّبَيْن | with both good employees |
| | لِجُنْدِيَّيْن تُرْكِيَّيْن | to/for two Turkish soldiers |
| | فِي الْمُشْكِلَتَيْن الْمُعَقَّدَتَيْن | in both complex problems |

**141. Table 30: Sound Plurals of Nouns and Adjectives, Indefinite and Definite.** Sound (i.e. regular) plural case-endings are shown below. There are two sound plural patterns, feminine and masculine. The feminine sound plurals have a different indefinite and definite pattern; the masculine sound plurals are the same for both indefinite and definite words.

Table 30a: Feminine Sound Plural, Indefinite/Definite.

**Indefinite**

| Gender, An./Inan. | Nominative | Accusative and Genitive | |
|---|---|---|---|
| 1. Uninflected word-ending, consonant: nom. ـاتٌ... -ātun, acc./gen. ـاتٍ... -ātin: | | | |
| inanimate masc. | مَحَلَّاتٌ | مَحَلَّاتٍ | places |
| 2. Uninflected word-ending ـة... : nom. ـاتٌ... -ātun, acc./gen. ـاتٍ... -ātin: | | | |
| inanimate fem. | مَرَّاتٌ | مَرَّاتٍ | times |
| animate fem. | زَمِيلَاتٌ | زَمِيلَاتٍ | colleagues |
| animate fem. | طَيِّبَاتٌ | طَيِّبَاتٍ | good |
| animate fem. | صُحُفِيَّاتٌ | صُحُفِيَّاتٍ | journalists |
| animate fem. | مِصْرِيَّاتٌ | مِصْرِيَّاتٍ | Egyptian(s) |

**Definite**

| Gender, An./Inan. | Nominative | Accusative and Genitive | |
|---|---|---|---|
| 1. Uninflected word-ending, consonant: nom. ـاتُ... -ātu, acc./gen. ـاتِ... -āti: | | | |
| inanimate masc. | مَحَلَّاتُ | مَحَلَّاتِ | places |

| 2. Uninflected word-ending ة... : nom. ـَاتُ... -ātu, acc./gen. ـَاتِ... -āti: | | |
|---|---|---|
| inanimate fem. | مَرَّاتُ | مَرَّات | times |
| animate fem. | زَمِيلَاتُ | زَمِيلَات | colleagues |
| animate fem. | طَيِّبَاتُ | طَيِّبَات | good |
| animate fem. | صُحُفِيَّاتُ | صُحُفِيَّات | journalists |
| animate fem. | مِصْرِيَّاتُ | مِصْرِيَّات | Egyptian(s) |

There are two groups of words, according to their last written letter in the uninflected form of the singular. For words whose uninflected singular ends in a consonant, the plural ending is added directly to that consonant. An uninflected singular ending ة... is dropped before the plural ending is added.

There are also a few animate feminine nouns, ending in a consonant in the singular, which undergo a change before the feminine sound plural ending is added. Common examples are أُمّ 'mother', pl. أُمَّهَاتُ (etc.) and أُخْتُ 'sister', pl. أَخَوَاتُ (etc.). In some such words it is in fact the singular form, not the plural, which is anomalous; the plural shows a final radical no longer evident in the singular.

In short pronunciation, these case-endings are sounded only when a possessive suffix (147) is added.

This declension applies to the plural of:

- certain inanimate masculine nouns;
- most feminine animate and inanimate nouns;
- all adjectives qualifying animate feminine nouns or qualifying pronouns referring to such nouns;

It does not apply to any animate masculine nouns, or adjectives qualifying such nouns; or to adjectives qualifying inanimate nouns or pronouns referring to such nouns, of either gender.

The definite ending alone does not suffice to make the noun definite. See 132 for the three ways in which the noun is fully defined. All three ways demand definite case-endings.

The definite case-ending is added before any possessive suffix.

Further examples (definite examples with the article):

Nom.:          اِجْتِمَاعَاتُ   meetings

              الاِجْتِمَاعَاتُ   the meetings

              الصُّحُفِيَّاتُ   the journalists

السِّكْرِتيرَاتُ المِصْرِيّاتُ    the Egyptian secretaries

Acc.:    اجْتِمَاعَات    meetings

الصُّحُفِيّاتُ    the journalists

سِكْرِتيرَاتٍ مَسْؤُولاَتٍ    responsible secretaries

Gen.:    في الاجْتِمَاعَات    in/at the meetings

لِصُحُفِيّاتٍ    for journalists

لِلسِّكْرِتيرَاتِ المِصْرِيّاتِ    for the Egyptian secretaries

Table 30b: Masculine Sound Plural, Indefinite and Definite.

|  | Nominative | Acc./Gen. |  |
|---|---|---|---|
| 1. Uninflected ending, consonant: | مُشْرِفُونَ | مُشْرِفينَ | supervisors |
| nom. ـُونَ... -ūna, acc./gen. ـِينَ... -īna: | طَيِّبُونَ | طَيِّبينَ | good |
| 2. Uninflected word-ending ي... : nom. | صُحُفِيُّونَ | صُحُفِيّينَ | journalists |
| ـُّونَ... -yūna, acc./gen. ـِّينَ... -yīna: | وَطَنِيُّونَ | وَطَنِيّينَ | national |

There are two groups of words, according to their last written letter in uninflected form. An uninflected singular ending ي... becomes ـّي... before the plural ending ـُونَ\...ـينَ... is added.

In short pronunciation, the final ـَ... is not sounded.

This declension applies to both indefinite and definite nouns and adjectives of the following categories, in the plural:

- certain animate masculine nouns and certain adjectives qualifying such nouns or qualifying a pronoun referring to such a noun;
- certain adjectives qualifying a group of animate nouns of mixed gender, or qualifying a pronoun referring to such a group.

It does not apply to any feminine or any inanimate nouns, or any adjectives qualifying such nouns or qualifying a pronoun referring to such a noun.

As each word stands in this table, it is undefined. See 132 for the three ways in which the noun or adjective is fully defined. See 147 for the manner in which possessive suffixes are added to masculine sound plural nouns, and 148 for the manner in which a masculine sound plural noun is modified in construct.

Further examples (definite examples with the article):

Nom.:    مُوَظَّفُونَ    employees

المُوَظَّفُونَ    the employees

| | | |
|---|---|---|
| | الْمَأْمُورُونَ الإِيرَانِيُّونَ | the Iranian officials |
| Acc.: | مَأْمُورِينَ | officials |
| | الْمَأْمُورِينَ | the officials |
| | صُحُفِيِّينَ مَحَلِّيِّينَ | local journalists |
| Gen.: | مَعَ الْمُعَلِّمِينَ | with the teachers |
| | لِمُشْرِفِينَ | for supervisors |
| | لِلْمُشْرِفِينَ الْفَنِّيِّينَ | for the technical supervisors |

**142. Agreement of Adjectives.** Adjectives can assume either gender, and agree either fully (i.e. in gender, number, case and definition), or partly (i.e. in some of these characteristics) with the noun or pronoun which they qualify.

The feminine singular of regular adjectives is made by adding, to the last written letter of the masculine singular, the feminine ending ة..., to which are added the appropriate case-endings (see 137, 138, 140 and 141):

كَبِيرٌ  (m. indefinite nom. sing) } big

كَبِيرَةٌ  (f. indefinite nom. sing)

ة... added to a m. adjective ending in ي... gives يَّة... pronounced -īya*, to which are added the appropriate case-endings:

ضَرُورِيٌّ  (m. indefinite nom. sing) } necessary

ضَرُورِيَّةٌ  (f. indefinite nom. sing.)

* Strictly speaking, the masc. ending ي... is -iy, the fem. therefore -iyya; but in practice these endings are almost always pronounced –ī and -īya.

See 145, 153 and 154 for adjectives not conforming to this pattern.

See 140 for the dual, 141 for the sound plural, and 143 for broken plurals.

In making the adjective agree with its noun or pronoun, the following rules are observed regarding gender and number:

- The singular and dual forms of the adjective always agree in gender and number, there being no distinction between animate and inanimate.
- The masculine plural and feminine plural forms of the adjective are used to qualify only plural animate nouns (i.e. people); the masculine plural for an all-male group or a mixed group, the feminine plural only for an exclusively female group.
- For any inanimate plural noun or pronoun (irrespective of the gender of its singular), the inanimate plural form of the adjective is used; this form

is identical to that of the feminine singular.

An adjective used as a complement agrees in gender and number (under the rules given above) with the subject of the expression, but varies in case and definition:

الْقَضِيَّةُ عَاجِلَةٌ.    The matter is urgent.

كَانَ فُؤَادٌ الأَحْسَنَ.    Fuad was the best.

See 180 and 189 for the case and definition of the adjective in such expressions.

When the adjective is used other than as a complement, it follows and agrees with the noun which it qualifies, in every respect, i.e. gender and number (following the rules given above), and also in case and definition:

| | | |
|---|---|---|
| Nom.: | طَالِبٌ مُجْتَهِدٌ | a hard-working student |
| | التَّقْرِيرُ الْفَنِّيُّ | the technical report |
| | أَصْدِقَاءُ كُرَمَاءُ | generous friends |
| | حُكُومَاتٌ اشْتِرَاكِيَّةٌ | socialist governments |
| Acc.: | أُمًّا لَطِيفَةً | a kind mother |
| | الْوَثِيقَةَ الطَّوِيلَةَ | the long document |
| | الأُمَّهَاتُ الطَّيِّبَاتُ | the good mothers |
| | تَقَارِيرَ فَنِّيَّةً | technical reports |
| Gen.: | مَعَ مُتَظَاهِرَيْنِ غَاضِبَيْنِ | with two angry demonstrators |
| | فِي الْمُشْكِلَتَيْنِ الرَّئِيسِيَّتَيْنِ | in both (the) main problems |
| | مَعَ الْخُبَرَاءِ الْمَالِيِّينَ | with the financial experts |
| | ضِدَّ الْحَشَرَاتِ الضَّارَّةِ | against ('the') harmful insects |

These rules are valid for simple (i.e. one-word) adjectives. For compound adjectives and their agreement, see 160 and 163.

Since Arabic does not make our distinction between nouns and adjectives, all words which we regard as adjectives can also be used as nouns:

غَنِيٌّ    a rich man          الْفُقَرَاءُ    the poor

**143. Broken Plurals of Nouns and Adjectives.** Most masculine nouns, and a few feminine nouns, have an irregular or 'broken' plural. The same is true of many adjectives in the masculine (animate) plural form. The main broken plural measures are given below, with examples in nom. sing. and pl.; for the diptotes, see 144; for the forms ending in ی... see 145.

**أَفْعَالٌ:**

| | | | |
|---|---|---|---|
| رَقْمٌ أَرْقَامٌ | figure, number | شَخْصٌ أَشْخَاصٌ | person |
| سُوقٌ أَسْوَاقٌ | (m./f.) market | مَالٌ أَمْوَالٌ | property |
| وَقْتٌ أَوْقَاتٌ | time | | |

**فُعُولٌ:**

| | | | |
|---|---|---|---|
| بَحْثٌ بُحُوثٌ | discussion | شَكٌّ شُكُوكٌ | doubt |
| بَيْتٌ بُيُوتٌ | house | عَيْنٌ عُيُونٌ | (f.) eye |

**فُعَلَاءُ** (diptote, see 144):

| | | | |
|---|---|---|---|
| رَئِيسٌ رُؤَسَاءُ | chairman | وَزِيرٌ وُزَرَاءُ | minister |
| مُدِيرٌ مُدَرَاءُ | director | زَمِيلٌ زُمَلَاءُ | colleague |
| بَسِيطٌ بُسَطَاءُ | simple | لَطِيفٌ لُطَفَاءُ | kind (adj.) |

**فُعُلٌ:**

| | | | |
|---|---|---|---|
| كِتَابٌ كُتُبٌ | book | طَرِيقٌ طُرُقٌ | (m./f.) road |
| جَزِيرَةٌ جُزُرٌ | island | | |

**فُعْلٌ:**

| | |
|---|---|
| أَحْمَرُ حُمْرٌ | red (the m. s. form أَحْمَرُ is diptote) |

**فُعَلٌ:**

| | | | |
|---|---|---|---|
| صُورَةٌ صُوَرٌ | picture | دَوْلَةٌ دُوَلٌ | state (country) |
| أُمَّةٌ أُمَمٌ | nation | | |

**أَفْعُلٌ:**

| | | | |
|---|---|---|---|
| شَهْرٌ أَشْهُرٌ | month | نَهْرٌ أَنْهُرٌ | river |
| نَفْسٌ أَنْفُسٌ | (f.) soul | | |

**فَعَائِلُ** (diptote, derived words); **أَفَاعِلُ** (diptote, derived words); **فَعَالِلُ** (diptote, quadriliteral roots); **فَعَالِلَةٌ** (quadriliteral roots):

| | | | |
|---|---|---|---|
| زَبُونٌ زَبَائِنُ | client | أَجْنَبِيٌّ أَجَانِبُ | foreign |
| جَدْوَلٌ جَدَاوِلُ | schedule | أُسْتَاذٌ أَسَاتِذَةٌ | professor |

**فَوَاعِلُ** (diptote):

| | | | |
|---|---|---|---|
| بَاخِرَةٌ بَوَاخِرُ | steamship | دَائِرَةٌ دَوَائِرُ | directorate |

**فَعَالِيلُ** (diptote, derived words); **مَفَاعِيلُ** (diptote, derived words); **مَفَاعِلُ** (diptote, quadriliteral roots):

| | | | |
|---|---|---|---|
| مَكْتَبٌ مَكَاتِبُ | office; desk | مَبْلَغٌ مَبَالِغُ | amount |

مُشْكِلَةٌ مَشَاكِلُ    problem        مِفْتَاحٌ مَفَاتِيحُ    key

مَكْتُوبٌ مَكَاتِيبُ    letter        تِلْمِيذٌ تَلَامِيذُ    pupil

صَنْدُوقٌ صَنَادِيقُ    box

أَفْعِلَةٌ:

جَوَابٌ أَجْوِبَةٌ    answer        سُؤَالٌ أَسْئِلَةٌ    question

مِثَالٌ أَمْثِلَةٌ    example

فَعَلَةٌ:

مَاهِرٌ مَهَرَةٌ    skilled

فِعَالٌ:

جَبَلٌ جِبَالٌ    mountain        صَغِيرٌ صِغَارٌ    small; junior

كَبِيرٌ كِبَارٌ    big; senior        طَوِيلٌ طِوَالٌ    long

فِعَلٌ:

قِطْعَةٌ قِطَعٌ    piece

فِعْلَةٌ:

أَخٌ إِخْوَةٌ    brother (see 159)

أَفْعِلَاءُ (diptote):

صَدِيقٌ أَصْدِقَاءُ    friend        قَرِيبٌ أَقْرِبَاءُ    close

فُعَّالٌ:

تَاجِرٌ تُجَّارٌ    merchant        طَالِبٌ طُلَّابٌ    student

شَاطِرٌ شُطَّارٌ    cunning

فُعْلَانٌ:

بِلَادٌ بُلْدَانٌ    country        شُجَاعٌ شُجْعَانٌ    courageous

فِعْلَانٌ:

جَارٌ جِيرَانٌ    neighbour        نَارٌ نِيرَانٌ    fire

فَعِيلٌ:

حِمَارٌ حَمِيرٌ    donkey

فَعْلَى (invariable for case):

مَرِيضٌ مَرْضَى    sick

There are other patterns, less common.

**144. Table 31: Diptotes.** Diptote words have two forms for three cases, and no nunation. Diptote common nouns and diptote adjectives are diptote only in the indefinite form, declined as follows:

### Table 31a: Common Noun and Adjective Diptotes

| Nom. ´... -u | Acc./Gen. ´... -a | |
|---|---|---|
| مُدَرَاءُ | مُدَرَاءَ | directors |
| مَدَارِسُ | مَدَارِسَ | schools |
| مَفَاتِيحُ | مَفَاتِيحَ | keys |
| وَسَائِلُ | وَسَائِلَ | means |
| جَدَاوِلُ | جَدَاوِلَ | schedules |
| عَصَافِيرُ | عَصَافِيرَ | birds |
| كَسْلَانُ | كَسْلَانَ | lazy (m. sing.) |
| أَحْمَرُ | أَحْمَرَ | red (m. sing.) |

### Table 31b: Proper Noun Diptotes

| | Nominative | Acc./Gen. | |
|---|---|---|---|
| 1. Uninflected form of the | مِصْرُ | مِصْرَ | Egypt |
| | بَارِيسُ | بَارِيسَ | Paris |
| word ending in a consonant: | يَزِيدُ | يَزِيدَ | Yazid |
| | أَشْرَفُ | أَشْرَفَ | Ashraf |
| | مَرْيَمُ | مَرْيَمَ | Maryam |
| nom. ´... -u, acc./gen. ´... -a | رَمَضَانُ | رَمَضَانَ | Ramadan |
| 2. Uninflected ending ة... : | مَكَّةُ | مَكَّةَ | Mecca |
| nom. ´... -tu, acc./gen. ´... -ta | لُطْفِيَّةُ | لُطْفِيَّةَ | Lutfiya |

The diptote case-endings are:

- uninflected ending in a consonant: nom. ´... -u, acc./gen. ´... -a (most common-noun and adjective diptotes).
- uninflected ending in ة... : nom. ´... -tu, acc./gen. ´... -ta (almost all are proper-noun diptotes).

In short pronunciation, the case-endings are not sounded. ة... is pronounced -a.

The main groups of adjectives and common nouns which are diptote when indefinite are:

- All nouns and adjectives, singular or plural, masculine or feminine, with final ء ا... , where neither letter is (or represents) a radical. But if either of these letters is a radical (e.g. in اِبْتِدَاءٌ 'beginning', root بدأ), the noun is not diptote, see 137, 138, 140 and 141.

- Broken plurals with the measures مَفَاعِلُ , فَعَائِلُ , مَفَاعِيلُ or فَعَالِيلُ : see 143 for further examples.
- Masculine singular adjectives with the uninflected ending ...اَنُ whose feminine singular ends in ...ىَ . NB: The feminine form is not diptote but invariable for case; see 145.
- Masculine singular adjectives in the elative measure أَفْعَلُ\أَفْعَلُ (i.e. comparatives and those denoting colours and physical defects, see 153 and 161 respectively).

When such nouns are made definite by any means, they are regular. See 132, 138, 147 and 148.

Most proper nouns are also diptote, although they have definite meaning. The main groups of diptote proper nouns are:

- Feminine names.
- Names of verbal origin with an elative or tense form*.
- Names ending in ...اَنُ .
- Most foreign names.

There are other diptote names which cannot be categorised.

Proper nouns are almost always pronounced short in all cases.

* Some important proper nouns having other verbal forms (e.g. زَيْدٌ , مُحَمَّدٌ ) are not diptote but follow the declension shown in Table 27, para. 137.


**145. Indeclinable Nouns and Adjectives.** A small number of nouns and adjectives has no endings for case. The most important words of this group are singular words ending in ...ى :

- When the ...ى represents the final radical, the word has ...ىً in the indefinite form and ...ىَ in the definite form:

all cases:        مَقْهىً\اَلْمَقْهَى    a/the café

                  مُسْتَشْفىً\اَلْمُسْتَشْفَى    a/the hospital

- When the ...ى does not represent a radical, the word is invariable for case and definition, and there is no nunation:

all cases:        ذِكْرَى(الـ)    a/the memory

                  كَسْلَى    lazy (f. s. of كَسْلاَنُ , diptote, see 144)

                  اَلْكُبْرَى    the greatest (f. s., superlative, see 154)

...ى is written only finally; when followed by a suffix, it becomes ا :

ذِكْرَاهُ  his memory

فِي مَقْهَاهُمْ  in their café

When ى is added to ي the combination is written يَا... . The word remains invariable for case:

الدُّنْيَا  the world (from f. s. superlative, no pl.)

In words of this type the ى becomes ي before a dual or sound plural ending is added. Not all have sound plurals:

| Nom.: | مَقْهَيَانِ | two cafés |
|---|---|---|
| | مُسْتَشْفَيَانِ | two hospitals |
| | مُسْتَشْفَيَاتٌ | hospitals |
| | الذِّكْرَيَاتُ | the memories |
| | مَقَاهٍ\الْمَقَاهِي | (the) cafés (anomalous declension, 162) |

For the nouns and adjectives invariable for case, short and full pronunciation are the same. Further, in the short pronunciation of such words, ىً... is pronounced -ā and ... is pronounced -ī , for both indefinite and definite forms.

**146.  Table 32: Demonstrative Adjectives.** The demonstrative adjectives ('this, that' etc., also called demonstrative pronouns) are:

| Singular, all cases | | Animate plural | |
|---|---|---|---|
| masc. | fem./inan. pl. | m./f., all cases | |
| هٰذَا | هٰذِهِ | هٰؤُلَاءِ | this/these |
| ذٰلِكَ | تِلْكَ | أُولٰئِكَ \(أُولَائِكَ) | that/those |

| | Dual | | |
|---|---|---|---|
| | masculine | feminine | |
| Nom. | هٰذَانِ | هَاتَانِ | these two, |
| Acc./Gen. | هٰذَيْنِ | هَاتَيْنِ | both these |
| Nom. | ذَانِكَ | تَانِكَ | those two, |
| Acc/Gen. | ذَيْنِكَ | تَيْنِكَ | both those |

The small 'alif pointed on some of the words is pronounced like medial ...ٰ..., -ā-. The alternative plural form أُولَائِكَ is seldom encountered.

The demonstrative adjective normally precedes the noun which it qualifies; the noun carries the definite article:

Nom::           هٰذِهِ الْوَثِيقَةُ    this document

                هٰذَانِ الشَّخْصَانِ   these two people

Acc.:           أُولٰئِكَ الطُّلَّابَ    those students

Gen.:        فِي هَاتَيْنِ الرِّسَالَتَيْنِ    in both these letters

Following the general rule, the final ا of هٰذَا is pronounced short before the
hamzat al-waṣl (see 28) of the article following it:

فِي هٰذَا التَّقْرِيرِ    fī hā<u>dh</u>a t-taqrīr*i*   in this resolution/report

When a demonstrative adjective qualifies the last noun of a construct (see 148), it
precedes that noun, interrupting the construct:

مُسَوَّدَةُ هٰذَا التَّقْرِيرِ    the draft of this report

But when the demonstrative qualifies any other noun of the construct, it follows
the whole expression:

مُسَوَّدَةُ التَّقْرِيرِ هٰذِهِ    this draft of the report

even if this leads to ambiguity:

أَخْذُ نَصِّ التَّقْرِيرِ هٰذَا    { this acceptance of the text of the report,
                                      the acceptance of this text of the report

A demonstrative is the only adjective permitted to interrupt a construct, and then
only to qualify its last noun.

The demonstrative is also used as a pronoun, i.e. to denote an implied noun
(with which it must agree as far as possible):

نُفَضِّلُ هٰذِهِ.    We prefer this one.

When the gender of the noun is unknown (e.g. in some questions), a masculine
form is commonly used:

مَا هٰذَا؟    What is this?

See 180 for the demonstrative as subject of an equation.

**147. Table 33: Possessive Adjective Suffixes.** The possessive
adjectives (also called possessive or genitive pronouns) 'my', 'your' etc., take
the form of a suffix:

|                   | Singular |      | Plural |      |
| ----------------- | -------- | ---- | ------ | ---- |
| 1st person m./f.  | ي...     | my   | نَا... | our  |
| 2nd person m.     | كَ...    | your | كُمْ...| your |
| 2nd person f.     | كِ...    | your | كُنَّ...| your |

| 3rd person m. | ‏ـهُ‏... | his/its | ‏ـهُمْ‏... | their* |
| 3rd person f. | ‏ـهَا‏... | her/its, their** | ‏ـهُنَّ‏... | their* |

|  | Dual |
| --- | --- |
| 2nd person m./f. | ‏ـكُمَا‏... of you both |
| 3rd person m./f. | ‏ـهُمَا‏... of them both*** |

\* animate plural;  \*\* inanimate plural;  \*\*\* animate or inanimate. See 134.

These are the same as the direct object or accusative pronoun suffixes (see 166), except for the 1st person singular.

The 1st person plural suffix ‏ـنَا‏... is used also for the 1st person dual. The 2nd and 3rd persons masculine plural suffixes ‏ـكُمْ‏... and ‏ـهُمْ‏... are used to denote animate plural masculine possessors or those of mixed gender; the 2nd and 3rd persons feminine plural suffixes ‏ـكُنَّ‏...and ‏ـهُنَّ‏... are used to denote only animate plural feminine possessors.

Since possession makes the noun definite, these suffixes are attached to the definite case-ending of the possessed noun (or, for a noun with no case-ending, to its definite form). Certain forms of the noun are modified before the suffix is attached:

- The uninflected ending ‏ـة‏... is rewritten ‏ـتـ‏... (since ‏ة‏ cannot appear in the middle of a word).
- Dual and masculine sound plural nouns lose their final syllable ‏نِ‏... or ‏نَ‏... respectively.
- The indeclinable ending ‏ـى‏... is rewritten ‏ـا‏... (since ‏ى‏ cannot appear in the middle of a word).

Further, some of the suffixes are modified when attached to certain endings. Allowing for these modifications, the suffixes are attached as follows:

- The 1st person plural suffix ‏ـنَا‏... 'our', all the 2nd person suffixes 'your', and the 3rd person feminine singular/inanimate plural suffix ‏ـهَا‏... 'her/its/their' are attached in the form shown in the table given above:

Nom.:     ‏مَكْتَبُكِ\مَكْتَبُكَ‏     your (m./f.) office

‏شَرِكَتُنَا‏     our company

‏مُهَنْدِسَاهُمْ‏     both their engineers

‏امْتِيَازَاتُهَا‏     its concessions

‏مُشْرِفُوكَ‏     your supervisors

Acc.:              مَكْتَبَكَ        your office

                  وَثِيقَتَكُمْ       your document

                  زُمَلاءَنَا        our colleagues

                  زَمِيلَيْنَا       both our colleagues

                  مُلاَحَظَاتِنَا     our comments

                  مُهَنْدِسِينَا      our engineers

                  تَوَلِّيَهَا        her assumption of office

Gen.:             فِي مَكْتَبِكَ      in your office

                  لأَصْدِقَائِنَا     to/for our friends

                  فِي رِسَالَتِكُمْ    in your letter

                  مَعَ زَمِيلاَتِهَا   with her colleagues

                  لِمُهَنْدِسَيْكُمْ    to/for both your engineers

                  لِمُهَنْدِسِيهَا     to/for its engineers

all three cases:      ذِكْرَاهَا      her memory

See 118, 137, 138, 140, 141, and 143.

• When the 1st person sing. suffix ي... 'my' is attached to a singular or
broken plural noun whose uninflected ending is a consonant or ة... 
(modified to ت... , see above), the case-ending is dropped:

All three cases: مَكْتَبِي   my office        رِسَالَتِي   my letter

                  جَارِي   my neighbour        رِسَالاَتِي   my letters

• After the endings or modified endings ا... , ي... or يَ... the 1st person
singular suffix is يَ... . The ي of this ending combines with an immediately preceding ي as ...:

Nom.:             مُوَظَّفَايَ       both my employees

                  رِسَالَتَايَ       both my letters

Nom./Gen.:        تَوَلِّيَّ        my assumption of office

Acc./Gen.:        مُوَظَّفَيَّ       both my employees

                  رِسَالَتَيَّ       both my letters

all three cases:      ذِكْرَايَ      my memory

Further, the nominative case-ending of masculine sound plural nouns also becomes ...ي before the 1st person suffix is attached. This gives us the combination ...يَّ for all three cases:

all three cases:          مُوَظَّفِيَّ          my employees

- After the case-ending ... or an ending or modified ending written with ي (howsoever pronounced), the 3rd person suffixes ...هُ, ...هُمَا, ...هُمْ and ...هُنَّ become ...هِ , ...هِمَا , ...هِمْ and ...هِنَّ respectively. After any other ending they retain the form shown in Table 33 earlier in this paragraph:

| Nom.: | مَكْتَبُهُ | his/its office |
| | وَظَائِفُهُمْ | their jobs |
| Nom./Gen.: | تَوَلِّيهِ | his assumption of office |
| Acc.: | وَظِيفَتَهُ | his job |
| | وُزَرَاءَهُمْ | their ministers |
| Acc./Gen.: | جَوَازَاتِهِمْ | their passports |
| | مُشْرِفَيْهِ | both his supervisors |
| | مُشْرِفِيهِ | his supervisors |
| Gen.: | فِي قِسْمِهِ | in his department |
| | فِي رِسَالَتِهِنَّ | in their letter |
| | فِي رِسَالَاتِهِنَّ | in their letters |
| | لِعَلِّمَيْهِمْ | to/for both their teachers |
| | لِعَلِّمِيهِمْ | to/for their teachers |
| all three cases: | مَقْهَاهُ | his café |

- When hamzat al-waṣl (28) follows the suffixes ...هُمْ or ...كُمْ , these become ...هُمُ and ...كُمُ in full pronunciation:

| Nom.: | طَلَبُهُمُ الرَّسْمِيُّ | their official request |
| Acc.: | طَلَبَهُمُ الرَّسْمِيَّ | their official request |
| Gen.: | مِنْ طَلَبِكُمُ الرَّسْمِيِّ | from your official request |

- When hamzat al-waṣl follows the modified suffix ...هِمْ (see above), the suffix becomes respectively ...هُمُ or ...هِمُ in full pronunciation:

| Nom.: | تَوَلِّيهِمُ\...يهِمُ الرَّسْمِيُّ | their official assumption of office |
| Acc./Gen.: | حَسَبَ رِسَالَتَيْهِمُ الْعَاجِلَتَيْنِ | according to their two urgent letters |

The possessive adjective or genitive suffixes are also used after prepositions and after the base-word ...إِيَّا (see 167 and 173).

**148. Construct ( الإِضَافَةُ ).** A construct is an expression consisting of two or more nouns and showing the association between them; often, but not always, that of possession. A construct may be definite or indefinite in meaning. We examine the two-noun construct first.

In the two-noun construct:

- the first noun has a definite ending, but is not explicitly defined, i.e. it cannot carry either the article or a possessive suffix. It stands in the case demanded by its function in the sentence.

- the last noun is always in the genitive case, definite or indefinite according to the meaning of the whole expression. If definite, the last noun is explicitly defined (i.e. carries a definite article or a possessive suffix, unless it is a proper noun not normally carrying either.) It is this last noun which determines whether the whole expression is definite or indefinite in meaning. (But see 154 for an exception to this rule.)

- the only adjective which may interrupt the expression is a demonstrative ( هٰذا etc., see 146) preceding and qualifying the last noun.

Examples (the grammatical case shown is that of the first noun, since the last noun is always genitive):

| | | |
|---|---|---|
| Nom.: | كُتُبُ الطَّالِب | the student's books |
| | عِلْمُ الهَنْدَسَة | engineering science (*the* science of engineering) |
| | مُدِيرُ بَنْك | a bank manager |
| | فِنْجَانُ شَايٍّ | a cup of tea* |
| Acc.: | صَادِرَات شَرِكَتِه | his company's exports |
| | حَلَّ هٰذه المُشْكِلَة | the solution of/to this problem |
| | مُشْرِفَ نَوْبَة | a shift supervisor |
| | مَصَالِحَ مِصْرَ | Egypt's interests |
| Gen.: | في وَظِيفَة المُشْرِف | in the supervisors' job |
| | في عِرَاق اليَوْم | in today's Iraq |
| | بِجِهَاز حَفْر | with a drilling rig |

(* But 'a kilo of tea' (i.e. a measurement) is كِيلُو مِنَ الشَّايِّ , see 172)

A dual noun loses its final ن... , and a masculine sound plural noun its final ن... , when followed by another word in construct. The resultant final long vowel

(ي...\ـُو...\ـا...) is pronounced short before a following hamzat al-waṣl, under the normal rule. The vowel is still written long. The diphthong ـَي... of the dual becomes ـَي... (see 28) before a following hamzat al-waṣl:

Nom.:   مُمَثِّلُو الْوِكَالَةِ    *mumaththilu l-wikālati*    the agency's representatives

Acc.:   نُسْخَتَيْ بَيَانِهِمْ    *nuskhatay bayānihim*    both copies of their statement

نُسْخَتَيِ الْبَيَانِ    *nuskhatayi l-bayāni*/nuskhatay al-bayān
both copies of the statement

Gen.:   مَعَ مُهَنْدِسِي الْبِتْرُولِ    *ma' a muhandisi l-bitrouli*   with the petroleum engineers

بِجِهَازَيْ حَفْرٍ    *bi-jihāzay ḥafrin*    with two drilling rigs

A construct may have more than two nouns, in a 'string'. The rules apply to each noun accordingly, i.e. a middle noun, like the first noun, cannot be explicitly defined; but, like the last noun, it stands in the genitive case. In a definite construct, each noun except the last one is deemed to be defined by its successor:

نَصُّ طَلَبِ التَّعْوِيضِ    the text of the compensation claim

فِي مُسَوَّدَةِ تَقْرِيرِ أَحْمَدَ    in the draft of Ahmad's report

أَنْبَاءُ حَادِثِ مُرُورٍ    news of a traffic accident

A construct may be multiple, with two nouns linked by وَ 'and' or أَوْ 'or':

أَعْضَاءُ الْحُكُومَةِ وَالْمُعَارَضَةِ
(the) members of the government and (of the) opposition

حَجْمُ أَوْ وَزْنُ الشَّحْنِ    the volume or weight of the load

In fact each of these is an ellipsis of two constructs.

The latter of these two multiple constructs (i.e. with two first elements) is modern usage. Earlier usage preferred restatement with a possessive suffix for such a construct:

حَجْمُ الشَّحْنِ أَوْ وَزْنُهُ    'the volume of the load or its weight'

In short pronunciation (see 30), the ending ة... of any noun, other than the last one, of a construct is pronounced -at, irrespective of case:

مُهِمَّة اللَّجْنَةِ    *mahammatu l-lajnati*/mahammat al-lajna   the committee's task

Since no adjective other than a demonstrative may interrupt the construct, any adjective which is not a complement must follow the whole construct, irrespective of which noun it qualifies:

أُسْتَاذُ جَامِعَةٍ سَابِقٌ    a former university professor

سَيَّارَةُ الْمُدِيرِ الرَّسْمِيَّةُ    the director's official car

even if this leads to ambiguity:

مَعَ مُديرِ البَنْكِ المِصْرِيِّ   with the Egyptian bank manager

(who or what is Egyptian?)

Ambiguity may be avoided by recasting with لِ 'to/for', avoiding the construct:

مَعَ المُدير المِصْرِيِّ لِلبَنْك   with the Egyptian manager of the bank

مَعَ المُدير لِلبَنْكِ المِصْرِيِّ   with the manager of the Egyptian bank

The structure with لِ is also used to avoid an over-long 'string' construct:

تَفَاصِيلُ بَرْنَامَجِ الشَّرِكَة لِلتَّدْريب   details of the company's training programme

or: تَفَاصِيلُ بَرْنَامَجِ التَّدْريبِ لِلشَّرِكَة (better than: تَفَاصِيلُ بَرْنَامَجِ تَدْريبِ الشَّرِكَة)

Certain set expressions have the form of a construct with as first element an adjective (which may be a participle):

كِبَارُ المُوَظَّفِينَ   senior staff          فَائِقُ الاحْتِرَامِ   great ('excellent') respect

كِبَارُ مُوَظَّفِيهِمْ   their senior staff          بِوَافِرِ الشُّكْرِ   with profuse thanks

The expressions with the article are indefinite, despite appearances.

All can be recast as a noun + adjective:

المُوَظَّفُونَ الكِبَارُ   the senior staff          ضُبَّاطُهُمُ الصِّغَارُ   their junior officers

## 149. Collective Nouns.

**149. Collective Nouns.** Many living creatures, natural substances and artisanal products are designated by a collective noun, masculine singular and with no plural, standing for the whole group or species. Examples (see 137 and 138 for the declension):

| | | | | | |
|---|---|---|---|---|---|
| إِبْلٌ | camels | خَيْلٌ | horses | بَقَرٌ | cattle |
| سَمَكٌ | fish | دَجَاجٌ | chickens | نَمْلٌ | ants |
| نَحْلٌ | bees | ذُبَابٌ | flies | تُفَّاحٌ | apples |
| عِنَبٌ | grapes | تَمْرٌ | dates | تِينٌ | figs |
| مَوْزٌ | bananas | كَرَزٌ | cherries | حَبٌّ | grains, seeds |
| شَجَرٌ | trees | بَيْضٌ | eggs | وَرَقٌ | foliage; paper |
| طُوبٌ | bricks | بَلَاطٌ | tiles | | |

The unit of most of these nouns is expressed by adding the feminine ending ة...
(for the declension, see 137, 138, 140 and 141):

- with sound plural:

| | | | | | |
|---|---|---|---|---|---|
| بَقَرَةٌ | cow | دَجَاجَةٌ | chicken | نَمْلَةٌ | ant |

| | | | | | |
|---|---|---|---|---|---|
| نَحْلَةٌ | bee | ذُبَابَةٌ | fly | تُفَّاحَةٌ | apple |
| تِينَةٌ | fig | مَوْزَةٌ | banana | كَرَزَةٌ | cherry |
| حَبَّةٌ | grain, seed | بَيْضَةٌ | egg | طُوبَةٌ | brick |

- with broken plural; some with both sound and broken plurals:

سَمَكَةٌ أَسْمَاكٌ fish    عِنَبَةٌ أَعْنَابٌ grape(s)

شَجَرَةٌ؛ شَجَرَاتٌ\أَشْجَارٌ tree(s)/kinds of tree    تَمْرَةٌ تُمُورٌ date(s)

بَلَاطَةٌ بَلَاطَاتٌ\أَبْلِطَةٌ tile(s)    وَرَقَةٌ وَرَقَاتٌ\أَوْرَاقٌ leaf(ves)/sheet(s) of paper

Some important mammals have a unit noun from a different root. The following examples have a broken plural (for the declension, see 137, 138 and 140):

حِصَانٌ خُصُنٌ\أَخْصِنَةٌ horse(s)    جَمَلٌ جِمَالٌ\أَجْمَالٌ camel(s)

**150. Negation of Nouns and Adjectives.** Various devices exist to make nouns and adjectives negative.

A useful negative compound noun can be formed with the noun عَدَمُ 'lack' in construct (see 148) with a definite verbal noun (see 53):

عَدَمُ الثَّقَافَة lack of culture

عَدَمُ خِبْرَتِه his inexperience

لِعَدَمِ الِاهْتِمَام through inattention

أَوْقَفُوا الْمَشْرُوعَ لِعَدَمِ التَّمْوِيل. They stopped the project for lack of financing.

With a non-verbal noun, we interpose a neutral verbal noun such as وُجُودٌ 'existence':

مُشْكِلَتُنَا الْكُبْرَى هِيَ عَدَمُ وُجُودِ الْمَوَادِّ الأَوَّلِيَّةِ اللَّازِمَة.

Our greatest problem is lack of the necessary raw materials.

The adjectival equivalent is عَدِيمٌ (sound plural), with the same construction:

عَدِيمُ الثَّقَافَة uncultured, lacking culture

The noun غَيْرُ 'other' is used to negate a following adjective (including participles) in the genitive, making a construct which can be interpreted as a noun or adjective, depending on context:

غَيْرُ مَعْرُوفٍ unknown

غَيْرُ مُشَارِكِينَ non-participating, non-participants

Following the rules of the construct, when the expression is made definite, the article is prefixed to its last word:

لِلْمُرَشَّحِينَ غَيْرِ النَّاجِحِينَ  for the unsuccessful candidates

See 152 for the use of اَلْغَيْرُ , غَيْرُهُ etc. as a definite noun, and 172 for the preposition غَيْرَ .

A few relative adjectives and their derived abstract nouns (135, 136) are negated with the prefixed particle لَا :

لَاسِلْكِيٌّ  wireless (adjective)

الْمُوَاصَلَاتُ اللَّاسِلْكِيَّةُ  wireless telegraphy ('communications')

اللَّامَرْكَزِيَّةُ  decentralisation

لِسُلُوكِهِمِ اللَّاإِنْسَانِيِّ*  for their inhuman behaviour

(* two adjacent 'alifs in this word, in breach of the normal rule)


**151. Quasi-, Semi-.** Compound nouns and adjectives having the meaning 'quasi-', 'semi-' and the like are constructed with the nouns شِبْهُ (pl. أَشْبَاهُ) 'likeness' and نِصْفُ (pl. أَنْصَافُ) 'half', in construct (see 148) with either a noun or an adjective. These two words can be regarded as prefixes in this usage; note that the definite is made in the same way as with غَيْرُ 'un-' (150.):

شِبْهُ رَسْمِيٍّ  quasi-official, semi-official

فِي شِبْهِ الْجَزِيرَةِ الْعَرَبِيَّةِ  in the Arabian peninsula

مُعْطَيَاتُ نِصْفُ مُعَالَجَةً  half-processed data


**152. All, Some, Same, Other, Both, Any.** The nouns كُلٌّ, جَمِيعٌ, بَعْضٌ, نَفْسٌ (pl. أَنْفُسٌ) ذَاتٌ (pl. ذَوَاتُ), غَيْرٌ , كِلَا and the pronoun أَيٌّ\أَيَّةٌ are used adjectivally as follows:

• كُلٌّ a whole:
  - in singular indefinite construct (see 148), 'each/every':

    ... يَعْرِفُ كُلُّ طَالِبٍ  Every student knows ...

  - in singular definite construct, 'all of/the whole':

    ... يَعْرِفُ كُلُّ الصَّفِّ  The whole class knows ...

  - in plural definite construct or with a plural possessive adjective suffix 'all (of)':

    يَعْرِفُ كُلَّ الطُّلَّابِ.  He knows all (the) students.

    تُسَاعِدُ كُلَّ طَالِبَاتِهَا.  She helps all her students.

    كُلُّنَا  all of us

كُلّ is grammatically masculine singular; but it is used as if it were plural, when the meaning demands it:

عِنْدَ كُلِّ هٰؤُلَاءِ الطُّلَّابِ الْجُدُدِ   with all these new students

كُلُّ الْمُرَشَّحِينَ الَّذِينَ ...   all the candidates who ...

إِنَّ كُلَّ الْمُرَشَّحِينَ وَصَلُوا.   All the candidates have arrived.

وَصَلَتْ كُلُّ الطَّالِبَاتِ.   All the students arrived. (verbal statement, see 183)

كُلُّهُمْ حَاضِرُونَ.   All of them are present.

Note also related structures:

- الْكُلُّ  the whole, everybody/everything, all (plural):

هٰذَا مُفِيدٌ لِلْكُلِّ.   This is useful to all.

- كُلُّهُ  (etc.) following and in apposition to a definite noun:

فِي الشَّوَارِعِ كُلِّهَا   in all the streets ('in the streets, all of them')

فِي الصَّفِّ كُلِّهِ   in the whole class

• جَمِيعٌ  a whole: This word is used exactly as is كُلّ in its (animate or inanimate) plural meaning, 'all':

يَعْرِفُ جَمِيعَ الطُّلَّابِ الْجُدُدِ.   He knows all the new students.

هٰذَا مُفِيدٌ لِلْجَمِيعِ.   This is useful to all.

• بَعْضٌ  a part:

- in definite construct or with a possessive adjective suffix, 'some (of)':

بَعْضُ الْوَقْتِ\وَقْتِكَ   some of the/your time

لِبَعْضِ الْمَنْدُوبِينَ   for some of the delegates

بَعْضُهُمْ   some of them

- after a preposition, 'each other':

افْتَرَقُوا عَنْ بَعْضٍ.   They separated ('from each other').

- repeated, in the plural; the first with the possessive suffix, the second indefinite, 'each other':

كَانُوا يَشُكُّونَ بَعْضُهُمْ فِي بَعْضٍ.   They used to doubt each other.

بَعْضٌ is grammatically masculine singular; but it is used as if it were plural, when the meaning demands it:

بَعْضُ الْمَنْدُوبِينَ الْأَجَانِبِ رَفَضُوهُ.   Some of the foreign delegates rejected it.

• نَفْسٌ, pl. أَنْفُسٌ  soul:

- following and in apposition to a noun or pronoun (including an implied pronoun), '-self' (as an emphatic or reflexive pronoun):

هُوَ نَفْسُهُ قَالَهُ.    He said it himself.

كَانُو يَشُكُّون في أَنْفُسهِمْ.    They doubted themselves.

- in the singular, in definite construct with a singular, dual or plural noun, 'the same':

في نَفْسِ الأَوْقَاتِ.    at the same times

- ذَاتٌ , pl. ذَوَاتٌ essence, identity:

This word is used exactly as is نَفْسٌ :

لِذَاتِ الْغَرَضِ    for the same purpose

- غَيْرٌ other: with the article or a possessive suffix, the noun often being best translated with an English plural, 'others':

لَيْسَ غَيْرَهُ.    There is no ('its') other/There are no others.

حَاوِلْ أَنْ تُسَاعِدَ الْغَيْرَ في نَفْسِ الْوَقْتِ.

          Try to help others at the same time.

See 150 for the use of غَيْر to negate nouns and adjectives, and 172 for the preposition غَيْر 'other than', also used to negate adverbs (176).

- كِلا (masc.), كِلْتَا (fem.) both:

This word is used only in definite construct with a dual noun (when it is invariable for case) or with a dual possessive adjective suffix (when it is declined, see 147). Since the dual already means 'both', this word is used mainly for emphasis:

لِكِلا الْمُدِيرَيْنِ    to/for both (the) directors

بَيْنَ كِلْتَا الْحُكُومَتَيْنِ    between both governments

بَيْنَ كِلْتَيْهِمَا    between both of them

A verb of which it is the subject, or an adjective qualifying it, is usually singular, NB:

كِلاهُمَا وَصَلَ أَمْس.    They both ('Each of them') arrived yesterday.

كِلاهُمَا غَنِيٌّ.    They are both rich.

- أَيٌّ (masc.), أَيَّةٌ (fem.) any:

See 169. This word is also used in construct with a singular indefinite noun to mean 'any':

لِأَيِّ غَرَضٍ   for any purpose

فِي أَيَّةِ سَاعَةٍ   at any hour

**153. Comparative Degree of Adjectives.** The comparative adjective
('bigger, better') is always indefinite.

Simple adjectives (i.e. neither relative, nor participial from an increased verbal
form, nor similarly derived) have a comparative form based on the so-called
'elative' measure أَفْعَلُ, with variants as follows. The elative comparative
measure is diptote (see 144). The following examples are nominative; the
positive degree is shown first:

- sound, assimilated, hollow roots, أَفْعَلُ:

| | | | | | | | |
|---|---|---|---|---|---|---|---|
| كَبِيرٌ | big | أَكْبَرُ | bigger | قَصِيرٌ | short | أَقْصَرُ | shorter |
| سَهْلٌ\سَهِلٌ | easy | | | أَسْهَلُ | easier | | |
| وَاسِعٌ | wide | أَوْسَعُ | wider | وَاطِئٌ | low | أَوْطَأُ | lower |
| طَوِيلٌ | long | | | أَطْوَلُ | longer | | |
| (positive degree not used) | | | | أَمْيَزُ عَلَى | preferable to | | |

- doubled roots, أَفْعَلُ:

جَدِيدٌ new   أَجَدُّ newer     هَامٌّ important   أَهَمُّ more important

- defective roots, أَفْعَلُ :

عَلِيٌّ high   أَعْلَى higher (invariable for number and case, see 145)
(This is not a relative adjective (see 135); ي is the final radical.)

The elative comparative form is invariable for gender or number:

وَثِيقَةٌ أَطْوَلُ   a longer document

فِي شُؤُونٍ أَهَمَّ   in more important matters

إِنَّ الْأَرْقَامَ أَوْطَأُ.   The figures are lower.

The comparative of derived adjectives (e.g. relative, participial from Forms II-X,
etc.) is expressed with the the elative أَكْثَرُ 'more' or أَشَدُّ 'stronger' followed
by the indefinite accusative form of the abstract noun (verbal noun if the adjective
is a participle) denoting the quality:

إِجْرَاءَاتٌ ضَرُورِيَّةٌ   necessary measures

إِجْرَاءَاتٌ أَكْثَرُ ضَرُورَةً   more necessary measures ('measures greater in necessity')

لِأَشْخَاصٍ مُثَقَّفِينَ   for cultured people

لِأَشْخَاصٍ أَشَدَّ ثَقَافَةً    for more cultured people ('people stronger in culture')

Decreasing comparison of both simple and derived adjectives is expressed with أَقَلُّ (itself the elative comparative of قَلِيلٌ 'little, few') and the indefinite accusative of the appropriate abstract or verbal noun:

أَسْئِلَةٌ أَقَلُّ أَهَمِّيَّةً    less important questions

مَعَ عُمَّالٍ أَقَلَّ اجْتِهَادًا    with less industrious workers

Equal comparison ('as ... as') does not entail the comparative; it is expressed with مِثْلَ 'like' and the adjective in the positive degree:

لَيْسَ غَنِيًّا مِثْلَكَ.    He is not as rich as ('not rich like') you.

'Than' is مِنْ as a preposition (i.e. before a noun or pronoun), or مِمَّا as a conjunction (i.e. before a clause):

إِنَّ الْجِنْسَ أَهَمُّ مِنَ الثَّمَنِ.    The quality is more important than the price.

يَعْرِفُ هُوَ أَكْثَرَ مِمَّا أَنَا أَعْرِفُ بِخُصُوصِه.    He knows more than I do about it.

When the comparative is the complement of a verb of being, becoming or similar, an alternative structure is to use a verb indicating increase or decrease:

زَادَ الْحِوَارُ صَرَاحَةً.    The dialogue became more frank.

                     ('... increased in frankness')

For the expression 'The more ..., the more...', see 197.

**154. Superlative Degree of Adjectives.** The superlative ('biggest, best') is expressed by making the comparative (see 153) definite, either by placing the comparative form in indefinite construct (see 148) with its noun (NB: the expression has definite meaning, in breach of the rule):

أَهَمُّ مَصْنَعٍ    the most important factory

لِأَقْصَرِ مُدَّةٍ    for the shortest period

أَشَدُّ تِلْمِيذٍ اجْتِهَادًا.    the hardest-working pupil

or by attaching a possessive adjective suffix (see 147):

مَعَ أَسْهَلِهَا    with the easiest of them

or by using it as a normal adjective, following and agreeing with a definite noun:

الْمَصْنَعُ الْأَهَمُّ    the most important factory

فِي الْمَصْنَعِ الْأَهَمِّ    in the most important factory

With derived adjectives it is the أَكْثَرُ or أَشَدُّ which is made definite:

الأَشْخَاصُ الأَكْثَرُ ثَقَافَةً the most cultured people

The elative superlative adjective, being definite, is no longer diptote (see 144).

Certain elative superlatives have a broken feminine form on the measure فُعْلَى (or variants thereof), which form must be used whenever the adjective agrees in gender with a feminine or inanimate plural noun. Common examples are given below (masculine/feminine, the latter invariable for number and case (see 145)):

- sound roots:

الكُبْرَى الأَكْبَرُ biggest     الصُّغْرَى الأَصْغَرُ smallest

الحُسْنَى الأَحْسَنُ best     العُظْمَى الأَعْظَمُ greatest

الفُضْلَى الأَفْضَلُ best

- hollow roots:

الطُّولَى الأَطْوَلُ longest

- defective roots (masculine also indeclinable):

الدُّنْيَا* الأَدْنَى lowest     العُلْيَا* الأَعْلَى highest

* ى becomes ا... after ـيـ... .

في المَصَانِعِ الصُّغْرَى in the smallest factories

هٰذِهِ هِيَ الصُّغْرَى. These are/This is the smallest.

The feminine elative superlatives are often found in set expressions such as:

الدُّوَلُ الكُبْرَى the superpowers

آسِيَا الصُّغْرَى Asia Minor

some of which are also used, contrary to the rule, indefinitely:

دَوْلَةٌ\دُوَلٌ كُبْرَى a superpower, superpowers

These superlatives can form definite masculine and feminine sound plurals to denote implied animate plural nouns, when the meaning permits it:

لِلْحُسْنَوَاتِ في الصَّفِّ for the best (girls) in the class

مِنْ جَمِيعِ طُلَّابِنَا هُمُ الأَفْضَلُونَ. Of all our students they are the best.

A few superlatives also form a broken masculine plural with special meaning:

الأَكَابِرُ the great (from أَكْبَرُ )

عَظَائِمُ الأُمُورِ awesome matters (from أَعْظَمُ from عَظِيمٌ)

'As ... as possible' with adjectival meaning is expressed with a quasi-superlative construction:

طَلَمْبَةٌ أَقْوَى مَا يُمْكِنُ a pump as powerful as possible/the strongest possible pump

See 178 for the commoner use of this construction in adverbial expressions.

**155. First, Last, Other.** Three important adjectives build elative forms with a feminine and an animate plural; they are used in the manner of comparatives and superlatives (153 and 154):

|        | singular | dual | animate plural | |
|--------|----------|------|----------------|---|
| masc.  | أَوَّلُ   | أَوَّلَانِ | أَوَّلُونَ | first |
| fem.   | أُولَى * | أُوَّلَتَانِ | أُوَّلَيَاتُ | |
| masc.  | آخِرُ    | آخِرَانِ | آخِرُونَ | last |
| fem.   | آخِرَةُ * | آخِرَتَانِ | آخِرَاتُ | |
| masc.  | آخَرُ    | آخَرَانِ | أُخَرُ\آخَرُونَ | other |
| fem.   | أُخْرَى * | آخَرَتَانِ | أُخَرُ\أُخْرَيَاتُ | |

\* also inanimate plural

The first two words, أَوَّلُ (etc.) and آخِرُ (etc.) are mostly used definitely, i.e. like superlatives. They are diptote (144).

أَوَّلُ مُرَشَّحٍ\المُـرَشَّحُ الأَوَّلُ    the first candidate (m.)

أَوَّلُ مُرَشَّحَةٍ\المُـرَشَّحَةُ الأُولَى    the first candidate (f.)

المُـرَشَّحَاتُ الأَوَّلِيَاتُ    the first candidates (f.)

Similarly for آخَرُ 'other', except that this word is often also used indefinitely, i.e. like a comparative. In this form it is also diptote:

شَخْصٌ آخَرُ    someone else          آخَرُ مَرَّةٍ    the other time

مَرَّةٌ أُخْرَى    another time          المَرَّةُ الأُخْرَى    the other time

Note also the following structures, with a broken plural, having special meaning:

فِي أَوَّلِ السَّنَةِ    at the beginning of the year

فِي أَوَائِلِ السَّنَةِ    early in the year

فِي آخِرِ الشَّهْرِ    at the end of the month

فِي أَوَاخِرِ الشَّهْرِ    late in the month

**156. Better and Worse.** The masculine nouns خَيْرٌ 'good' and شَرٌّ 'evil' can be used in an equation (180) or a construct (148) to express the comparatives or superlatives 'better/best' or 'worse/worst' respectively:

هٰذَا خَيْرٌ مِنْ ذٰلِكَ.   This is better than that.

خَيْرُ نَتِيجَةٍ   a better result

بِشَرِّ النَّتَائِجِ   with the worst results ('... of the results')

**157. Nouns of Place, Activity, Instrument.** Many nouns related to activity or situation are derived from Form I of verbs (see 37). Some have sound plurals, some broken (and possibly diptote, see 144) plurals.

<u>Place.</u> The place in which something happens may have the measure مَفْعَلٌ\مَفْعَلَةٌ (with variants for doubled or hollow roots):

| Root/Connotation | | Singular | Plural | |
|---|---|---|---|---|
| شغل | work | مَشْغَلٌ | مَشَاغِلُ | workshop |
| صنع | fabricate | مَصْنَعٌ | مَصَانِعُ | factory |
| حكم | judge | مَحْكَمَةٌ | مَحَاكِمُ | lawcourt |
| طير | fly | مَطَارٌ | مَطَارَاتٌ | airport |

<u>Activity.</u> The activity may have the measure فِعَالٌ\فِعَالَةٌ , the person pursuing it فَعَّالٌ* ; plurals are sound:

| Root/Connotation | | Activity | | Person | |
|---|---|---|---|---|---|
| طبخ | cook | طِبَاخَةٌ | cookery | طَبَّاخٌ | cook |
| لحم | weld | لِحَامٌ | welding | لَحَّامٌ | welder |

(* This is the intensive active participle of verbs of Form I, now mostly found in this usage. An exception is the word فَعَّالٌ itself, 'effective'.)

<u>Instrument.</u> The instrument used may have the measure مِفْعَالٌ\مِفْعَلَةٌ :

| Root/Connotation | | Singular | Plural | |
|---|---|---|---|---|
| فتح | open | مِفْتَاحٌ | مَفَاتِيحُ | key |
| نشف | dry | مِنْشَفَةٌ | مَنَاشِفُ | towel |

A few instruments have the feminine form of the the intensive active participle of Form I (see above), with a sound plural:

| Root/Connotation | | Singular | Plural | |
|---|---|---|---|---|
| برد | cold | بَرَّادَةٌ | بَرَّادَاتٌ | refrigerator |
| سير | travel | سَيَّارَةٌ | سَيَّارَاتٌ | car |

Certain passive participles of increased forms of verbs can denote the place of the activity:

| | | | |
|---|---|---|---|
| اِئْتَمَرَ يَأْتَمِرُ | VIII (see 67) to deliberate, | مُؤْتَمَرٌ | conference |
| اخْتَبَرَ يَخْتَبِرُ | VIII to test, | مُخْتَبَرٌ | laboratory |
| اِنْقَلَبَ يَنْقَلِبُ | VII to be overthrown, | مُنْقَلَبٌ | place of overthrow, one's 'Waterloo' |
| اِسْتَوْصَفَ يَسْتَوْصِفُ | X (see 95) to consult (medically), | مُسْتَوْصَفٌ | clinic |
| اِسْتَرَاحَ يَسْتَرِيحُ | X (see 101) to rest, | مُسْتَرَاحٌ | lavatory |

**158. Diminutive Nouns and Adjectives.** Some nouns and adjectives have a diminutive form, built on the measures فُعَيْلٌ\فُعَيْلَةٌ or فُعَيِّلٌ\فُعَيِّلَةٌ (triliteral roots), فُعَيْلِلٌ or فُعَيْلِيلٌ (quadriliteral roots):

| | | | | | | | |
|---|---|---|---|---|---|---|---|
| وَلَدٌ | boy | وُلَيْدٌ | little boy | بَحْرٌ | sea | بُحَيْرَةٌ | lake |
| كَلْبٌ | dog | كُلَيْبٌ | puppy | كِتَابٌ | book | كُتَيِّبٌ | booklet |
| صَغِيرٌ | small | صُغَيِّرٌ | tiny | بُسْتَانٌ | garden | بُسَيْتِينٌ | small garden |

**159. أَبٌ 'ab etc.** The nouns أَبٌ 'father', أَخٌ 'brother' and حَمٌ 'father-in-law' are sometimes anomalous.

They are regular in the following circumstances (only أَبٌ is shown):

- when used indefinitely, see 132:

Nom. أَبٌ , Acc. أَبًا , Gen. أَبٍ  a father

- when used with the definite article or with the 1st person singular possessive adjective suffix ي... 'my' (in which latter circumstance the case-ending is dropped), see 138 and 147:

Nom. الأَبُ, Acc. الأَبَ, Gen. الأَبِ the father; all cases أَبِي my father
When the noun is followed by another noun in construct (see 148), or when it carries any possessive adjective suffix other than the 1st person sing. ي... 'my', the three definite case-endings are replaced by the corresponding long vowel (Nom. و... for ُ... , Acc. ا... for َ... , Gen. ي... for ِ... ):

Nom.:      أَخُو زَمِيلِي    my colleague's brother

               أَخُوهُ    his brother

Acc.:      أَبَا هٰذَا الطَّالِبِ    this student's father

               حَمَاهَا    her father-in-law

Gen.:      لِأَخِيهِ    to/for his brother

لِأَبِي الطَّالِب to/for the student's father

In the dual, a final-radical و, absent in the singular, is restored. With this, the dual is regular (see 140): Nom. أَبَوَانِ , Acc./Gen. أَبَوَيْنِ .

The plurals are broken:

Nom. أَحْمَاءٌ إِخْوَةٌ آبَاءٌ ; Acc. أَحْمَاءَ إِخْوَةً آبَاءً ; Gen. أَحْمَاءٍ إِخْوَةٍ آبَاءٍ

The plurals ending in ...اء are not diptote; the ء represents the otherwise obsolete final radical.

إِخْوَةٌ means 'brothers' (in a family). We have also إِخْوَانٌ 'brethren' (members of a fraternity or community).

**160. Table 34: <u>dhū</u> etc.** The anomalous noun ذُو , meaning 'possessing' or 'characterised by' exists only in the definite form. It has both masculine and feminine forms. The masculine singular declines like the anomalous form of أَبٌ (see 159):

| Singular | Nominative | Accusative | Genitive |
|---|---|---|---|
| masculine | ذُو | ذَا | ذِي |
| feminine* | ذَاتُ | ذَاتَ | ذَاتِ |

| Dual** | Nominative | Accusative/Genitive |
|---|---|---|
| masculine | ذَوَا | ذَوَيْ |
| feminine | ذَوَاتَا | ذَوَاتَيْ |

| Animate Pl. | Nominative | Accusative/Genitive |
|---|---|---|
| masculine | ذَوُو | ذَوِي |
| feminine | ذَوَاتُ | ذَوَاتِ |

* also inanimate plural.  ** animate and inanimate. See 134.

This noun is always used in construct (see 148), which acts as a compound adjective:

Nom.:      مَسْأَلَةٌ ذَاتُ أَهَمِّيَّةٍ     a matter of importance; an important matter

Acc.:      سَيِّدَةً ذَاتَ ثَقَافَةٍ     a cultured lady

           طَبِيبًا ذَا شَجَاعَةٍ     a courageous doctor

Gen.:   بِالطُّلُمْبَاتِ ذَاتِ الْقُوَّةِ الْكُبْرَى     with the highest-powered pumps

مَعَ الْمُحَامِي ذِي الْخِبْرَةِ الْمُنَاسِبَةِ   with the lawyer having the appropriate
experience

Note:

- The last element of the construct agrees in definition with the qualified noun.
- The final long vowel found in some of the forms is pronounced short before the definite article (hamzat al-waṣl), see 28.

**161. Adjectives of Colour and Defect.** Most adjectives denoting colour or physical defect have the elative measure (see 153) in the singular, and have a broken animate plural used for both genders. The indefinite singular is diptote (see 144), except for one important indeclinable form. Important examples are:

| singular | | dual | | animate plural | |
|---|---|---|---|---|---|
| masc. | fem.* | masc. | fem. | masc. + fem. | |
| أَحْمَرُ | حَمْرَاءُ | أَحْمَرَانِ | حَمْرَاوَانِ | حُمْرٌ | red |
| أَسْوَدُ | سَوْدَاءُ | أَسْوَدَانِ | سَوْدَاوَانِ | سُودٌ | black |
| أَبْيَضُ | بَيْضَاءُ | أَبْيَضَانِ | بَيْضَاوَانِ | بِيضٌ | white |
| أَطْرَشُ | طَرْشَاءُ | أَطْرَشَانِ | طَرْشَاوَانِ | طُرْشٌ | deaf |
| أَعْوَجُ | عَوْجَاءُ | أَعْوَجَانِ | عَوْجَاوَانِ | عُوجٌ | bent |
| أَجَشُّ | جَشَّاءُ | أَجَشَّانِ | جَشَّاوَانِ | جُشٌّ | hoarse |
| أَعْمَى** | عُمْيَاءُ | أَعْمَيَانِ | عُمْيَاوَانِ | عُمْيٌ | blind |

\* also inanimate plural. See 134.          \** invariable for case.

The following are also declined like أَحْمَرُ : أَخْضَرُ green; أَزْرَقُ blue; أَصْفَرُ yellow; أَعْرَجُ lame; أَخْرَسُ dumb.

Comparatives and superlatives are formed as for derived adjectives (see 153 and 154). The abstract nouns used for this structure are formed as follows:

- all colours except those with hollow roots (i.e. weak middle radical); measure فُعْلَةٌ : أَكْثَرُ\أَشَدُّ زُرْقَةً bluer
- colours with hollow roots; measure فَعَالٌ :

  أَكْثَرُ\أَشَدُّ سَوَادًا blacker          أَكْثَرُ\أَشَدُّ بَيَاضًا whiter

- physical defects; measure فَعَلٌ : أَكْثَرُ\أَشَدُّ طَرَشًا deafer

**162. Anomalous Plurals.** A few nouns have an anomalous broken plural declined on the pattern of the masculine singular defective active participles (see 117). Important examples are:

يَدٌ (f.) hand,    pl. أَيَادٍ\أَيَادِيًا    (indef. nom.+ gen.; acc.)

الأَيَادِي\الأَيَادِيَ    (def. nom.+ gen.; acc.)

أَرْضٌ (f.) land,    pl. أَرَاضٍ\أَرَاضِيًا    (indef. nom.+ gen.; acc.)

الأَرَاضِي\الأَرَضِيَ    (def. nom.+ gen.; acc.)

**163. Improper Annexation (الإِضَافَةُ غَيْرُ الحَقِيقِيَّة).** Certain compound adjectives consist of an adjective (which may be a participle) followed by a defined genitive noun, in a form similar to the construct (see 148):

سَرِيعُ البَدِيهَة    quick-witted ('quick the wit')

دَائِمُ العَجْز    permanently disabled

The annexation (i.e. agreement) is called improper because the adjectival element of the compound agrees with the 'wrong' noun:

مُؤَسَّسَةٌ كَثِيرَةُ المَال    a wealthy foundation

قَرْضٌ مُنْخَفِضُ الفَائِدَةُ    a soft ('reduced-interest') loan

بِوَاسِطَة طُلْمِبَات عَالِيَّة الضَغْط    by means of high-pressure pumps

فِي اتِّفَاقِيَّة مَحْدُودَة الأَجَل    in a limited-term agreement

We have the same phenomenon nearer home: 'Elle avait l'air contente', a correct sentence in which, however, it is logically not she (f.), but her appearance (m.), which should be described as happy.

The Arabic examples given above are all indefinite. In the definite form, all three words (one adjective, two nouns) are made definite:

المُؤَسَّسَةُ الكَثِيرَةُ المَال    the wealthy foundation

قَرْضُهُمُ المُنْخَفِضُ الفَائِدَةُ    their soft loan

بِوَاسِطَة هذِه الطُلْمِبَات العَالِيَّة الضَغْط    by means of these high-pressure pumps

However, we occasionally encounter definite expressions in which the adjectival element is left undefined:

فِي اتِّفَاقِيَّتِنَا (الـ)مَحْدُودَة الأَجَل    in our limited-term agreement

**164. Apposition.** When the two objects of a doubly transitive verb (33) are in apposition, i.e. have the same identity, the second object must be indefinite:

انْتَخَبُوا صَدِيقَهُ رَئِيسًا.    They elected his friend chairman/president.

In some examples, the apposition can be alternatively expressed with the preposition كَ 'like', 'as':

رَحَّبُوا بِي صَدِيقًا\كَصَدِيقٍ.     They greeted me as a friend.

The structure with the second noun in the indefinite accusative is found also in certain set phrases with e.g. بِصِفَة 'in the capacity of':

بِصِفَتِهِ مَنْدُوبًا     in his capacity as delegate

# 13. Pronouns

**165.** **Table 35. Subject Pronouns.** The subject or nominative pronouns are:

|  | Singular | | Plural | |
|---|---|---|---|---|
| 1st person m./f. | أَنَا | I | نَحْنُ | we |
| 2nd person m. | أَنْتَ | you | أَنْتُمْ | you |
| 2nd person f. | أَنْتِ | you | أَنْتُنَّ | you |
| 3rd person m. | هُوَ | he/it | هُمْ | they* |
| 3rd person f. | هِيَ | she/it/they** | هُنَّ | they* |

|  | Dual | |
|---|---|---|
| 2nd person m./f. | أَنْتُمَا | both of you |
| 3rd person m./f. | هُمَا | both of them*** |

\* animate; \*\* inanimate; \*\*\* animate or inanimate. See 134.

The 1st person plural pronoun نَحْنُ is used also for the dual. The 2nd and 3rd persons masculine plural pronouns أَنْتُمْ and هُمْ are used to denote animate plural masculine nouns or nouns of mixed gender; the 2nd and 3rd persons feminine plural pronouns أَنْتُنَّ and هُنَّ are used to denote only animate plural feminine nouns.

The subject pronoun is used:

- In an equation: see 180.
- To emphasise: the subject or object (direct or prepositional, see 33) of a verb; or a noun governed by a preposition; or a possessive adjective suffix (see 147):

  أَنَا أَخَذْتُهُ.   *I* took it.

  لَيْسَ هُوَ مَسْؤُولاً.   *He* is not responsible.

  سَأَلُونِي أَنَا.   They asked *me*.

  يَعْتَمِدُونَ عَلَيْنَا نَحْنُ.   They are relying on *us*.

  فِي قِسْمِهِ هُوَ   in *his* department

- After the conjunction وَ in a clause of circumstance (see 196).
- In an ellipsis with no other indication of the subject:

مَنِ الَّذِي كَتَبَهُ؟ – أَنَا.   Who wrote it? I (did).

(مَنْ becomes مَنِ before hamzat al-waṣl; see 28.)

- After إِلَّا 'except' in an exceptive sentence (see 201).

The subject pronoun is usually omitted when its identity is otherwise clear, and no emphasis is required:

كَتَبْتُهُ.   I wrote it.

**166. Table 36. Direct Object Pronoun Suffixes.** The direct object or accusative pronouns take the form of a suffix, identical to the possessive or genitive suffixes (see 147) except for the 1st person singular:

|  | Singular |  | Plural |  |
|---|---|---|---|---|
| 1st person m./f. | ...نِي | me | ...نَا | us |
| 2nd person m. | ...كَ | you | ...كُمْ | you |
| 2nd person f. | ...كِ | you | ...كُنَّ | you |
| 3rd person m. | ...هُ | him/it | ...هُمْ | them* |
| 3rd person f. | ...هَا | her/it/them** | ...هُنَّ | them* |

|  | Dual |  |
|---|---|---|
| 2nd person m./f. | ...كُمَا | both of you |
| 3rd person m./f. | ...هُمَا | both of them*** |

\* animate;  ** inanimate;  *** animate or inanimate. See 134.

The 1st person plural suffix ...نَا is used also for the dual. The 2nd and 3rd persons masculine plural suffixes ...كُمْ and ...هُمْ are used to denote animate plural masculine objects or objects of mixed gender; the 2nd and 3rd persons feminine plural suffixes ...كُنَّ and ...هُنَّ are used to denote only animate plural feminine objects.

The suffix is attached to the full form of the verb of which it is the direct object. Certain forms of the verb are modified before the suffix is attached:

- The 2nd person masculine plural ending ...تُمْ of the perfect tense becomes ...تُمُو .
- The ending ...وا of the 3rd person masculine plural perfect, subjunctive and jussive tenses, and of the masculine plural of the imperative, loses its silent ا in writing. The pronunciation is unchanged.
- The ending ...ىَ becomes ...ا .

Further, certain suffixes are modified when attached to certain verb-endings. Allowing for these modifications, the suffixes are attached as follows:

- The 1st person suffixes نِي... 'me' and نَا... 'us', all the 2nd person suffixes 'your', and the 3rd person feminine singular/inanimate plural suffix هَا... 'her/its/their' are attached in the form shown in the table:

فَهِمَنِي     he understood me

هَلْ فَهِمَكَ؟     Did he understand you?

أَسْمَعُهَا     I hear her

شَكَرُوكُمْ     they thanked you

نَشْكُرُهُمْ     we thank them

رَفَضْتُمُوهَا     you refused it/them

يَنْسَاهُ     he forgets it

- After the 2nd person feminine singular ending تِ... of the perfect tense, and after any verbal ending (whether personal ending or final radical) ـِي... or ـَيْ... (but not ـَا... ), the 3rd person suffixes هُ..., هُمَا..., هُمْ... and هُنَّ... become هِ... , هِمَا... , هِمْ... and هِنَّ... respectively. After any other ending they retain the form shown in Table 36 above:

كَتَبْتَهُ     you (masc.) wrote it

كَتَبْتِهِ     you (fem.) wrote it

لاَ تُذَكِّرِيهِ     do not (fem.) remind him

يَضْرِبُهُ     he hits it

يَرْمِيهِ     he throws it

نَسِيَهُمْ     he forgot them

لِكَيْ تَرَاهُمْ     so that you (masc.) see them

لِكَيْ تَرَيْهِمْ     so that you (fem.) see them

In all of the aforegoing, full and short pronunciation are identical.

- When hamzat al-waṣl (see 28) follows the suffixes هُمْ... or كُمْ... in the same phrase, these become respectively هُمُ... and كُمُ... in full pronunciation:

رَأَيْنَاهُمُ الْيَوْمَ.     We saw them today.

سَأَلْنَاكُمُ السُّؤَالَ كِتَابَةً.     We asked you the question in writing.

- When hamzat al-waṣl follows the modified suffix هِم... (see above) in the same phrase, the suffix becomes ...هِمْ or ...هِمِ in full pronunciation:

سَيُنَادِيهِمِ الآنَ.  He will call them now.

- See 182 for the use of these suffixes after conjunctions of the أَنَّ group, to denote the subject of the verb in a nominal sentence.

**167. Table 37: Independent Direct Object Pronouns.** The independent direct object or accusative pronouns take the form of a base word إِيَّا... suffixed with the appropriate possessive or prepositional object suffix (147, 173):

|              | Singular |          | Plural   |         |
|--------------|----------|----------|----------|---------|
| 1st person m./f. | ( إِيَّايَ | me   | إِيَّانَا | us )   |
| 2nd person m. | ( إِيَّاكَ | you  | إِيَّاكُمْ | you ) |
| 2nd person f. | ( إِيَّاكِ | you  | إِيَّاكُنَّ | you ) |
| 3rd person m. | إِيَّاهُ | (him)/it | ( إِيَّاهُمْ | them*) |
| 3rd person f. | إِيَّاهَا | (her)/it/them** | ( إِيَّاهُنَّ | them*) |

|              | Dual |          |
|--------------|------|----------|
| 2nd person m./f. | ( إِيَّاكُمَا | both of you ) |
| 3rd person m./f. | إِيَّاهُمَا | both of them*** |

* animate; ** inanimate; *** animate or inanimate. See below, and 134.

Although these pronouns exist in all persons, in modern practice one seldom finds other than the 3rd persons inanimate in use, after a verb with two pronoun objects (see 33):

سَأَلُوهُمْ إِيَّاهُ.  They asked them it.

أَعْطَانِي إِيَّاهُ.  He gave it/them to me.

The last example can also be أَعْطَانِيهِ .

**168. Table 38: Relative Pronouns.** The relative pronouns ('who', 'whom', 'which', 'that', also called relative conjunctions) are all in the 3rd person. They are:

|                     | Masculine | Feminine |
|---------------------|-----------|----------|
| Singular, all cases | ٱلَّذِي    | ٱلَّتِي *  |
| Dual**, nominative  | ٱللَّذَانِ | ٱللَّتَانِ |
| acc. and gen.       | ٱللَّذَيْنِ | ٱللَّتَيْنِ |

| | | |
|---|---|---|
| Animate pl., all cases | اَلَّذِينَ | اللَّوَاتِي |

\* also inanimate plural; \*\* animate or inanimate. See 134.

The ‏لّ‎ found in some of the forms is pronounced -ll-, exactly like the standard ‏لّ‎ in the other forms. The pronoun starts with hamzat-al-waṣl; its initial vowel is ‏اِ...‎ when the pronoun begins the phrase or sentence, and is dropped altogether after a word ending with a vowel in the same phrase. See 28.

The relative pronoun agrees as far as possible with its antecedent (the word to which it relates). It is used only when the antecedent is a definite noun, or, in certain circumstances, a pronoun.

The relative pronoun is used as it stands, when it is the subject of its own verb (i.e. the verb in the same clause):

اَلْمَأْمُورُ الَّذِي أَصْدَرَ الْبَيَانَ مَوْجُودٌ.

The official who issued the statement is present.

إِنَّ الرِّسَالَةَ الَّتِي وَصَلَتِ الْيَوْمَ تُسَاعِدُنَا كَثِيراً.

The letter which arrived today helps us greatly.

When the relative pronoun is the direct or prepositional object of its own verb, the antecedent is reiterated in the relative clause by attaching the appropriate direct object suffix (see 166) to the verb, or the prepositional object suffix (see 173) to the preposition, respectively:

الرِّسَالَاتُ الَّتِي تَسَلَّمْنَاهَا أَمْسِ

the letters which we received ('them') yesterday

الْحُكُومَةُ الَّتِي مُعْتَمَدٌ لَدَيْهَا السَّفِيرُ

the government to which the ambassador is accredited ('to it')

When the antecedent is a pronoun, the masculine singular pronoun مَنْ 'who' or مَا 'what' (see 169) is used to express both antecedent and relative pronoun in one. In relative clauses of this kind, reiteration is optional for a direct object but obligatory for a prepositional object. Instead of مَنْ we can use the relative pronoun itself, with no antecedent:

Subject: اَلَّذِي \ مَنْ يَتَكَلَّمُ كَذٰلِكَ يَكْذِبُ.  He who/Whoever talks like that is lying.

Dir. Obj.:        لَمْ أَفْهَمْ مَا قَالَ\قَالَهُ.

I did not understand what/that which he said ('it').

Prep. Obj.: هٰذَا (هُوَ) مَا يُصِرُّونَ عَلَيْهِ. This is what they are insisting on.

One of the prepositions expressing possession (لِ , مَعَ , عِنْدَ, see 174) may be used, with reiteration of the antecedent, to express 'who has' (etc.):

هٰذَا هُوَ الْمُتَخَصِّصُ الَّذِي عِنْدَهُ الْخِبْرَةُ الْمَطْلُوبَةُ.

This is the specialist who has ('with whom is') the required experience.
When مَنْ or مَا is the prepositional object of the main verb, we attach it to the
appropriate preposition:

تَعَجَّبْنَا مِمَّا حَدَثَ.    We were astonished at what happened.

سَتَدْفَعُ الشَّرِكَةُ لِمَنْ يُقَدِّمُ الشَّهَادَةَ.

The company will pay ('to') him/anyone who presents the certificate.

سَتَدْفَعُ الشَّرِكَةُ لِمَنْ لَدَيْهِ الشَّهَادَةُ.

The company will pay ('to') him/anyone who has the certificate.

لِنَطْلُبِ الْمُسَاعَدَةَ مِمَّنْ يَفْهَمُ الْمَسْأَلَةَ.

Let us seek help from (someone) who understands the matter.
The construction مَا ... مِنْ 'what(ever) ... of' followed by a definite noun, is
commonly used as an indefinite relative expression of the following type:

نَسْتَعْمِلُ مَا عِنْدَنَا مِنَ الْوَسَائِلِ.    We shall use whatever means we have/such

means as we have ('what we have of means').
When the antecedent is not a noun or pronoun but the whole preceding clause,
the usual relative pronoun or conjunction is الْأَمْرُ الَّذِي   '(that) which'. An
expression of circumstance with وَ(ذٰلِكَ) (196) can also be used in this context:

نَجَحَتِ التَّجْرِبَةُ الْأَمْرُ الَّذِي\وَذٰلِكَ أَفَادَنَا كَثِيرًا.

The experiment succeeded, which (fact) benefited us greatly.

يُقَرِّرُونَ أَنَّ الْأَرْقَامَ إِيجَابِيَّةٌ الْأَمْرُ الَّذِي\وَأَنَا أَشُكُّ فِيهِ.

They report that the figures are positive, which I doubt.
When the antecedent is an indefinite noun, the relative pronoun is omitted. All the
other rules associated with a noun antecedent apply:

Subject:   مُقَرِّرٌ يَعْرِفُ الْمِنْطَقَةَ   a correspondent who knows the region

Dir. Obj.:   مُقَرِّرٌ لَا نَعْرِفُهُ   a correspondent (whom) we do not know ('him')

Prep. Obj.: مُقَرِّرٌ نَعْتَمِدُ عَلَيْهِ   a correspondent on whom we rely

('whom we rely on him')

Prep.:   مُقَرِّرٌ لَهُ فَهْمُ الْأَزْمَةِ   a correspondent who has understanding of the crisis
After an indefinite antecedent, when the relative clause is an equation (180), we
interpose the subject pronoun:

أَعْرِفُ شَخْصًا هُوَ غَنِيٌّ جِدًّا.    I know a person who ('he') is very rich.
The subject pronoun is also used, together with the relative, in sentences of the
kind 'It is/was I who ...':

الرَّئِيسُ هُوَ الَّذِي قَدْ تَكَلَّمَ.  It is/was the chairman who spoke.

نَحْنُ الَّذِينَ نَطْلُبُ.  It is we who are asking. ('We are who ...')

A negative passive verb in an indefinite relative clause can often express an English adjective of the form 'un...able/in...able':

حِكَايَةٌ لاَ تُنْسَى  an unforgettable story

In English a relative pronoun which is either the direct or the prepositional object of its own verb may be omitted at will ('a man (whom) I trust ...', 'the money (which) we live on ...'). The rule for omitting the relative pronoun in Arabic is binding, and applies differently.

**169. Interrogative Pronouns.** All interrogative pronouns are singular. Most are only masculine, and invariable for case:

مَنْ  who(m) ...?        مَاذَا، مَا  what ...?        كَمْ  how much/many...?

أَيُّ  (masc.), أَيَّةُ  (fem.) which ...?

لِمَنْ  whose ...?        مَنْ  (in construct) whose ...?

A question beginning with one of these words does not have هَلْ or أ (see 184), since it cannot be answered with 'yes' or 'no'.

The interrogative pronouns may introduce either direct or indirect questions (see 184 and 186). They are used as follows:

- مَنْ may be subject or direct object of the verb in its clause, or can be governed by a preposition. For the subject of the verb in a longer question, the relative interrogative structure is usually preferred; see 170.

مَنْ يَعْرِفُ؟  Who knows?

سَأَلْنَاهُ مَنْ يَزُورُ.  We asked him who he was ('is') visiting.

مَنْ زُرْتَ؟  Whom did you visit?

مَعَ مَنْ بَحَثْتَ الْمَوْضُوعَ؟  With whom have you discussed the subject?

لاَ يُهِمُّ مَعَ مَنْ بَحَثَهُ.  It does not matter with whom he discussed it.

- مَاذَا\مَا may be subject or direct object of the verb in its clause, or can be governed by a preposition:

مَا الأَسْهَلُ لَكَ؟  What is ('the') easiest for you?

أُرِيدُ أَنْ أَعْرِفَ مَاذَا حَدَثَ.  I want to know what happened.

مَاذَا أَجَابَ؟  What did he reply?

قُولُوا لَنَا مَاذَا أَجَابَ.  Tell us what he replied.

مِنَ الْوَاضِحِ مِمَّنْ سَمِعُوهُ.    It is clear from whom they have heard it.

See 172 for the forms عَمَّا , مِمَّا , عَمَّنْ and مِمَّنْ .

For the subject of an interrogative equation with a noun as complement, the
expression مَا هِيَ\مَا هُوَ\مَا is often preferred; see 180.

- كَمْ may be subject or direct object of the verb in its clause, or can be
  governed by a preposition.

كَمْ كَلَّفَنَا ؟    How much did it cost us?

أَعْلَنُوا كَمْ سَيُكَلِّفُ.    They announced how much it will/would cost.

كَمْ يُرِيدُ الزَّبُونُ؟    How much does the customer want?

بِكَمِ اشْتَرَوُا الامْتِيَازَ ؟    For how much did they buy the concession?

لَمْ يُعْلِنُوا بِكَمِ اشْتَرَوْهُ. 

     They did not announce for how much they bought it.

كَمْ is used also before a noun, often giving adjectival meaning. The
noun is in the accusative singular, irrespective of its grammatical function
and logical number:

كَمْ نَائِبًا صَوَّتَ؟    How many deputies voted?

An alternative structure, used before a noun denoting something which
cannot be counted, is كَمْ مِنْ :

كَمْ مِنَ الْوَقْتِ ظَلَّ هُنَا ؟    How long ('How much time') did he stay here?

- أَيٌّ\أَيَّةٌ is the only declinable interrogative pronoun (see 137 for
  declension). It may occupy any function in the sentence.

أَيٌّ مِنَ الْمُدَرَاءِ يَحْضُرُ؟    Which of the directors is attending?

Often the masculine is used for the feminine, especially when the latter is
separated from its noun:

قُلْ لِي أَيًّا مِنَ الْمُدُنِ تَزُورُ.    Tell me which of the cities you (will) visit.

أَيٌّ\أَيَّةٌ is also used quasi-adjectivally, with a singular noun, in indefinite
construct (see 148):

إِنَّهُ غَيْرُ مَعْرُوفٍ أَيُّ مُدِيرٍ يَحْضُرُ.    It is not known which director will attend.

أَيَّةَ سِكْرِتِيرَةٍ وَظَّفْتُمْ؟    Which secretary did you recruit?

لِأَيِّ غَرَضٍ يَسْتَعْمِلُونَهَا ؟    For which/what purpose do they use it/them?

See 152 for the use of أَيٌّ\أَيَّةٌ as an indefinite pronoun, 'any'.

- The pronoun لِمَنْ 'whose ...?' is used only as subject of an equation, 'Whose is ...?':

لِمَنْ هٰذَا المَلَفُّ؟          Whose is this file?

سَأَلْتُ لِمَنْ هٰذَا المَلَفُّ.

I asked whose file this is/was ('whose is/was this file').

'Whose ...?' in any other use, including adjectival, is مَنْ in construct with a preceding noun:

أَخَذْتَ مَلَفَّ مَنْ؟          Whose file ('The file of whom') did you take?

**170. Relative Interrogative.** Direct or indirect questions beginning with the interrogative pronoun مَنْ 'who(m) ...?' (see 169) are sometimes better expressed by adding a relative clause; the whole question then begins ... مَنِ الَّذِي (see 28 for the kasra after مَنْ). For all but the simplest questions, this relative interrogative structure is preferred when the pronoun is subject or direct object of the verb in the same clause, or when the pronoun is governed by one of the prepositions expressing possession ('Who has ...?'), لِ , مَعَ , عِنْدَ (see 174):

Subject:          مَنِ الَّذِي قَالَ هٰذَا ؟          Who ('is it who') said this?

(مَنْ قَالَ هٰذَا ؟ Qui est-ce qui a dit cela?) (preferred by many to

إِنَّنِي أَعْرِفُ مَنِ الَّذِي قَالَ هٰذَا.          I know who said this.

Dir. Obj.:          مَنِ الَّذِي اسْتَقْبَلَهُ الْوَزِيرُ؟

Whom did the minister receive? ('Who is it whom the minister received?')

Prep., possession:          مَنِ الَّذِي عِنْدَهُ\مَعَهُ\لَهُ الخِبْرَةُ الْوَاجِبَةُ؟

Who has the necessary experience?

يَجِبُ أَنْ نَكْتَشِفَ مَنِ الَّذِي عِنْدَهُ خِبْرَةٌ كَافِيَةٌ.

We must discover who has sufficient experience.

When مَنْ is governed by a preposition not expressing possession, the simple interrogative structure is normally used:

Prep.:          مِمَّنْ طَلَبُوهُ؟          Whom did they ask for it? ('From whom did they ask it?')

**171. Indefinite Pronouns.** The nouns أَحَدٌ 'one' and شَيْءٌ 'thing' are used as indefinite pronouns.

In an affirmative sentence, أَحَدٌ means 'someone', and شَيْءٌ 'something':

اتَّصَلَ أَحَدٌ بِالْمُدِيرِ.          Someone has contacted the director.

سَمِعْتُ أَحَدًا يَقُولُ هٰذَا.

سَمِعْتُ أَحَدًا قَالَ هٰذَا.     }      I heard someone say that.

حَدَثَ شَيْءٌ غَيْرُ مُتَوَقَّعٍ.      Something unexpected happened.

تَعَجَّبْنَا مِنْ شَيْءٍ فِي تَقْرِيرِهِ.      We were surprised at something in his report.

In a negative sentence, the two words mean 'nobody' and 'nothing' respectively. As subject of a negative sentence they are best put into categorical negation (see 200) followed by the indefinite relative construction (168):

لَا أَحَدَ يَعْرِفُ هٰذَا.      Nobody knows that ('There is nobody who …').

لَا شَيْءَ يُؤَثِّرُ أَكْثَرَ عَلَى السُّوقِ.      Nothing affects the market more.

لَا أَطْلُبُهُ مِنْ أَحَدٍ.      I ask it of nobody.

لَمْ نَشْتَرِ شَيْئًا.      We bought nothing.

أَحَدٌ has a feminine form إِحْدَى which is invariable for case. These pronouns are used for 'one of …' (animate or inanimate), in a definite construct (see 148) or with a possessive suffix:

مَعَ إِحْدَى زَمِيلَاتِنَا      with one of our colleagues

لِأَحَدِهِمْ\لِإِحْدَاهُنَّ\لِإِحْدَاهَا      for one of them (masc./fem./inanimate)

We also find the same meaning expressed by repetition of the noun:

وِكَالَةٌ مِنْ وِكَالَاتِهِمْ      ('an agency of their agencies') one of their agencies

See 210 for 'one' as a number, which has a different form.

See 152 for the indefinite pronoun 'any'.

See 203 for indefinite noun expressions used as indefinite pronouns.

# 14. Prepositions

**172. General.** The commonest prepositions are shown below.

| | | |
|---|---|---|
| فِي in | عَلَى on | إِلَى to; for |
| لِ to; for | مِنْ* from | عَنْ from; about |
| دُونَ\بِدُونِ without | مَعَ with (accompanied by) | بِ in; with (by means of) |
| دَاخِلَ inside | خَارِجَ outside | ضِدَّ against |
| أَمَامَ\قُدَّامَ before; in front of | وَرَاءَ\خَلْفَ behind | بَيْنَ between; among |
| فَوْقَ above | تَحْتَ below | حَوْلَ\حَوَالَى around; about |
| عِنْدَ at; in the presence of | لَدَى at; in the presence of | مِثْلَ like |
| بَعْدَ after | قَبْلَ before | خِلَالَ during |
| طُولَ for the duration of | جَنْبَ (janba) beside | عَبْرَ through; beyond |
| بِسَبَبِ because of | بِالرَّغْمِ مِنْ* despite | بِخُصُوصِ concerning |
| غَيْرَ except; other than | بِغَيْرِ without | تُجَاهَ opposite |
| حَتَّى until; as far as | مُنْذُ since | كَ like, as |

All prepositions except one, shown in 201, govern the genitive case:

ضِدَّ الحُكُومَةِ against the government

بَعْدَ الاِجْتِمَاعِ after the meeting

* See 28. مِنْ becomes مِنِ before a word beginning with ...ا (hamzat al-waṣl):

مِنِ ابْنِي mini bnī from my son

and مِنَ before the definite article:

مِنَ اللَّجْنَةِ mina l-lajnati from the committee

in both of which the vowel of the hamzat al-waṣl of the following word is dropped. That is the approved pointing, which can, however, be ignored when reading unpointed text, since by pronouncing min in all situations, including before a following vowel, we automatically have the right pronunciation:

مِن ابني\من اللّجنة min ibnī/min al-lajnati from my son/the committee

Note also:

• مِمَّنْ , مِمَّا (for مِنْ مَنْ , مِنْ مَا , مَنْ) from whom/what

عَمَّنْ , عَمَّا (for عَنْ مَنْ , عَنْ مَا , عن) about whom/what

• مِنْ in partitive expressions or measurements = 'of':

جُزْءٌ مِنَ المُشْكِلَة    part of the problem

كِيلُو مِنَ السُّكَّرِ    a kilo of sugar

(not to be confused with e.g. فِنْجَانُ شَايٍ 'a cup of tea', see 148)

- مِثْلَ هٰذَا الـ... 'such (a) ...', 'a ... like this':

فِي مِثْلَ هٰذِهِ الأَزْمَة    in such a crisis/in a crisis like this

Arabic has few prepositions originating as such. The prepositions ending in ...ْ are in fact accusative nouns used as prepositions (in most instances, their principal modern use). Similarly, the derivation of the compound prepositions like بِالرُّغْمِ مِن and بِسَبَبِ is clear from their form. The final ...ْ or ... of such prepositions is dropped in short pronunciation when no pronoun suffix (see 173 below) is added.

**173. Prepositional Object Pronoun Suffixes.** Prepositional object or genitive pronouns (i.e. pronouns governed by a preposition) take the form of a suffix; these are the same suffixes, and subject to the same provisions, as the possessive adjective suffixes (see 147). When used to express prepositional objects, the suffixes have the meaning in English 'me', you', 'him' etc. In addition, the following provisions apply:

- Any short vowel ending a preposition is dropped before the 1st person singular suffix ...ي :

| | | | |
|---|---|---|---|
| مَعَ | with: | مَعِي | with me |
| ضِدَّ | against: | ضِدِّي | against me |
| لِ | to: | لِي | to me |
| بِ | with, in: | بِي | with me |

- The prepositions مِنْ and عَنْ double their final ن before the 1st person singular suffix ...ي :

مِنِّي\عَنِّي    from me

- The prepositional ending ...ى becomes ...يْ before a prepositional object suffix; ...ى + the 1st person sing. suffix ...ي becomes ...يَّ :

| | | | |
|---|---|---|---|
| إِلَى | to: | إِلَيْكُمْ | to you |
| عَلَى | on: | عَلَيَّ | on me |

- The preposition لِ 'to' becomes لَ... before all suffixes except that of the first person singular (see above):

لَهَا  to her        لَهُنَّ  to them

- After any preposition (other than لِ ) ending ...ِ , ...ِي or ...َيْ , the 3rd person suffixes ...هُ , ...هُمَا , ...هُمْ and ...هُنَّ become respectively ...هِ , ...هِمَا , ...هِمْ and ...هِنَّ . After any other ending these suffixes retain the form shown in Table 33 (para. 147):

بِهِ  in him/it                       بِهِمْ  in them

عَلَيْهَا  on her/it/them             فِيهِ  in him/it

إِلَيْهِ  to him            لَدَيْهِ  before him, in his presence

- The preposition بَيْنَ 'between' governs two concepts, not one. If either of the concepts is a pronoun, بَيْنَ is repeated:

بَيْنَ مِصْرَ وَلُبْنَانَ  between Egypt and Lebanon

*but:*    بَيْنِي وَبَيْنَ السَّفِيرِ  between the ambassador and me

بَيْنَنَا وَبَيْنَكُمْ  between you and us

- The prepositions حَتَّى 'until/as far as' and كَ 'like/as' do not take pronoun suffixes.

**174. To Have.** The concept 'to have' is not ordinarily expressed with a verb but with one of the prepositions عِنْدَ , لِ , مَعَ or لَدَى followed by the noun or the prepositional object pronoun suffix (see 173 and 166) denoting the possessor. The prepositions most commonly used are عِنْدَ and لِ :

عِنْدَ الْبَنْكِ الأَمْوَالُ الْمُنَاسِبَةُ.

The bank has ('In the bank's possession are') the appropriate funds.

لِلْخَبِيرِ عِلْمٌ وَاسِعٌ فِي الأَمْرِ.   The expert has wide knowledge in the matter.

مَعَ means more 'on the possessor's person':

كَانَتْ مَعَهُ الآلَاتُ اللَّازِمَةُ.

He had (with him) the necessary equipment ('instruments').

لَدَى implies attribution, and is used more with abstract than concrete ideas:

لَيْسَ لَدَيْهِ فَهْمٌ كَافٍ لِلْقَضِيَّةِ.   He has not sufficient understanding of the case.

# 15. Adverbs

**175. Derivation.** Most simple adverbs have the form of the indefinite accusative singular of the adjective or noun from which they are derived. This is the 'adverbial accusative'. When the derivation is from an adjective, the masculine is taken as base:

| | | | |
|---|---|---|---|
| جَدِيدٌ | new | جَدِيدًا | recently |
| كَثِيرٌ | much | كَثِيرًا | much |
| رَسْمِيٌّ | official | رَسْمِيًّا | officially |
| فَوْرٌ | boiling (noun) | فَوْرًا | immediately |
| مَثَلٌ | example | مَثَلًا | for example |
| عَادَةٌ | custom | عَادَةً | usually |
| صَبَاحٌ | morning | صَبَاحًا | in the morning, a.m. |

The original adjective may be a participle, or the original noun a verbal noun:

| | | | |
|---|---|---|---|
| مَكْتُومٌ | confidential | مَكْتُومًا | confidentially |
| تَقْرِيبٌ | approximation | تَقْرِيبًا | approximately |
| إِكْرَامٌ | deference | إِكْرَامًا ل | in honour of |
| نِيَابَةٌ | deputyship | نِيَابَةً عَنْ | deputising for |

ابْتِدَاءٌ beginning    ابْتِدَاءً initially    ابْتِدَاءً مِنْ with effect from

كَتَبُوا لِي رِسَالَةً مَكْتُومَةً. They wrote me a confidential letter.

(adjective qualifying a noun)

كَتَبُوا لِي رِسَالَةً مَكْتُومًا. They wrote me a letter confidentially.

(adverb modifying a verb)

The adverbial accusative ending is always pronounced, even in short pronunciation (30).

Some adverbial ideas are expressed with a preposition-plus-noun phrase. Some have a definite noun, some indefinite:

| | | | |
|---|---|---|---|
| سُهُولَةٌ | ease | بِسُهُولَة | easily ('with ease') |
| قَصْدٌ | purpose | عَنْ قَصْد | purposely |
| ضَبْطٌ | ḍabṭun/ẓabṭun* precision | | |
| | بِالضَّبْط | bi-ḍ-ḍabṭi/bi-ẓ-ẓabṭi | precisely (with precision') |

\* In the root ضبط the ض is very commonly pronounced as ظ ẓ .

Many adverbial expressions are formed with a noun phrase such as بِصُورَةٍ or بِشَكْلٍ plus the appropriate adjective, 'in a ... manner'. This is especially common when the original adjective is relative or participial:

بِصُورَةٍ عَامَّةٍ     in general

بِصُورَةٍ رَسْمِيَّةٍ     officially (cf. رَسْمِيًّا above)

بِشَكْلٍ مُمْتَازٍ     excellently

See 203 for the use of مَا in indefinite expressions, some of them adverbial.

Often, an absolute object (see 204) qualified by an adjective is best understood in English as an adverb or adverbial expression:

أَجَابُوا جَوَابًا شَدِيدًا.     They replied sternly ('They replied a stern reply').

**176. Negation.** Simple adverbs are most commonly negated with the preposition غَيْرَ 'other than'. The adverb keeps its form:

رَسْمِيًّا officially     غَيْرَ رَسْمِيًّا unofficially

With compound adverbs formed with بِصُورَةٍ (see 175 above), the noun غَيْرُ is used as in 150:

بِصُورَةٍ غَيْرِ مَقْبُولَةٍ     in an unacceptable manner

These two structures can be used whenever appropriate. A more limited structure, found only in a few set forms, consists of putting the preposition بِ before a categorical negation (see 200):

بِلاَ شَكٍّ     undoubtedly

**177. Interrogative Adverbs.** The main interrogative adverbs are:

كَيْفَ how          مَتَى when

أَيْنَ where          لِمَاذَا\لِمَ why

In addition to these, prepositional phrases can be constructed with interrogative pronouns (see 169) and used as interrogative adverbial expressions, e.g.:

لِأَيِّ غَرَضٍ     for what purpose

بِكَمْ مِنَ الرِّبْحِ     with how much profit

Interrogative adverbs and interrogative adverbial expressions introduce direct or indirect questions (see 184 and 186). No other interrogative introductory word is needed:

مَتَى يَبْدَأُ الْمُؤْتَمَرُ؟     When does the conference begin?

أَعْلَنُوا مَتَى يَبْدَأُ الْمُؤْتَمَرُ.

They announced when the conference would ('will') begin.

خلالَ أَيَّةِ فَتْرَةٍ رَفَضُوا التَّعْوِيضَ؟

During which period did they refuse compensation?

A sentence of this last kind can also be expressed with a relative interrogative (see 170) beginning الَّتِي ... هِيَ مَا\الَّذِي ... هُوَ مَا 'what is?' (*qu'est-ce qui* ...?):

مَا هِيَ الفَتْرَةُ الَّتِي رَفَضُوا التَّعْوِيضَ خِلاَلَهَا ؟

('What is the period during which ...?')

### 178. Comparative and Superlative Degrees of Adverbs. Properly speaking, adverbs cannot be made comparative or superlative as they stand.

For common simple adverbs, i.e. in the adverbial accusative, the accusative elative comparative of the original adjective (see 153) is used also adverbially:

| | | | |
|---|---|---|---|
| كَثِيرًا | much | أَكْثَرَ | more |
| قَلِيلاً | little | أَقَلَّ | less |
| شَدِيدًا | severely | أَشَدَّ | more severely |

For the rest, a prepositional phrase must be used (see 175 above); either with a noun qualified by أَكْثَرَ :

بِسُهُولَةٍ easily    بِسُهُولَةٍ أَكْثَرَ more easily

or with بِصُورَةٍ and a comparative adjective:

سَرِيعًا quickly    بِصُورَةٍ أَسْرَعَ more quickly

'as ... as possible' with adverbial meaning is expressed as follows:

بِأَسْرَعَ مَا يُمْكِنُ as soon/fast as possible

بِأَكْثَرَ مَا يُمْكِنُ as much as possible

See 154 for a similar construction with adjectival meaning.

Superlatives must also be stated indirectly. One acceptable formula is a qualified comparative, 'better/more (etc.) than all':

تَتَكَلَّمُ بِصُورَةٍ أَفْضَلَ مِنَ الجَمِيعِ. She speaks (the) best ('better than all').

# 16. Syntax

**179. General.** Chapters 4 to 15, 17 and 18 include those points of syntax, i.e. sentence-building, which can conveniently be covered there. This chapter covers those which cannot.

**180. Equations.** The simplest Arabic sentences have no verb. Examples:

أَحْمَدُ كَاتِبٌ.　Ahmad is a clerk.

هِيَ ذَكِيَّةٌ.　She is intelligent.

الْوَكَالَةُ هُنَا.　The agency is here.

الْمُدِيرُ غَائِبٌ.　The director is absent.

هٰذِهِ الْقَضِيَّةُ صَعْبَةٌ.　This case is difficult.

هٰذِهِ مُلاَحَظَاتٌ شَخْصِيَّةٌ فَقَطْ.　These are only personal comments.

نَحْنُ ضِدَّ دَفْعِ الإِضَافَةِ.　We are against payment of the supplement.

In such sentences, which we can for convenience call 'equations', we have:

- a definite subject,
- no verb, but an inferred meaning 'to be' ('am/is/are') in present time,
- an indefinite complement, i.e. an expression completing the meaning by identifying the subject ('a clerk'), describing it ('intelligent') or locating it ('here').

Definite equations also exist, in which both subject and complement are defined. In these, the subject is usually a pronoun; if it is a noun, it is usually restated with the corresponding pronoun:

هُوَ الأَوَّلُ.　It is the first.

الْمُدِيرُ هُوَ رَئِيسُ اللَّجْنَةِ.　The director is the committee chairman.

أَكْبَرُ مُشْكِلَةٍ هِيَ التَّمْوِيلُ.　The greatest problem is financing.

In a definite equation beginning 'This is the .../These are the ...' (with an article), we must restate with a pronoun. If the complement is otherwise defined, then the restatement is not obligatory:

هٰذَا هُوَ التَّقْرِيرُ.　This is the report.

(هٰذَا التَّقْرِيرُ is not a sentence; it means 'this report ...', see 146.)

هَلْ هٰذَا هُوَ التَّقْرِيرُ؟　Is this the report?

*but:*　هٰذَا (هُوَ) تَقْرِيرِي.　This is my report.

هٰذِهِ (هِيَ) مُلاَحَظَاتُ الْخُبَرَاءِ.    These are the experts' comments.

The personal pronoun is similarly used to restate an interrogative pronoun which is the subject of a definite equation:

مَا هُوَ بَرْنَامَجُ الْيَوْمِ؟    What is today's programme?

مَا هِيَ مُشْكِلَتُنَا الْأَشَدُّ؟    What is our most severe problem?

مَنْ هُوَ الْمَسْؤُولُ؟    Who is the responsible person?

The last example can also be expressed with a relative interrogative (see 170) plus the personal pronoun:

مَنِ الَّذِي هُوَ الْمَسْؤُولُ؟    ('Qui (est-ce) qui (est) le responsable?')

In an equation of the 'There is/are .... here is/are ...' type with an indefinite subject, the complement is put first, with no verb as usual:

فِي الْمِينَاءِ سَفِينَةٌ.    There is a ship in the harbour.

This is traditional usage. In modern usage it is common to add يُوجَدُ\تُوجَدُ 'is found' in such sentences:

فِي جِهَازِ التَّقْطِيرِ يُوجَدُ عَيْبٌ كَهْرَبَائِيٌّ.

There is an electrical fault in the distillation plant.

يُوجَدُ\تُوجَدُ are respectively the 3rd person singular masculine and feminine/ inanimate plural imperfect passive forms of وَجَدَ يَجِدُ I, 'to find' (assimilated, see 95).

Equations are always in present time-sequence, and always affirmative. The past or future equivalents, or the negative, of such sentences require the use of either the verb كَانَ 'to be' or لَيْسَ 'not to be', for which see 189.

An equation making a statement counts as a nominal sentence; see 182 below.


**181.  Statements.** Sentences consisting of a statement may take the form of a nominal sentence (see 182 below) or a verbal sentence (see 183 below).


**182.  Nominal  Sentences.** In a nominal sentence, the subject (which may be a noun or a subject pronoun, see 165) stands earlier than its verb, as in English. In the simplest nominal sentence making a statement, the subject is in the nominative case, and the verb agrees with it in gender, number and person (nouns being 3rd person). The rules of agreement given in para. 35 apply:

الْوَفْدُ وَصَلَ أَمْسِ.    The delegation arrived yesterday.

الْأَعْضَاءُ رَفَضُوا الاِقْتِرَاحَ.    The members rejected the proposal.

نَحْنُ رَفَضْنَاهُ.   *We* rejected it.

Equations (see 180) also count as nominal sentences:

المُديرُ غَائِبٌ.   The director is absent.

هيَ ذَكِيَّةٌ.   She is intelligent.

When the statement is the main clause of the sentence, it is frequently introduced by the conjunction إنَّ . This word adds no meaning; it merely announces that a statement follows. The subject then stands in the <u>accusative</u> case:

إنَّ الوَفْدَ وَصَلَ أَمْسِ.   The delegation arrived yesterday.

إنَّ الأَعْضَاءَ رَفَضُوا الاقْتِرَاحَ.   The members rejected the proposal.

When the subject is a pronoun, it is suffixed to the conjunction:

إنَّنَا رَفَضْنَاهُ.   We rejected it.

In the statements with an explicit verb (i.e. other than equations), the structure with إنَّ is often considered to be better style.

An equation can also be introduced by إنَّ ; the complement remains in the nominative:

إنَّ المُديرَ غَائِبٌ.   The director is absent.

إنَّهَا ذَكِيَّةٌ.   She is intelligent.

إنَّ is one of the so-called أَخَوَاتُ أَنَّ 'sisters of 'anna' (i.e. cognates or derivatives of the conjunction أَنَّ 'that'). The important sisters of أَنَّ are:

| إنَّ (studied here) | أَنَّ that | (وَ)لٰكِنَّ but |
|---|---|---|
| لأَنَّ because | كَأَنَّ as if, as though | |

The same rules apply for all the sisters: subject in the accusative (suffixed if a pronoun), complement (if any) in the nominative:

لأَنَّ اللَّجْنَةَ رَفَضَت الاقْتِرَاحَ   because the committee has rejected the proposal

ولٰكِنَّ المُديرَ غَائِبٌ   but the director is absent (This is an equation.)

The sisters have alternative forms with the first person object pronoun suffixes:

إنَّني\إنّي\الأَنَّني\الأَنّي   that I ..., because I ...

إنَّنَا\إنَّا\الأَنَّنَا\الأَنَّا   that we ..., because we ...

See 185 for the use of أَنَّ and كَأَنَّ , and another use of إنَّ , in indirect speech.
See 198 for the use of لأَنَّ .

Nominal sentences also exist as direct or indirect questions. See 184 and 186.

**183. Verbal Sentences.** In a verbal sentence making a statement, the verb stands earlier than its subject. When the subject is a noun, the verb agrees in gender and person (always 3rd) with it, but not in number; it is always singular, irrespective of the number of the subject:

وَصَلَ الْوَفَدُ أَمْسِ.     The delegation arrived yesterday.

رَفَضَ الْأَعْضَاءُ الِاقْتِرَاحَ.     The members rejected the proposal.

اتَّفَقَ الْجَانِبَانِ عَلَيْهِ.     Both sides agreed on it.

An inanimate plural verb counts as grammatically singular:

اتَّفَقَتِ الْوُفُودُ عَلَيْهِ.     The delegations agreed on it.

When the subject of the verb is an implied pronoun (1st, 2nd or 3rd person), the statement counts as verbal, but the verb agrees fully with its subject, since the latter is built into the verb:

وَصَلْنَا\وَصَلَا\وَصَلُوا أَمْسِ.     We/They both/They arrived yesterday.

Since equations (see 180) have no verb, they cannot feature in verbal statements. The examples given above contain simple (one-word) verbs. When the tense is compound (see 47 to 49), or there are two verbs (see 190, 191 and 196), only the first element of the compound verb or the first of the two verbs may stand early and be in the singular. The rest of the compound verb, or the second verb, follows the subject, and therefore agrees fully with it:

كَانَ الْمُدَرَاءُ يَبْحَثُونَ الْمَوْضُوعَ.     The directors were discussing the matter.

كَانَتِ الْوُفُودُ قَدْ بَحَثَتْهُ قَبْلًا.     The delegations had discussed it earlier.

بَدَأَ الْحَفَّارُونَ يَسْتَبْدِلُونَ الْمِثْقَبَ.     The drillers began to replace the bit.

يُرِيدُ الْمَنْدُوبُونَ أَنْ يُؤَكِّدُوا وَضْعَهُمْ.     The delegates wish to confirm their position.

كَانَ الْمَنْدُوبُونَ قَدْ بَدَأُوا يَدْرُسُونَ الْمَوْضُوعَ.

The delegates had begun to study the matter.

أَوْقَفَ الْحَفَّارُونَ عَمَلِيَّاتِ الْحَفْرِ وَفَحَصُوا الْمُشْكِلَةَ.

The drillers stopped drilling operations and examined the problem.

أَجَابَ الْمُمَثِّلُونَ يُشِيرُونَ إِلَى الْوَضْعِ الِاقْتِصَادِيِّ.

The representatives replied (by) pointing to the economic situation.

Verbal sentences also exist as direct or indirect questions. See 184 and 186.

**184.  Direct Questions.** Questions are always introduced by an interrogative word. For direct questions requiring the answer 'yes' or 'no', the interrogative particles هَلْ and أ are most commonly used, the former mainly for affirmative questions. The rules for nominal and verbal sentences (182, 183) apply:

هَلْ حَضَّرُوا التَّقْرِيرَ؟     Have they prepared the report?

أَلَمْ يَتَسَلَّم المَنْدُوبُونَ الوَثَائِقَ؟     Have the delegates not received the documents?

In a question, 'or' and 'or not' are respectively أَمْ and أَمْ لَا or أَوْ and أَوْ لَا :

أَوَافَقْتُمْ عَلَيْهِ أَمْ لَا؟     Have you agreed to it or not?

أَ , as a one-letter word, is written with the next word (see 17). Its initial hamza is almost always written, for clarity. Before hamzat al-waṣl, هَلْ becomes هَلِ .

'Yes/no' questions may be equations (see 180):

هَلْ هُوَ ذَكِيٌّ؟     Is he intelligent?

هَلِ السَّفِيرُ مَوْجُودٌ؟     Is the ambassador present?

هَلْ هِيَ المُؤَلِّفَةُ؟     Is she the author?

Direct questions expecting an answer other than 'yes' or 'no' are introduced by the appropriate interrogative pronoun or adverb, for which see 169 and 177.

For indirect questions, see 186.

**185. Indirect Speech: Statement.** Indirect statement is introduced by the conjunction إِنَّ or أَنَّ 'that'. This conjunction may not be omitted, unlike English usage ('He says (that) he is ill'.).

After the verb قَالَ يَقُولُ I, 'to say' we use إِنَّ :

يَقُولُ إِنَّ الجَوَابَ مُرْضٍ.     He says (that) the answer is satisfactory.

After all other verbs of speech, the introductory conjunction is أَنَّ :

يُعْلِنُونَ أَنَّ الطَّائِرَةَ مُتَأَخِّرَةٌ.     They are announcing that the aircraft is delayed.

See 182. The subject following أَنَّ or إِنَّ stands in the accusative; if a pronoun, it is suffixed:

يَقُولُ إِنَّهُ يَفْهَمُ الوَثِيقَةَ.     He says (that) he understands the document.

In indirect speech, the verb of the report is in the tense of the original expression. If the reported part is an equation (see 180) it remains so. There is no 'sequence of tenses' as in English:

أَعْلَنُوا أَنَّ الطَّائِرَةَ مُتَأَخِّرَةٌ.     They announced that the aircraft was ('is') delayed.

أَكَّدْتُ أَنَّنِي تَسَلَّمْتُ الوَثِيقَةَ.     I confirmed that I (had) received the document.

قَالَ إِنَّ الجَوَابَ مُرْضٍ.     He said (that) the answer was ('is') satisfactory.

When the verb of speech takes a prepositional object, the preposition is put immediately before the conjunction:

أَخْبَرُونَا بِأَنَّهُمْ سَيُرْسِلُونَ الشَّحْنَ بِالطَّرِيقِ الجَوِّيَّةِ.

They informed us that they would ('will') send the load by air.

The rules of indirect statement apply also to other sentences where the statement is dependent upon a verb not of speech but of perception:

اِعْتَقَدْتُ أَنَّهُمْ مَسْرُورُونَ.    I thought that they were pleased.

When the indirect statement is an equation after certain verbs of perception or speech such as:

| | | | |
|---|---|---|---|
| ظَنَّ يَظُنُّ | I, to suppose | عَرَفَ يَعْرِفُ\عَلِمَ يَعْلَمُ | I, to know |
| اِعْتَقَدَ | VIII to believe | اِدَّعَى | VIII to allege |
| زَعَمَ يَزْعُمُ | I, to claim | وَجَدَ يَجِدُ | I, to discover |

the sentence can be recast, as shown below:

ظَنَنْتُ أَنَّهُمْ مَسْرُورُونَ.    I supposed that they were pleased.

ظَنَنْتُهُمْ مَسْرُورِينَ. →    'I supposed them pleased.'

Note here:

- the conjunction is dropped,
- the subject of the equation goes into the definite accusative if a noun, or is suffixed if a pronoun,
- any noun complement goes into the indefinite accusative.

This is similar to the structure for verbs with two direct objects, see 164.

The conjunction كَأَنَّ 'as if, as though', a sister of أَنَّ (see 182), also follows the tense rules of indirect statement and is best examined here:

تَكَلَّمَتْ كَأَنَّهَا تَعْرِفُ الْمَوْضُوعَ.    She spoke as if she knew ('knows') the subject.

أَنَّ also introduces clauses of the type 'It is/was ... that', which in Arabic are constructed with مِنَ الـ ... أَنَّ, as follows (the tense rules of indirect speech do not apply):

مِنَ الْوَاضِحِ أَنَّ الْمُشْرِفَ هُوَ الْمَسْؤُولُ.

       It is clear that the supervisor is responsible.

مِنَ الْمَعْرُوفِ أَنَّ السَّوَّاقَ غَابَ أَمْسِ.

       It is known that the driver was absent ('absented himself') yesterday.

A similar pattern is:

اَلْمُهِمُّ هُوَ أَنَّهُ نَجَحَ نَجَاحًا كَامِلاً.

       The important thing is that he has succeeded completely.

أَنَّ is used in this structure for facts or alleged facts; see 190 for 'It is ... that' in expressions not of fact but of probability or desirability.

The indirect statement clause can be replaced by a definite verbal noun (in construct if necessary, see 148), giving similar meaning:

أَكَّدُوا أَنَّهُمْ يَرْفُضُونَ الاقْتِرَاحَ.    They confirmed that they rejected the proposal.

أَكَّدُوا رَفْضَهُمْ لِلاقْتِرَاحَ.    They confirmed their rejection of the proposal.

**186. Indirect Speech: Questions.** Indirect questions expecting the answer 'yes' or 'no' are introduced by one of the conjunctions هَلْ or إِذَا (مَا) 'whether'. The rules for nominal and verbal sentences (182, 183) apply. See 184 above for the tense or time-sequence of the question-clause:

إِنَّا لاَ نَعْرِفُ هَلْ هُوَ مَوْجُودٌ.    We do not know whether he is present.

لَمْ يُؤَكِّدُوا (مَا) إِذَا سَيَحْضُرُونَهُ.

They did not confirm whether they would/will attend it.

لاَ نَعْرِفُ هَلِ اتَّفَقَ النُّوَّابُ أَمْ لاَ.

We do not know whether the deputies agreed or not.

(هَلْ becomes هَلِ before hamzat al-waṣl, see 184.)

The indirect question may itself depend on a direct question:

هَلْ أَكَّدُوا إِذَا سَيَحْضُرُونَ؟    Did they confirm whether they would/will attend?

Indirect questions not expecting the answer 'yes' or 'no' are introduced by the appropriate interrogative pronoun (see 169) or adverb (177). The rules for the time-sequence still apply:

لاَ يَعْرِفُ مَا حَدَثَ لَهُ.    He does not know what happened to him.

شَرَحَتْ لَنَا لِمَاذَا تَسْتَقِيلُ.    She explained to us why she was ('is') resigning.

**187. Indirect Speech: Command and Request.** Indirect command or request is expressed with one of the conjunctions

أَنْ   that                    أَلاَّ   that ... not

and a verb in the (imperfect) subjunctive tense:

أَمَرْنَا النُّوبَةَ أَنْ تَبْدَأَ الإِنْتَاجَ.    We ordered the shift to start production.
                                               ('... that it start ...')

يَطْلُبُونَ مِنَّا أَلاَّ نُوقِفَ الْبَحْثَ.    They are asking us not to stop the search.

See 190 for other uses of these conjunctions followed by the subjunctive.

The indirect command can be replaced by a definite verbal noun (in construct if necessary, see 148), giving similar meaning:

إِنَّنَا نَطْلُبُ أَنْ تَدْفَعُوا الْعِلاَوَةَ.    We demand that you pay the allowance.

إِنَّنَا نَطْلُبُ دَفْعَ الْعِلاَوَةِ.    We demand payment of the allowance.

**188. Conjunction and Particle فَ** . The conjunction and particle فَ
deserves study. As a one-letter word, it is joined to the next word (see 17).

It is often used to join two equal clauses. In this use it can mean 'and then', 'and
so' , 'for', 'since':

نَادَيْتُهُ فَجَاءَ بِاتِّجَاهِي.    I called him and (so) he came up to me.

قَدْ نَسُوا تَمْوِيلَ الْمَصَارِيفِ الرَّأْسِيَّةِ فَفَشَلَتِ الْعَمَلِيَّةُ.

They had forgotten to finance the overheads, so the operation failed.

لِنَبِعِ الآنَ فَالظُّرُوفُ مُوَافِقَةٌ.

Let us sell now, since conditions are favourable.

سَيَرْسُبُ فَهُوَ كَسْلاَنٌ.    He will fail, for he is lazy.

لَسْتُ مُتَأَكِّداً فَهٰذَا مُعَقَّدٌ.    I am uncertain, for this is complicated.

لاَ تَتَرَدَّدُوا فَإِنَّنَا مُسْتَعِدُّونَ.    Do not hesitate; ('for') we are ready.

فَ is obligatory where the sentence is introduced by one of these expressions:

أَمَّا    as for    بِالنِّسْبَةِ لِ\فِيمَا يَتَعَلَّقُ بِ\فِيمَا يَخْتَصُّ بِ    concerning

أَمَّا الْقَامُوسُ فَإِنَّهُ مُفِيدٌ جِدّاً.    As for the dictionary, it is very useful.

بِالنِّسْبَةِ لِلْمَصَارِيفِ الْجَارِيَةِ فَمَا هُوَ رَأْيُكُمْ؟

Concerning the running costs, what is your view?

فِيمَا يَتَعَلَّقُ بِالرَّأْسْمَالِ ذِي الأَخْطَارِ فَإِنِّي أَقْتَرِحُ بِخُصُوصِ هٰذَا الْبَنْدِ ...

In the matter of the risk capital, for this chapter I propose …

In this use فَ is not directly translatable.

See 46 for فَ before a jussive verb, and 194 for فَ beginning the main clause of
a real condition.

**189.    Complemented Verbs.** Certain intransitive verbs require a following
complement, i.e. an element completing the meaning. They are verbs of being,
seeming or becoming; we may call them the complemented verbs. The
complement is put into the <u>accusative</u> case. Common verbs of this type are:

كَانَ    I, to be (hollow, see 103)

لَيْسَ    I, not to be  (hollow, see 103)

صَارَ يَصِيرُ    I, to become (hollow, see 103)

ظَلَّ يَظَلُّ    I, to remain (doubled, see 86)

دَامَ يَدُومُ    I, to persist; still to be (hollow)

بَقِيَ يَبْقَى    I, to remain (defective, see 110)

مَا عَادَ لاَ يَعُودُ  I, to be no longer (hollow)

مَا زَالَ لاَ يَزَالُ  I, still to be (hollow; this verb conjugates
like خَافَ يَخَافُ I, see 103)

Examples:

كَانُوا مَوْجُودِينَ*.  They were present.

صَارَ الْوَضْعُ مُعَقَّدًا بَعْدَ اسْتِقَالَتِه.

The position became complicated after his resignation.

مَا زَالُوا مُتَأَكِّدِينَ مِنْ حَقِيقَة حِكَايَتِنَا.

They were still convinced of the truth of our account.

* This is the past equivalent of an equation (see 180).

كَانَ , while regular in its conjugation, is anomalous in its use:

• When not dependent on another verb, and present time is intended, it is
  omitted altogether, giving us an equation:

هُوَ مَرِيضٌ.  He is sick.

• Its imperfect tense has present-time meaning only when it depends on
  another verb (see 190 and 191):

أَوَدُّ أَنْ أَكُونَ هُنَاكَ.  I want to be there.

أُفَضِّلُ أَنْ يَكُونَ الْجَوَابَ إِيجَابِيّاً.  I prefer that the answer should be positive.

When not dependent on another verb, its imperfect has future meaning,
giving us the future equivalent of an equation:

إِنّا نَكُونُ مَعَكُمْ.  We shall be with you.

يَكُونُ الْحَلُّ بَسِيطًا.  The solution will be simple.

See 47 to 49 for the use of كَانَ in compound tenses.

لَيْسَ is also anomalous in that it exists only in the perfect tense, with present
meaning. It has no participle, imperative or verbal noun. It gives us the negative
equivalent of an equation. It can also be used as a prepositional verb, with بِ :

لَيْسَ مُؤَهَّلاً.  He is not qualified.

لَيْسُوا بِخُبَرَاءَ.  They are not experts.

The complemented verbs are called by Arabs أَخَوَاتُ كَانَ 'the sisters of kāna'.

See 182, the sisters of أَنَّ . The sisters of أَنَّ have their subject in the accusative
and their complement in the nominative, while the sisters of كَانَ have the exact
opposite. In a sentence containing both structures, each rule applies in turn:

إِنَّ الْمَنْدُوبِينَ كَانُوا غَائِبِينَ.  The delegates were absent.

Many complemented verbs can be used as auxiliary verbs; see 191.

### 190. Expressions of Purpose, Potential, Obligation, Uncertainty

**etc..** Certain verbs denoting potential, purpose, obligation, volition and the like, followed by one of the conjunctions

أَنْ   that          أَلَّا   so that ... not

+ a verb in the subjunctive, will convey the meaning of the English auxiliary-plus-infinitive structure (e.g. 'He can speak Arabic.', 'We permit them to go.', 'What may we reply?'). Common verbs introducing such expressions are:

| | | |
|---|---|---|
| اسْتَطَاعَ يَسْتَطِيعُ | X (hollow) | can, to be able |
| حَاوَلَ يُحَاوِلُ | III (hollow) | to try |
| فَضَّلَ يُفَضِّلُ | II (sound) | to prefer |
| سَمَحَ يَسْمَحُ لِ | I, (sound) | to permit |
| (كَانَ) يُرِيدُ * | IV (hollow) | to want |
| (كَانَ) يَجِبُ * | I, (assimilated) | must, to have to |
| (كَانَ) يَجُوزُ * | I, (hollow) | may, might, to be permitted/possible |
| (كَانَ) يُمْكِنُ * | IV (sound) | may, might, to be likely/possible |
| (كَانَ) يَنْبَغِي * | VII (defective) | ought to, to be fitting |

* For these five verbs the continuous perfect (see 47) is used instead of the perfect for past time.

لَا يَسْتَطِيعُ أَنْ يَتَكَلَّمَ الْعَرَبِيَّةَ.   He cannot ('that he') speak Arabic.

يُحَاوِلُ الْحَفَّارُونَ أَنْ يُصْلِحُوا الْمِثْقَبَ.   The drillers are trying to repair the bit.

أُفَضِّلُ أَلَّا أُشَارِكَ.   I prefer not to participate.

كُنَّا نُرِيدُ أَنْ يَنْفِيَ الِادِّعَاءَ.   We wanted him to ('that he') deny the allegation.

Alternatively the conjunction-plus-subjunctive structure can be replaced by a definite verbal noun (in construct if necessary, see 148), giving the same meaning:

لَا يَسْتَطِيعُ تَكَلُّمَ الْعَرَبِيَّةِ.   'He is not capable of the speaking of Arabic.'

يُحَاوِلُ الْحَفَّارُونَ إِصْلَاحَ الْمِثْقَبِ.   'The drillers are attempting the repair of the bit.'

كُنَّا نُرِيدُ نَفْيَهُ لِلِادِّعَاءِ.   'We wanted his denial of the allegation.'

See 54 for the use of the verbal noun with direct and prepositional objects.

The verbs يَجِبُ , يَجُوزُ , يُمْكِنُ and يَنْبَغِي are impersonal expressions as they stand, always in the third person masculine singular:

يَجِبُ أَنْ يَسْتَمِرَّ الحَفْرُ.

يَجِبُ اسْتِمْرَارُ الحَفْرِ.

The drilling must continue.

كَانَ يُمْكِنُ فَشَلُ المَشْرُوعِ. The project might have failed.

The personal attachment of these expressions can be reinforced thus:

- with يَجِبُ\يَنْبَغِي :     add عَلَى + the person,

- with يَجُوزُ\يَنْبَغِي :     add لِ + the person,

- with يُمْكِنُ :        add the person as direct object,

as either noun or pronoun-object suffix, in all three situations.

(كَانَ) يَجِبُ عَلَى القِسْمِ أَنْ يَتَدَخَّلَ\التَدَخُّلُ.

The department has to/had to intervene.

هَلْ يَجُوزُ لَهُمْ أَنْ يَسْتَأْنِفُوا الحَفْرَ التَجْرِيبِيَّ\اسْتِئْنَافُ الحَفْرِ التَجْرِيبِيِّ؟

Might they resume experimental drilling?

لاَ يُمْكِنُنَا أَنْ نَدْفَعَ الزِّيَادَةَ\دَفْعُ الزِّيَادَةِ. It is not possible for us to pay the increase.

يَنْبَغِي عَلَيْهِ أَنْ يَدْفَعَ\الدَّفْعُ. He ought to pay.

The idea of obligation can also be expressed non-verbally, with the preposition عَلَى plus noun or suffixed pronoun, plus أَنْ or a definite verbal noun:

عَلَى الرَّئِيسِ أَنْ يُوضِحَ مَوْقِفَهُ. The chairman must ('It is for the chairman to') clarify his position.

عَلَيْهِ إِيضَاحُ مَوْقِفِه. It is for/up to him to clarify his position.

The construction أَنْ or its negative أَلاَّ with the verb in the subjunctive is also used after verbs expressing anticipatory feelings such as hope, doubt, fear etc., and after expressions of probability, desirability etc.:

شَكُّوا فِي أَنْ تَكْفِيَ الأَمْوَالُ. They doubted that the funds would suffice.

نَخَافُ أَلاَّ يَفْهَمَ القَضِيَّةَ. We fear that he may/does not understand the case.

مِنَ الضَّرُورِيِّ أَنْ تَحْضُرَ. It is essential that you (should) attend.

آمُلُ أَنْ تَكُونَ النَتَائِجُ سَلْبِيَّةً. I hope that the results are ('may be') negative.

(We cannot use an equation (180) in this last example, since we need a subjunctive verb.)

The hope/doubt/fear etc. may relate to a presumed event in the past, in which case the rare future perfect tense is used:

آمُلُ أَنْ يَكُونُوا قَد نَجَحُوا. I hope they ('will') have succeeded.

See 185 for the pattern 'It is ... that' applying to statements of fact. See 187 for the use of these conjunctions in indirect command or request.

Expressions of purpose with a much wider choice of main verb, corresponding to e.g. 'I did it in order that/to …', are introduced by one of the conjunctions

لِ\الأَنْ\كَيْ\لِكَيْ    so that; in order to

حَتَّى    until        لِئَلاَّ    lest, so that … not

اِسْتَكْشَفُوا الْحَقْلَ لِكَيْ يُحَضِّرُوا الْحَفْرَ التَّجْرِيبِيَّ.

They explored the field in order to prepare experimental drilling.

يَجِبُ عَلَيْنَا أَنْ نَمْنَحَ الْوَكَالَةَ تَمْوِيلاً إِضَافِيًّا لِئَلاَّ يَتَأَخَّرَ الْمَشْرُوعُ.

We must grant the agency additional funds so that the project is not delayed.

لِنَنْتَظِرْ حَتَّى يَنْشُرُوا الأَرْقَامَ.    Let us wait until they publish the figures.

In such sentences also we can replace the conjunction-plus-verb structure with a preposition and a definite verbal noun. Common prepositions used are:

لِ    for        مِنْ أَجْلِ\فِي سَبِيلِ    for (the sake of)

اِسْتَكْشَفُوا الْحَقْلَ لِتَحْضِيرِ\مِنْ أَجْلِ تَحْضِيرِ الْحَفْرِ التَّجْرِيبِيِّ.    They explored the

field in order to prepare ('for the preparation of') experimental drilling.

See 197 for the use of the conjunction حَتَّى with a verb in an indicative (mostly perfect) tense, reporting a fact.

**191. Verbs used as Auxiliaries.** Certain verbs can be used as auxiliary verbs, followed by a dependent verb in the imperfect (indicative) tense, with no conjunction. Common verbs used in this manner include:

بَدَأَ يَبْدَأُ    I, to begin (hamzated)

أَخَذَ يَأْخُذُ    I, to begin (hamzated)

كَادَ يَكَادُ    I, almost to (do) (hollow; this verb conjugates like

خَافَ يَخَافُ    I, see 103)

اِسْتَمَرَّ يَسْتَمِرُّ    X to continue (doubled, see 86)

تَرَكَ يَتْرُكُ    I, to let (sound)

وَدَعَ يَدَعُ    I, to let (assimilated)

جَعَلَ يَجْعَلُ    I, to oblige (sound)

and some complemented verbs (see 189), sometimes with a different meaning:

ظَلَّ يَظَلُّ    I, to remain (doing)

دَامَ يَدُومُ    I, still to (do)

عَادَ يَعُودُ    I, to (do) again

صَارَ يَصِيرُ  I, to begin

The auxiliary verb may be in any tense, or in the imperative; but the dependent verb is always in the imperfect (indicative) tense:

بَدَأَ يَسْتَجْوِبُ الشَّاهِدَ.  He began to interrogate the witness.

لاَ تَسْتَمِرَّ تَطْلُبُ مَا هُوَ غَيْرُ مُمْكِنٍ.  Do not continue to demand what is impossible.

عَادُوا يَقْرَأُونَ التَّقْرِيرَ.  They re-read the report.

The examples above have the same subject for both verbs. The verbs of letting or obliging have a direct object which becomes the subject of the second verb:

لَمْ يَدَعُونَا\يَتْرُكُونَا نَدْخُلُ.  They would ('did') not let us in ('enter').

إِنَّكَ تَرَكْتَ الْمُشْكِلَةَ تَتَعَقَّدُ.  You have allowed the problem to get complicated.

The second verb in the auxiliary expression can be replaced by a definite verbal noun (in construct if necessary, see 148), giving similar meaning:

بَدَأَ اسْتِجْوَابَ الشَّاهِد.  He began the interrogation of the witness.

See 183 for the agreement of the auxiliary verb in verbal sentences.

**192. Participial Verb.** It is common to use an active participle instead of a tense, to indicate an action. The participle agrees with the subject in the manner described in 52:

هِيَ مُسَافِرَةٌ الْيَوْمَ.  She is travelling today.

الْمُرَشَّحُ جَالِسٌ فِي قَاعَةِ الانْتِظَارِ.  The candidate is sitting in the waiting room.

The participle used in this manner has present meaning unless preceded by a perfect form of كَانَ (which gives us an equivalent of the continuous perfect).

See also the use of the participle in expressions of circumstance (196).

An active participle can be used instead of a tense in a relative expression, similarly to English usage:

... السَّيِّدَةُ الْمُسَافِرَةُ\الَّتِي تُسَافِرُ الْيَوْمَ  The lady (who is) travelling today ...

... السَّيِّدَةُ الْمُسَافِرَةُ\الَّتِي كَانَتْ تُسَافِرُ\الَّتِي سَافَرَتْ أَمْسِ

The lady travelling/who was travelling/who travelled yesterday ...

**193. Simultaneous Verbs.** In the following type of sentence, situated in the past, we have the comparatively rare phenomenon of أَنْ followed by the perfect tense:

بَدَأَ خِطَابَهُ بِأَنْ أَشَارَ إِلَى تَجْدِيدِ اتِّفَاقِنَا.

He began his speech by referring to the renewal of our agreement. This could also be stated with an expression of circumstance (see 196):

بَدَأَ خِطَابَهُ مُشِيراً \ (وَهُوَ) يُشِيرُ إِلَى تَجْدِيدِ اتِّفَاقِنَا .

**194. Conditional Sentences.** We distinguish between real or possible conditions ('If he comes …') and unreal or impossible conditions ('If I were rich …', 'Had we known …').

<u>Real Conditions</u>. Real conditions are mostly introduced by the conjunction إِذَا 'if'. The verb after إِذَا is in the perfect tense; the perfect of كَانَ is used if the clause would otherwise have no verb, and the continuous perfect for those verbs whose perfect is little used (e.g. كَانَ يُرِيدُ, 190). The verb in the main (i.e. non-conditional) clause may be in the perfect or in the tense demanded by logic, or in the imperative; if the first word in this clause is anything other than an affirmative verb in the perfect or imperfect (without سَ \ سَوْفَ ), or if it is لَيْسَ, then it has فَـ... prefixed to it:

إِذَا شَارَكْتُمْ كَانَ \ يَكُونُ أَسْهَلَ عَلَيْنَا .

If you participate it will be easier for us.

إِذَا أَضْرَبُوا رَفَضْنَا \ نَرْفُضُ \ فَسَنَرْفُضُ طَلَبَ التَّعْوِيضِ .

If they strike we shall reject the compensation claim.

إِذَا أَضْرَبُوا فَلَنْ نَدْفَعَ طَلَبَ التَّعْوِيضِ .

If they strike we shall not pay the compensation claim.

إِذَا كَانَ عِنْدَكَ جَدْوَلُ الْعَمَلِ فَأَرْسِلْهُ لِي .

If you have the agenda, send it to me.

إِذَا كُنْتَ تُرِيدُ مُسَاعَدَتَنَا فَلاَ تَتَرَدَّدْ أَنْ تَطْلُبَهَا \ فِي طَلَبِهَا .

If you want our help do not hesitate to ask for it/in asking for it.

إِذَا شَارَكْتُمْ فَأَنَا مَعَكُمْ .

If you participate, I am with you.

إِذَا أَضْرَبُوا فَإِنَّ رَدَّ الْفِعْلِ يَكُونُ شَدِيداً .

If they strike the reaction will be severe.
When the condition follows the main clause, then any particle فَـ... is dropped:

أَرْسِلْ لِي جَدْوَلَ الْعَمَلِ إِذَا كَانَ عِنْدَكَ .

Send me the agenda, if you have it.
The sentences shown above are all in present or future time-sequence, which is natural for real conditions. For the rarer real conditions in past time-sequence, the verb in the conditional clause is made pluperfect with كَانَ قَدْ :

إِذَا كَانَ قَدْ قَالَ هٰذَا فَهُوَ كَذَبَ \ يَكْذِبُ .

If he said that, he was/is lying.
A negative condition in the perfect is expressed by لَمْ + the jussive (not مَا + perfect); the non-conditional clause has the negative form appropriate to its verb:

إِذَا لَمْ يُضْرِبُوا فَلَنْ نَرْفُضَ طَلَبَ التَّعْوِيضِ .

If they do not strike we shall not refuse the compensation claim.

Real conditions are also, less commonly, introduced by the conjunction اِنْ 'if'. The verbs in both the conditional clause and the main clause then stand in the perfect, or the jussive, or one in each tense:

إِنْ أَضْرَبُوا رَفَضْنَا\إِنْ يُضْرِبُوا نَرْفُضْ طَلَبَ التَّعْوِيضِ.

If they strike we shall reject the compensation claim.

Apart from the different rules for the tenses, the rules for إِذَا apply also to اِنْ.

Real conditions expressing a stipulation can also be introduced by:

بِشَرْطِ أَنْ\عَلَى شَرْطِ أَنْ\عَلَى أَنْ   on condition that, provided that

In such sentences the verb in the conditional clause is introduced by أَنْ, which means it must stand in the subjunctive; the verb in the non-conditional clause has the tense demanded by logic:

سَنَدْفَعُ التَّعْوِيضَ عَلَى شَرْطِ أَنْ يَسْتَأْنِفُوا العَمَلَ.

We will pay the compensation provided they resume work.

Unreal Conditions. Unreal conditions are introduced by the conjunction لَوْ 'if'. The verb in the conditional clause stands in the perfect (كَانَ where the clause would otherwise have no verb, continuous perfect for a verb not normally used in the perfect, as with إِذَا). The verb in the non-conditional clause is mostly perfect, but can also be pluperfect with كَانَ قَدْ. It usually carries the particle لَ...:

لَوْ عَرَفْتُ لَأَخْبَرْتُكَ.   If I knew I would tell you.

لَوْ أَضْرَبُوا لَكُنَّا رَفَضْنَا طَلَبَ التَّعْوِيضِ.

If they had struck we would have rejected the compensation claim.

When the two clauses are reversed in order, the particle لَ... can be dropped:

أَخْبَرْتُكَ لَوْ عَرَفْتُ.   I would tell you, if I knew.

The conditional verb negates with لَمْ + jussive; the non-conditional verb with مَا(لَ) + perfect:

لَوْ لَمْ يُؤَيِّدْنَا لَمَا نَجَحَ المَشْرُوعُ.

If he had not supported us the project would not have succeeded.

The condition may be a nominal sentence (182); it is then introduced by لَوْ أَنْ:

لَوْ أَنَّ المَجْلِسَ أَيَّدَنَا لَكَانَ الوَضْعُ أَوْضَحَ.

If the council had supported us the position would be clearer.

'Unless' is expressed as 'if … not' with a real condition:

إِذَا لَمْ يَسْتَثْمِرْ فَوْرًا يَخْسَرْ فُرْصَةً مُمْتَازَةً.   Unless he invests/If he does not invest immediately he will lose an excellent opportunity.

See also 209 for another formula for 'unless'.

A request expressed as a condition is treated as an unreal condition:

لَكُنَّا مَمْنُونِينَ لَوْ تَفَضَّلْتُمْ بِالاتِّصَالِ بِنَا.

        We would be grateful if you would please contact us.

The ellipsis 'If not/otherwise/or else' is وَإِلاَّ :

لَنَسْتَعْجِلْ وَإِلاَّ فَنَتَأَخَّرُ.    Let us hurry or else we shall be late.

Occasionally a condition can be expressed with a prepositional phrase (e.g. فِي حَالَة 'in the event of', عَلَى شَرْطِ 'on condition of') and a verbal noun instead of a conjunction + clause:

فِي حَالَةِ ثِقْلٍ نَوْعِيٍّ عَالٍ    if the specific gravity is high ('in the event of a ...')

'But for' is expressed with لَوْ لاَ with a nominative noun or a pronoun suffix, followed by a verb in the perfect tense:

لَوْ لاَ مُسَاعَدَتُهَا لَفَشِلَ.    But for her help it would have failed.

لَوْ لاَهَا لَكَانَ الْوَضْعُ مَيْؤُوسًا. But for her, the situation would have been desperate.

See 186 for 'if' meaning 'whether' in indirect questions. See 185 for 'as if'.

**195. Concessive Sentences.** Sentences expressing concession ('Although ...') are introduced by conjunctions (some of them derived from pronouns or adverbs) such as

(حَتَّى) وَلَوْ   even if; even though      مَعَ أَنَّ   although

مَنْ   whoever      مَهْمَا   whatever

أَيْنَمَا   wherever    كَيْفَمَا   however    مَتَى مَا   whenever

After حَتَّى وَلَوْ the verb rules for unreal conditions apply (see 194); after مَهْمَا those for real conditions:

حَتَّى وَلَوْ كَانَت الْعَمَلِيَّةُ صَعْبَةً قُمْنَا بِهَا.

       Even though the operation is difficult, we are undertaking it.

مَهْمَا كَانَت الظُّرُوفُ فَسَنَسْتَمِرُ. Whatever the conditions (are), we shall continue.

'whatever' used adjectivally is مَهْمَا ... مِنَ الـ... :

مَهْمَا سَأَلْتَ مِنَ الأَسْئِلَة يَسْتَحِي.

       Whatever ('of') questions you ask, he will be ashamed.

مَعَ أَنَّ follows the rules of أَنَّ (see 182):

مَعَ أَنَّ الطَّقْسَ يَسُوْءُ نَسْتَمِرُ فِي الْبَحْثِ.

       Although the weather is worsening we shall continue the search.

After the other conjunctions the tense is dictated by logic:

كَيْفَمَا يَعْمَلْ لَنْ يُرَقُّوهُ. However he works they will not promote him.

Concession can also be expressed with a preposition such as بِالرُّغْمِ مِنْ 'despite'
and a verbal noun, instead of a conjunction + clause:

بِالرُّغْمِ مِنْ إِخْلاَصِهِ ... Despite his sincerity… (= Although he is sincere…)

**196. Expressions of Circumstance (أَلْحَالُ).** Expressions of circumstance
show a state or action accompanying the main verb. There are three common
types:

- Accusative of circumstance. An accompanying state or action can be
  expressed with the indefinite accusative of the appropriate noun, adjective or
  active participle:

  رَجَعَ غَنِيًّا. He came back rich.

  عَرَفْتُهُ طَالِبًا. * I knew him as a student.

  (i.e. when I was *or* when he was)

  أَضَافَ قَائِلاً إِنَّ ... He added ('saying') that …

  تَلْفَنُوا طَالِبِينَ مُسَاعَدَتَنَا. They telephoned requesting our help.

  غَادَرُوا بَيْرُوتَ مُتَوَجِّهِينَ إِلَى دِمَشْقَ. They left Beirut heading for Damascus.

(* Can be recast with عَرَفْتُهُ كَطَالِبٍ . : كَ See 172.)

- Verb of circumstance. Alternatively, a simultaneous action can be expressed
  with a verb; this verb stands in the imperfect (indicative) tense, irrespective
  of the time-sequence of the sentence:

  تَلْفَنُوا يَطْلُبُونَ مُسَاعَدَتَنَا. They telephoned requesting our help.

  سَمِعْتُهَا تُغَنِّي. I heard her sing(ing).

- Clause of Circumstance. Such clauses are introduced by the conjunction وَ ,
  which then has temporal sense ('when, while') or concessive sense
  ('whereas, while').

  Sometimes the وَ is not directly translatable. It is followed by:

  - subject + imperfect/active participle/equation, for a simultaneous
    action:

    دَخَلَتْ وَالأَطْفَالُ يَنَامُونَ\نَائِمُونَ.
                She came in while the children were sleeping/asleep.

    كَتَبَ رِسَالَةً وَهُوَ يَطْلُبُ\طَالِبٌ نُقُوداً. He wrote a letter, asking for money.

    عَرَفْتُهُ وَهُوَ طَالِبٌ. I knew him when/while he was a student.

عَرَفْتُهُ وَأَنَا طَالِبٌ.   I knew him when/while I was a student.

- subject + قَدْ + perfect tense for a previous action:

عَرَفْتُهُ وَ(هُوَ) قَدْ تَرَكَ وَظِيفَتَهُ.   I knew him when he (had) left his job.

- لاَ + imperfect for a negated simultaneous action, or subject + لَيْسَ for a negated simultaneous state; or لَمْ + jussive for a negated previous action:

جَلَسَ وَلاَ يَقُولُ شَيْئًا.   He sat saying nothing/without saying anything.

خَرَجْنَا وَلَمْ يَصِلْ زَمِيلُنَا.   We left before our colleague arrived.

('while our colleague had not arrived')

Circumstantial وَ + pronoun subject can also have a non-identifying relative meaning, 'who (by the way) ...', 'which (incidentally) ...', 'while he/she/it is ...':

أُسْتَاذُنَا وَهُوَ لَيْسَ مِصْرِيًّا يَعْرِفُ القَاهِرَةَ مَعْرِفَةً كَامِلَةً.

Our professor, who is/although not Egyptian, knows Cairo thoroughly.

For another construction expressing simultaneous actions, 'by ...ing', see 193.


**197. Clauses of Time.** Clauses of time are mainly introduced by one of the following conjunctions:

| عِندَمَا when(ever) | قَبْلَ أَنْ before | بَعْدَ أَنْ after |
| بَيْنَمَا while | مُنْذُ أَنْ since | حَتَّى\إِلَى أَنْ until |
| طَالَمَا\مَا دَامَ as long as | لَمَّا when, after | حَالَمَا as soon as |
| | كُلَّمَا\حِينَمَا whenever | |

In referring to present or future time, قَبْلَ أَنْ is followed by the subjunctive; in referring to past time, it is followed by the perfect (indicative) tense:

سَنَنْظُرُ إِلَى نَمُوذَجِ الكُمْبِيُوتَرِ قَبْلَ أَنْ نُقَرِّرَ.

We shall look at the computer model before we decide.

نَظَرْنَا إِلَى نَمُوذَجِ الكُمْبِيُوتَرِ قَبْلَ أَنْ قَرَّرْنَا.

We looked at the computer model before we decided.

لَمَّا can refer only to past situations. It is followed by the perfect tense, often with pluperfect meaning:

لَمَّا جَدَّدْنَا البَرَامِجَ ...

After we (had) renewed the software ('the programmes') ...

حَتَّى with an indicative tense (usually the perfect) indicates time, not purpose:

اِنْتَظَرْنَا حَتَّى نَشَرُوهَا.  We waited until they published it/them.

See 190 for the use of حَتَّى with the subjunctive for 'until' in future time.

عِنْدَمَا with the imperfect tense can mean 'when' or 'whenever'; with the perfect 'when' (on one occasion):

عِنْدَمَا\حِينَمَا يَجِيءُ يُقَابِلُ مُمَثِّلِي العُمَّالِ.

Whenever he comes, he meets the shop stewards.

عِنْدَمَا يَصِلُونَ\وَصَلُوا ...  When they arrive(d) ...

بَعْدَ أَنْ is mostly followed by the perfect tense:

... بَعْدَ أَنْ نَظَرُوا إلَى البَرَامِجَ.  ... after they (have) looked at the software

كُلَّمَا is followed either by the perfect or the imperfect (indicative) tense; often the perfect has present meaning:

كُلَّمَا جَاءَ\يَجِيءُ يُقَابِلُ مُمَثِّلِي العُمَّالِ.

Whenever he comes, he meets the shop stewards.

كُلَّمَا also introduces so-called consecutive clauses, which are a mixture of time, reason and condition: 'The more ... the more ...'. In this meaning, both clauses have the verb in the perfect. Only the main clause contains a comparative:

كُلَّمَا تَأَخَّرْتَ وَجَدْتَهُ أَصْعَبَ.

The more you delay, the more difficult you will find it.

The remaining time conjunctions can be followed by any tense, as the sense demands:

... طَالَمَا أَصَرُّوا\يُصِرُّونَ عَلَى مِثْلَ هَذِهِ الشُّرُوطِ

as long as they insist(ed) on such conditions

... بَيْنَمَا نُحَضِّرُ\حَضَرْنَا المُسَوَّدَةَ  ... while we are/were preparing the draft

The time clause may precede or follow the clause on which it depends (لَمَّا clauses, however, usually precede). The rules for the tenses hold in both situations. A following main clause may be a nominal sentence (182); if so, it is introduced by فَإِنَّ :

بَعْدَ أَنْ انْتَهَتِ البُحُوثُ فَإِنَّ العُمَّالَ اسْتَأْنَفُوا عَمَلِيَّاتِهِم.

After the discussions ended, the workmen resumed their operations.

It is common to use a preposition + verbal noun instead of a conjunction + time clause, with the same meaning, and avoiding all choice of tense:

... بَعْدَ تَجْدِيدِ البَرَامِجِ  After renewing ('the renewal of') the software ...

... خِلَالَ تَحْضِيرِ المُسَوَّدَةِ  ... during the preparation of the draft

... خِلَالَ تَحْضِيرِنَا لِلمُسَوَّدَةِ  ... during our preparation of the draft

بَعْدَ انتِهَاءِ الْبُحُوثِ ...     After the end of the discussions ...

See 190 for a similar phenomenon with expressions of purpose etc. See 54 for the use of the verbal noun with a direct or prepositional object.

## 198. Clauses of Reason.

**198. Clauses of Reason.** Clauses of reason are commonly introduced by the conjunctions

لِأَنْ   because          حَيْثُ (أَنْ)\إِذْ (أَنْ)   since, as

The reason clause precedes or follows the main clause, depending on the conjunction. The verb may be in any tense:

- لِأَنْ : always follows. Sister of أَنْ , see 182.
- حَيْثُ (أَنْ) : usually follows, may precede.
- إِذْ (أَنْ) : may precede or follow.

غَابَ لِأَنْ أُمَّهُ كَانَتْ مَرِيضَةً.   He was absent because his mother was ill.

حَيْثُ (أَنَّهُ)\إِذْ (أَنَّهُ) لاَ يَعْرِفُ ...   Since he does not know, ...

We can replace the conjunction-plus-verb structure with a prepositional phrase, avoiding any choice of tenses:

غَابُوا بِسَبَبَ مَرَضِهِم.   They were absent because of ('their') illness.
                                  (= because they were ill)

**199. Topic and Comment** (الْجُمْلَةُ ذَاتُ الْوُجْهَيْنِ). This useful and common stylistic device permits us to emphasise a direct or prepositional object (the 'topic') by placing it first in the sentence, in the nominative case, followed by the statement or question (the 'comment') concerning it. The comment is a whole clause.

In reading aloud, we pause (with pause-form pronunciation if wished) before the comment:

الْمُعَاهَدَةُ ، صَدَّقَت الْحُكُومَةُ عَلَيْهَا الْيَوْمَ. 
                     The government ratified the treaty today.

الْبَنْدُ الثَّانِي رَفَضَهُ الْمَجْلِسُ.   The council rejected the second clause.

الْبَنْدُ الثَّانِي اتَّفَقُوا عَلَيْهِ.*   They agreed on the second clause.

* Because of the pause, likely to sound as 'al-band aṯ-ṯānī, ittafaqū ʿalayhi', in breach of the long vowel/hamzat al-waṣl rule.

For such sentences, English achieves the emphasis with the passive: 'The treaty was ratified by ...', 'The second clause was rejected by .../agreed on'. The topic and comment permits us to avoid an Arabic passive.

The topic may also be the last element of a construct (148), brought up front:

هٰذَا الْمَشْرُوعُ إِنْجَازُهُ عَاجِلٌ.    The implementation of this project is urgent.

(without emphasis: .إِنْجَازُ هٰذَا الْمَشْرُوعِ عَاجِلٌ )

Topic and comment is found in colloquial English: 'Harry, he's gone to Birmingham', 'Norma, don't know her'. In Arabic, topic and comment is good written style.

**200. Categorical Negation** (نَفْيُ الْجِنْسِ). The Arabic expression corresponding to 'There is no …' is known as categorical negation. It consists of the negative particle لا followed by the noun in the accusative indefinite singular form but without nunation:

لاَ شَكَّ فِي هٰذَا.    There is no doubt about this.

لاَ بُدَّ مِنْ أَنْ نَدْفَعَ الإِضَافَةَ.    There is no escaping that we pay the supplement.

In categorical negation, the case-ending of the noun is always pronounced, even in short form.

**201. Exceptive Sentences** (الْمُسْتَثْنَى): **Only.** The preposition إِلاَّ 'except' with a negative expression conveys the meaning 'only'.
In such a sentence, a noun governed by إِلاَّ stands not in the genitive, as with other prepositions, but in the case demanded by its own grammatical function:

لَمْ يَحْضُرْهُ إِلاَّ السَّفِيرُ.    Only the ambassador ('None but …') attended it.

لاَ أَعْرِفُ إِلاَّ الْقَائِمَ بِالأَعْمَال.    I know only the chargé d'affaires.

We cannot suffix a pronoun to إِلاَّ . The subject pronoun (165) is used, irrespective of grammatical function:

لَمْ يَحْضُرْهُ إِلاَّ هُوَ.    Only he attended it.

لاَ أَعْرِفُ إِلاَّ هُوَ.    I know only him.

إِلاَّ may be followed by a prepositional phrase:

لَنْ نَدْفَعَ إِلاَّ عَلَى أَسَاسِ عَقْدٍ.    We shall pay only on the basis of a contract.
                                         ('We shall not pay except on …').

لَمْ نَعْرِفْهَا إِلاَّ بِصَوْتِهَا.    We recognised her only by her voice.

لَمْ يَرْجِعُوا إِلاَّ بَعْدَ سَنَةٍ.    They did not return for a year.
                                   ('Ils ne sont revenus qu'après un an'.)

or a clause:

لاَ أَوَدُّ إِلاَّ أَنْ أُكَرِّرَ أَنْ ...    I only/I just wish to repeat that …

لَنْ نَنْجَحَ إلاَّ إذَا سَاعَدَنَا هُوَ. We shall succeed only if he helps us

(= We shall not succeed unless he helps us.)

Affirmative exceptive sentences also exist; they are rarer. A governed noun goes into the <u>accusative</u>; a governed pronoun stands in the subject form:

حَضَرَ الْجَمِيعُ إلاَّ السَّفِيرَيْنِ. Everybody attended except the two ambassadors.

أَعْرِفُ جَمِيعَهُمْ إلاَّ هُوَ. I know all of them except him.

See 225 for the use of إلاَّ with expressions of time.

**202. Expressions with the Verbal Noun.** A periphrasis with a verb + verbal noun is often preferred to a simple verb. Three important examples:

The perfect verb form تَمَّ\تَمَّتْ (تَمَّ يَتِمُّ I, 'to be completed', doubled, see 86) plus a definite verbal noun (often in construct (148)) expresses a completed past action or situation in the passive:

تَمَّ بَحْثُ الْمَوْضُوعِ. The matter was discussed.

تَمَّتْ دِرَاسَةُ التَّقْرِيرِ. The report was studied.

The perfect verb form جَرَى\جَرَتْ or the imperfect form يَجْرِي\تَجْرِي ( جَرَى يَجْرِي I, 'to flow', defective, see 110) plus a definite verbal noun (often in construct) expresses an ongoing action or situation in the passive:

جَرَتْ\تَجْرِي مُفَاوَضَةُ الطَّلَبِ أُسْبُوعًا كَامِلاً.

The demand was/is being negotiated for a whole week.

The verb قَامَ يَقُومُ بِ I, 'to undertake', hollow, in any tense or form, plus a definite verbal noun (often in construct) expresses the beginning and continuation of the action:

قُمْنَا بِحَفْرِ بِئْرٍ تَجْرِيبِيَّةٍ.

We drilled ('undertook the drilling of') an experimental well.

These three devices are common in journalism and professional reporting.

See 52 and 55 for the use of the passive of prepositional verbs like قَامَ يَقُومُ بِ.

**203. Expressions with Indefinite Nouns.** Indefinite pronoun and adverbial expressions can be constructed with the indefinite singular of certain nouns and adjectives, followed by the pronoun مَا (literally 'what'):

| | | | |
|---|---|---|---|
| شَخْصٌ مَا | somebody or other (nom.) | شَيْئًا مَا | something or other (acc.) |
| نَوْعًا مَا | somehow or other | لأَمْرٍ مَا | for some reason or other |
| يَوْمًا مَا | some day (in the future) | كَثِيراً مَا | often, as often as not |

كُلُّ وَجْهٍ مِنْ وُجُوهِ العَوْنِ الفَنِّي يُؤَيِّدُ اقْتِصَادَ الدُّوَلِ النَّامِيَةِ نَوْعًا مَا . Every single
aspect ('Every one of the aspects') of technical assistance helps
('supports') the economy of developing countries in one way or another.

... and    ... وَالوَاقِعُ أَنَّ الفَائِدَةُ غَيْرُ الُمَبَاشِرَةُ كَثِيرًا مَا تَزِيدُ عَنِ الفَائِدَةِ الُمَبَاشِرَةِ .
indeed the indirect benefit, as often as not, is bigger than ('exceeds') the direct.
The case-ending is always pronounced in such expressions, even in short
pronunciation.

**204. Absolute Object** (المَفْعُولُ المُطْلَقُ). A verb is often used together with
its verbal noun in the indefinite accusative, to complete or reinforce the sense of
the verb. This construction is called the absolute object:

سَأَلَنِي سُؤَالاً .    He asked me a question.

ادَّعَى ادِّعَاءً شَدِيدًا .    He made ('alleged') a severe allegation.

With a qualifying adjective, the expression may have adverbial force:

تَنْتَقِدُ الصُّحُفُ الحُكُومَةَ انْتِقَادًا مُسْتَمِرًّا .

The newspapers are continually criticising the government.
('criticising a continuous criticism')

تَعْرِفُ البَلَدَ مَعْرِفَةً مُفَصَّلَةً .    You know the town in detail.

The verb and verbal noun, although of the same root, need not be of the same
form (I to X):

تَفَاهَمَا (VI) فَهْمًا (I) كَامِلاً .    They understood each other completely.

The absolute object indefinite accusative ending is always pronounced, even in
short pronunciation.

An alternative type of absolute object can be made with كُلّ (see 152) in definite
construct, with the adverbial meaning 'fully':

أَيَّدُوهُ كُلَّ التَّأْيِيدِ ( = تَأْيِيدًا كَامِلاً )    They supported him fully.

**205. Table 39: Uses of the Accusative.** Of the three cases, the
accusative is the most versatile. This table summarises its principal uses, with
references to other paragraphs where appropriate:

| | Use | Example | Para. |
|---|---|---|---|
| 1 | Direct object: of a verb | كَتَبَ رِسَالَةً\الرِّسَالَةَ. كَتَبَهَا.<br>He wrote a/the letter. He wrote it. | 33/131 |
| | or of a verbal noun | فَهْمُ الخَبِيرِ الوَضْعَ. The expert's<br>understanding of the situation. | 54 |
| 2 | Subject of a verb after | أَعْتَقِدُ أَنَّ المَشْرُوعَ قَابَلٌ لِلتَّنْفِيذِ.<br>I believe that the project is feasible. | 182 |
| | أَنَّ or one of its sisters | إِنَّهُ جَدِيرٌ بِالإِنْجَازِ. – وَلَكِنَّهُ غِيرُ مُمْكِنٍ!<br>It is worth implementing. - But it is<br>impossible! | |
| 3 | Complement of a verb | كَانَ وَزِيرًا مَشْهُورًا.<br>He was a famous minister. | 189 |
| | (كَانَ or one of its sisters) | صَارَ الوَزِيرَ المَسْؤُولَ عَن البِيئَةِ.<br>He became the minister responsible<br>for the environment. | |
| 4 | Categorical negation | لاَ شَكَّ فِيهِ. There is no doubt of it. | 200 |
| 5 | Adverb | عَادَةً، مَثَلاً، سَرِيعًا، قَلِيلاً<br>usually, for example, quickly, little<br>عَمَلاً بِ\وَفْقًا لِ\بِنَاءً عَلَى<br>in accordance with | 175 |
| 6 | Comparison of derived<br>adjective | أَكْثَرُ تَخَصُّصًا more specialised | 153 |
| 7 | Comparison of simple<br>adverb | أَكْثَرَ، أَقَلَّ more, less | 178 |
| 8 | Accusative of circumstance | أَضَافَ قَائِلاً إِنَّ ... <br>He added ('saying') that … | 196 |
| 9 | Absolute object | احْتَجُّوا احْتِجَاجًا شَدِيدًا.<br>They protested strongly. | 204 |
| 10 | After كَم | كَمْ شَخْصًا؟ How many people? | 169 |
| 11 | After numbers ١١ to ٩٩ | مَعَ خَمْسَةٍ وَثَلاثِينَ ضَابِطًا<br>with thirty-five officers | 211-<br>213 |
| 12 | Elliptical expressions | شُكْرًا. عَفْوًا.<br>Thank you. I beg your pardon. | |
| 13 | Expressions of time | اليَوْمَ، الآنَ، يَوْمَ البَّتِ<br>today, now, on Saturday | 227 |

| 14 | Exclamations | مَا أَعْجَبَهُ!　　How strange! | 230 |
| | | مَا أَسْرَعَ مَا أَجَابُوا.<br>How quickly they replied. | |
| | | مَا أَشَدَّهُمُ اجْتِهَادًا.<br>How hardworking they are. | |
| 15 | Noun after إلاَّ in affirmative exceptive sentence | حَضَرَ الْجَمِيعُ إلاَّ الْوَزِيرَ.　Everybody attended except the minister. | 201 |

**206. Table 40: Uses of مَا.** This table summarises the principal uses of the word مَا , with references to other paragraphs:

| | Use | Example | Para. |
|---|---|---|---|
| 1 | Negative of the perfect<br>(some with special meaning) | مَا وَصَلُوا.　They have not arrived.<br>مَا زَالَ فَقِيرًا.　He remained poor. | 40<br>189 |
| 2 | 'what':<br>interrogative, 'what?'<br><br>relative, 'that which' | مَا هٰذَا؟　　　　　　　What is this?<br>مَا هُوَ الْغَرَضُ؟　What is the purpose?<br>كَرَّرُوا مَا قَالُوهُ فِي التَّقْرِيرِ.　They repeated what they said in the report. | 169<br><br>168 |
| 3 | Forming some conjunctions<br>(sometimes written like<br>a suffix) | مَا دَامَ\مَا لَمْ　　　　　as long as<br>كَمَا، بَيْنَمَا، عِنْدَمَا، كُلَّمَا، كَيْفَمَا<br>as, while, when, whenever, however | 197 |
| 4 | Indefinite expressions | شَخْصٌ مَا، يَوْمًا مَا<br>somebody, some day | 203 |
| 5 | Comparison,<br>'as ... as possible' | بِأَكْثَرَ مَا يُمْكِنُ　as much as possible | 154/<br>178 |
| 6 | Exclamations | مَا أَصْعَبَهُ.　How difficult it is. | 230 |

**207. Table 41: Alternative Structures:** Many structures have alternatives with similar meaning. The principal alternatives possible are shown below, with references to other paragraphs:

| | Alternatives | | Example | Para. |
|---|---|---|---|---|
| 1 | أَنْ + subjunctive | def. verbal noun | يَسْتَطِيعُ أَنْ يَكْتُبَ الرِّسَالَةَ.<br>يَسْتَطِيعُ كِتَابَةَ الرِّسَالَةِ.<br>He can write the letter.<br>نُرِيدُ أَنْ يَتَعَاوَنَ.<br>نُرِيدُ تَعَاوُنَهُ.<br>We want him to cooperate. | 190 |
| | (also indirect command/request) | | طَلَبْنَا أَنْ يَسْتَأْنِفُوا الْعَمَلَ.<br>طَلَبْنَا اسْتِئْنَافَ عَمَلِهِمْ. We demanded that they resume work. | 187 |
| 2 | أَلَّا + subjunctive | عدم + definite verbal noun | نَرْجُو أَلَّا يُدَخِّنُوا.<br>نَرْجُو عَدَمَ التَّدْخِينِ. We ask that they do not smoke. | 187 |
| 3 | كَيْ\لِكَيْ\حتَّى\ لِأَنْ + subjunctive | لِ + definite verbal noun | عَمِلْنَاهُ لِكَيْ نُوضِحَ الْوَضْعَ.<br>عَمِلْنَاهُ لِإِيضَاحِ الْوَضْعِ. We did it to clarify the situation. | 190 |
| 4 | أَنَّ\إِنَّ + indirect statement | def. verbal noun | أَخْبَرَهُمْ بِأَنَّهُ يَرْفُضُهُ.<br>أَخْبَرَهُمْ بِرَفْضِه إِيَّاهُ.<br>He told them he rejected it. | 185 |
| | | (verb of statement may change) | قَالَ إِنَّهُ غَيْرُ مُسْتَعِدٍّ لَهُ.<br>عَبَّرَ عَن عَدَمِ اسْتِعْدَادِه لَهُ. He said he was unprepared for it. | |
| 5 | conjunction + time clause | preposition + def. verbal noun | ... عِنْدَمَا\بَعْدَ أَنْ وَصَلُوا<br>... عِنْدَ\بَعْدَ وُصُولِهِمْ<br>... when/after they arrived | 197 |
| 6 | conjunction + clause of reason | لِ\مِن أَجل\بِسبب + def. verbal noun | ... لِأَنَّهُ غَابَ أَمْسِ<br>... بِسَبَبِ غِيَابَتِه أَمْسِ because he was absent yesterday | 198 |

| | | | | |
|---|---|---|---|---|
| 7 | conjunction + conditional clause | ... في حالة\على شرط + def. verbal noun | إِذَا احْتَجَّ ... <br> فَي حَالَةِ احْتِجَاجِهِ ... <br> If he protests ... | 194 |
| 8 | conjunction + concessive clause | بالرغم من + def. verbal noun | ... حَتَّى وَلَوْ أَنَّهَا كَانَتْ مَرِيضَةً <br> بِالرَّغْمِ مِنْ مَرَضِهَا ... <br> Although she is/was ill ... | 195 |
| 9 | imperfect active: simple tense | active participle | نَحْنُ نُغَادِرُ الْيَوْمَ. <br> نَحْنُ مُغَادِرُونَ الْيَوْمَ. <br> We are leaving today. | 192 |
| | continuous perfect tense | | كَانُوا يَجْلِسُونَ فِي الْمَحْكَمَةِ. <br> كَانُوا جَالِسِينَ فِي الْمَحْكَمَةِ. <br> They were sitting in court. | 47 |
| 10 | relative clause | participle: <br> active | النَّاسُ الَّذِينَ يُسَافِرُونَ إِلَى ... <br> النَّاسُ الْمُسَافِرُونَ إِلَى ... The <br> people (who are) travelling to... | 168/ 192 |
| | | passive of a transitive verb | الاتِّفَاقُ الَّذِي فُوِّضَ أَمْسِ ... <br> الاتِّفَاقُ الْمُفَاوَضُ أَمْسِ ... <br> The agreement (which was) negotiated yesterday ... | 168/ 52 |
| | | passive of a prepositional verb | الْمُسَوَّدَةُ الَّتِي اتُّفِقُوا عَلَيْهَا ... <br> الْمُسَوَّدَةُ الْمُتَّفَقُ عَلَيْهَا ... <br> The draft (they) agreed on ... | 168/ 52 |
| 11 | construct | لِ | سِيَاسَةُ الْبِلَادِ الْخَارِجِيَّةُ <br> السِّيَاسَةُ الْخَارِجِيَّةُ لِلْبِلَادِ <br> the country's foreign policy | 148 |
| 12 | auxiliary verb + imperfect | auxiliary verb + verbal noun | اسْتَمَرُّوا يُضْرِبُونَ. <br> اسْتَمَرُّوا بِإِضْرَابِهِمْ. <br> They continued to strike. | 191 |

| | | | | | |
|---|---|---|---|---|---|
| 13 | passive verb | | تمَّ، جرى\يجري<br>+ def. verbal noun | بُحثَ الـمَوْضُوعُ.<br>تَمَّ بَحْثُ الـمَوْضُوعِ. The<br>matter was discussed.<br>جرَى\يَجري بَحْثُ الـمَوْضُوعِ. The<br>matter was/is being discussed. | 55/<br>202 |
| 14 | active verb | | قَامَ ب\يَقُومُ ب<br>+ def. verbal noun | دَرَسُوا الـمَوْضُوعَ.<br>قَامُوا بِدِرَاسَةِ الـمَوْضُوعِ.<br>They studied the matter. | 202<br>163/ |
| 15 | relative<br>clause with<br>عند\لدى\ل | improper<br>annexation | ذو etc. | | مَصْرِفٌ لَدَيْهِ\لَهُ مَصَالِحُ دُوَليَّةٌ<br>مَصْرِفٌ دُوَليُّ مَصَالِحُهُ<br>مَصْرِفٌ ذُو مَصَالِحَ دُوَليَّةٍ a bank<br>with international interests | 168/<br>163/<br>160 |

The alternatives shown are not always usable in all contexts, nor are they always equivalent in style or meaning.

# 17. Numbers

**208. Numerals.** The written Arabic numerals are:

| | | | | |
|---|---|---|---|---|
| ٠ 0 | ١ 1 | ٢ 2 | ٣ 3 | ٤ 4 |
| ٥ 5 | ٦ 6 | ٧ 7 | ٨ 8 | ٩ 9 |

Handwritten forms are the same as print except:

٢ 2      ٣ or ٣ 3

Numbers are written from left to right:

١٢٤ 124          ٥٦٨٩٠٤ 5689·4

In Morocco, Algeria and Tunisia the European numerals are used.

**209. Cardinal Numbers - General.** The cardinal numbers are shown in Tables 42 to 45 (paras. 210 to 213) below. However, most people prefer to use the greatly simplified spoken forms of these numbers, shown in 214 below, even when reading from a text. For the 'official' written forms, the following general provisions apply to all :

- Forms said to be 'referring to masculine nouns' in the tables apply equally to animate plural nouns denoting groups of mixed gender, (as for adjectives, see 142, 2nd indent).
- All can be used in counting, i.e. as a noun, without a counted noun. **0** is used only in this manner. When the implied counted noun is unknown, the number stands in the form appropriate to a masculine noun.
- All but **0** can be used as a noun, with the counted noun in the form shown in the table. The whole expression may be definite or indefinite.
- All but **0** can be used as an adjective, following and qualifying the counted noun, which assumes the case appropriate to its function in the sentence; the number agrees with it in the manner shown.
- In a compound number preceding the counted noun, it is the last element of the compound which determines the form of the counted noun.
- An adjective agrees (see 142) with the <u>counted noun</u> if the expression is indefinite, and with the <u>number</u> (including with the latter's theoretical case and gender if it is invariable) if the expression is definite.
- Where a counted noun is said to be in a particular case, this is so irrespective of the noun's grammatical function in the sentence.
- The expression 'in its own case' means in the case demanded by the noun's grammatical function in the sentence.
- 'polarity' means reverse agreement, i.e. an apparently feminine number (ending in ة...) is used with a masculine noun; and an apparently

masculine number (i.e. not ending in ة...) is used with a feminine noun.
Further applications, specific to each group of numbers, are given in each table.

**210. Table 42: Cardinal Numbers** 0 to 10. See 209 above for general
provisions.
Number **0** is صِفْرٌ, pl. أَصْفَارٌ. It is used without a further noun. See also 223.
The following table shows the use of numbers **1** to **10**.

| Num- | Referring to: | | Use and form of the number |
|---|---|---|---|
| ber | m. noun | f. noun | |
| ١ | وَاحِدٌ | وَاحِدَةٌ | Sing.: 1. noun, in counting. 2. def./indef. adj. |
| ٢ | اثْنَانِ | اثْنَتَانِ | Dual: 1. noun, in counting. 2. def./indef. adj.* |
| ٣ | ثَلاَثَةٌ | ثَلاَثٌ | 1. Noun (diptote), in counting. |
| ٤ | أَرْبَعَةٌ | أَرْبَعٌ | 2. Def. or indef. noun, followed by counted noun in |
| ٥ | خَمْسَةٌ | خَمْسٌ | construct, in the <u>indefinite genitive plural</u>. |
| ٦ | سِتَّةٌ | سِتٌّ | Number stands in its own case, but has <u>polarity</u> |
| ٧ | سَبْعَةٌ | سَبْعٌ | of gender with the counted noun. |
| ٨ | ثَمَانِيَةٌ | ثَمَانٍ** | 3. Definite adjective, following definite counted |
| ٩ | تِسْعَةٌ | تِسْعٌ | noun. The definite counted noun stands in its |
| ١٠ | عَشَرَةٌ | عَشْرٌ | own case, and the definite number agrees in case |
| | | | but has <u>polarity</u> of gender with the counted noun. |

　* This number is used adjectivally only for emphasis.
　** ثَمَانٍ is declined like a defective active participle; see 117. It becomes
ثَمَانِي with a feminine counted noun.
See 178 for the indefinite pronoun expression 'one of ...'.
Examples of use:

| | | |
|---|---|---|
| 1: Nom.: | عُضْوٌ دَائِمٌ وَاحِدٌ | one permanent member |
| Acc.: | وَثِيقَةً وَاحِدَةً | one document |
| Gen.: | لِلدَّوْلَةِ الْحِيَادِيَّةِ الْوَاحِدَةِ | for the one neutral state |
| 2: Nom.: | تَقْرِيرَانِ فَنِّيَّانِ اثْنَانِ فَقَطْ | only two technical reports |
| Acc./Gen.: | (الـ)رِّسَالَتَيْنِ (الـ)اثْنَتَيْنِ | (the) *two* letters |
| 3-10: Nom.: | ثَلاَثَةُ مُمَثِّلِينَ رَئِيسِيِّينَ | three leading representatives |

الدُّوَلُ الكُبْرَى الأَرْبَعُ     }   the four big states
الأَرْبَعُ دُوَلِ الكُبْرَى

Acc.:    مَبَادِئُهُمُ الخَمْسَةَ    their five principles

سِتُّ نُقَط هَامَّة    six important points

Gen.:    مَعَ ثَمَانِيَةِ دِبْلُومَاسِيِّينَ    with eight diplomats

مِنَ الدُّوَلِ الصِّنَاعِيَّةِ السَّبْعِ    }   from the seven industrialised countries
مِنَ السَّبْعِ دُوَلِ الصِّنَاعِيَّةِ

**211. Table 43: Cardinal Numbers 11 to 19.** See 209 above for general provisions. The following table shows the use of numbers **11** to **19**.

| Num- ber | Referring to: | | Use and form of the number |
|---|---|---|---|
| | masc. noun | fem. noun | |
| ١١ | أَحَدَ عَشَرَ | إِحْدَى عَشْرَةَ | 1. Noun, in counting. |
| ١٢ | اثْنَا عَشَرَ | اثْنَتَا عَشْرَةَ | 2. Def. or indef. noun, followed by counted |
| ١٣ | ثَلَاثَةَ عَشَرَ | ثَلَاثَ عَشْرَةَ | noun in <u>indefinite accusative singular</u>. |
| ١٤ | أَرْبَعَةَ عَشَرَ | أَرْبَعَ عَشْرَةَ | Only the 2 of 12 is declined (as a dual); it |
| ١٥ | خَمْسَةَ عَشَرَ | خَمْسَ عَشْرَةَ | agrees in gender with the counted noun. |
| ١٦ | سِتَّةَ عَشَرَ | سِتَّ عَشْرَةَ | All other units, and all tens, are |
| ١٧ | سَبْعَةَ عَشَرَ | سَبْعَ عَشْرَةَ | invariable for case, units **3-9** having |
| ١٨ | ثَمَانِيَةَ عَشَرَ | ثَمَانِيَ عَشْرَةَ | polarity of gender with the counted noun. |
| ١٩ | تِسْعَةَ عَشَرَ | تِسْعَ عَشْرَةَ | 3. Definite adjective*, usage identical to that |
| | | | of nos. **3-9**; <u>except</u> that the 2 of **12** agrees |
| | | | as dual adj., units **3-9** having polarity. |

\* Only the units element of the compound is made definite.

Examples of use of **11** to **19**:

Nom.:    أَحَدَ عَشَرَ أُسْبُوعًا كَامِلاً    11 complete weeks

وِلَايَاتُنَا الاثْنَتَا عَشْرَةَ    our 12 provinces

Acc.:    الأَشْهُرُ الأَرْبَعَةَ عَشَرَ المَاضِيَّةُ    the last 14 months

خَمْسَ عَشْرَةَ جُنَيْهَةً مِصْرِيَّةً    £15 Egyptian

Gen.:    لِمُدَّةِ ثَمَانِيَةَ عَشَرَ عَامًا    for ('a period of') 18 years

$$\left.\begin{array}{r}\text{لِمُدَّةِ السَّنَوَاتِ التِّسْعَ عَشْرَةَ الْمُحَدَّدَةِ فِي الْعَقْدِ} \\ \text{لِمُدَّةِ التِّسْعَ عَشْرَةَ سَنَةً الْمُحَدَّدَةِ فِي الْعَقْدِ}\end{array}\right\}$$

for the 19 years

defined in the contract

**212. Table 44: Cardinal Numbers 20 to 99.** See 209 above for general provisions. The following table shows numbers **20** to **99**.

| No. | Referring to any noun | Use and form of the number |
|---|---|---|
| ٢٠ | عِشْرُونَ | Use is identical to that of numbers **13-19** |
| ٣٠ | ثَلَاثُونَ | (Table 43, para. 211 above) in all |
| ٤٠ | أَرْبَعُونَ | respects <u>except</u> that multiples of ten from |
| ٥٠ | خَمْسُونَ | **20** to **90** are declined like masculine |
| ٦٠ | سِتُّونَ | sound plurals (see 141), irrespective of |
| ٧٠ | سَبْعُونَ | the gender of the counted noun. The |
| ٨٠ | ثَمَانُونَ | number assumes its own case. |
| ٩٠ | تِسْعُونَ | |

| Number | Referring to: | | Use and form of the number |
|---|---|---|---|
| | masc. noun | fem. noun | |
| ٢١ | وَاحِدٌ وَعِشْرُونَ | وَاحِدَةٌ وَعِشْرُونَ | As for numbers **11** to **19**. Note the order |
| ٣٢ | اثْنَانِ وَثَلَاثُونَ | اثْنَتَانِ وَثَلَاثُونَ | of elements in compounds, each element |
| ٤٥ | خَمْسَةٌ وَأَرْبَعُونَ | خَمْسٌ وَأَرْبَعُونَ | following its own rules. Note also وَ. |
| ٦٧ | سَبْعَةٌ وَسِتُّونَ | سَبْعٌ وَسِتُّونَ | See 210 above for the use of the units |
| ٩٩ | تِسْعَةٌ وَتِسْعُونَ | تِسْعٌ وَتِسْعُونَ | element. See above for the tens. |

Examples of use of **20** to **99**:

Nom.:  عِشْرُونَ دِينَارًا   20 dinars

رِيَالَاتُهُ الْخَمْسُ وَالثَّلَاثُونَ   his 35 riyals

$$\left.\begin{array}{r}\text{Acc.: الْأَيَّامَ الْأَرْبَعِينَ الْمُعَيَّنَةَ تَحْتَ الْقَانُونِ} \\ \text{الْأَرْبَعِينَ يَوْمًا الْمُعَيَّنَةَ تَحْتَ الْقَانُونِ}\end{array}\right\}$$

the 40 days specified

under the law

قَرَأَ ثَمَانِينَ صَفْحَةً.   He read 80 pages.

Gen.: سُفَرَاءُ اثْنَتَيْنِ وَخَمْسِينَ دَوْلَةً   ambassadors of 52 countries

سُفَرَاءُ الدُّوَلِ الِاثْنَتَيْنِ وَالْخَمْسِينَ   the ambassadors of the 52 countries

في سِتَّةٍ وَسِتِّينَ جَدْوَلاً مُعَقَّدًا    in 66 complicated tables

**213. Table 45: Cardinal Numbers above 99.** See 209 above for general provisions. The following table shows numbers above 99.

| Number | Referring to any noun | Use and form of the number |
|---|---|---|
| ١٠٠ | مِئَةٌ\مائَةٌ [1] | 1. After numbers 3-9, مِئَةٌ stands in con- |
| ٢٠٠ | مِئَتَان | struct in the <u>indef. gen. sing.</u>, أَلْفٌ |
| ٣٠٠ | ثَلاَثُمِئَةٍ [2]\ثَلاَثُ مِئَةٍ | and مَلْيُونٌ in the <u>indef. gen. plural</u>. |
| ٤٠٠ | أَرْبَعُمِئَةٍ\أَرْبَعُ مِئَةٍ | 2. مِئَةٌ, أَلْفٌ and مَلْيُونٌ are declinable |
| ٥٠٠ | خَمْسُمِئَةٍ\خَمْسُ مِئَةٍ | nouns. |
| ٦٠٠ | سِتُّمِئَةٍ\سِتُّ مِئَةٍ | 3. مِئَةٌ is not used with numbers above **9**. |
| ٧٠٠ | سَبْعُمِئَةٍ\سَبْعُ مِئَةٍ | 4. Use of مِئَةٌ, أَلْفٌ and مَلْيُونٌ: |
| ٨٠٠ | ثَمَانِيمِئَةٍ\ثَمَانِي مِئَةٍ | • as noun, in counting. |
| ٩٠٠ | تَسْعُمِئَةٍ\تَسْعُ مِئَةٍ | • as def. or indef. noun, followed by |
| ١٠٠٠ | أَلْفٌ (pl. آلَافٌ) | counted noun in construct, in |
| ٢٠٠٠ | أَلْفَان | <u>indefinite genitive singular</u>. |
| ٣٠٠٠ | ثَلاَثَةُ آلَافٍ | • as definite adjective[3] following |
| ١٠٠٠٠٠٠ | مَلْيُونٌ (pl.[4] مَلاَيِينُ) | definite plural counted noun |
| ٢٠٠٠٠٠٠ | مَلْيُونَان | which is in its own case; the |
| ٣٠٠٠٠٠٠ | ثَلاَثَةُ مَلاَيِينَ | number agrees only in case. |

| Num-ber | Referring to: | | Use and form |
|---|---|---|---|
| | masc. noun | fem. noun | of the number |
| ١٣٢ | مِئَةٌ وَاثْنَان وَثَلاَثُونَ | مِئَةٌ وَاثْنَتَان وَثَلاَثُونَ | Use is as for com- |
| ٤٥٨ | أَرْبَعُمِئَةٍ وَثَمَانِيةٌ وَخَمْسُونَ | أَرْبَعُمِئَةٍ وَثَمَانٍ وَخَمْسُونَ | pounds **21** to **99** |
| ١٦٥٧ | أَلْفٌ وَسِتُّمِئَةٍ وَسَبْعَةٌ | أَلْفٌ وَسِتُّمِئَةٍ وَسَبْعٌ | (212 above), except |
| | وَخَمْسُونَ | وَخَمْسُونَ | that in definite mean- |
| ٢٢٦٦ | أَلْفَان وَمِئَتَان وَسِتَّةٌ وَسِتُّونَ | أَلْفَان وَمِئَتَان وَسِتٌّ وَسِتُّونَ | ing they are best |
| | | | used adjectivally[5]. |

1   مِئَةٌ\مائَةٌ (both spellings pronounced mi'a*tun*) has two plurals, مِئُونَ and (more common) مِئَاتٌ, declined respectively as masculine sound plural and feminine sound plural (see 141). They are used only for indeterminite numbers. Similarly, أَلْفٌ has an indeterminate plural أُلُوفٌ. These indeterminate plurals are used alone, or followed by مِنْ with a pronoun suffix, or مِنَ الـ... (etc.) with a noun:

Nom.:       مِئَاتٌ مِنْهُمْ     hundreds of them

Gen.:    مَعَ أُلُوفٍ مِنَ النَّاسِ    with thousands of people

2   The multiples of مِئَةٌ written as one word are commoner. The first element is declined in the same way in both forms.

3   In multiples of مِئَةٌ , أَلْفٌ and مَلْيُونٌ, only the first word of the compound (i.e. the units element) is made definite.

4   Diptote, see 144:   لِلْمَلَايِينَ مِنْهَا    for millions of them

مَلَايِينُ is used both indeterminately and determinately; see footnote [1] immediately above, and examples below.

5   i.e. following the counted noun, which then has its own case.

Examples of use of numbers above **99**:

Nom.:        مِئَةُ جُنْدِيٍّ    100 soldiers

الصَّفَحَاتُ الْمِئَةُ الأَحْسَنُ    the best 100 pages

مِئَتَانِ وَعِشْرُونَ فُوْلْتًا    220 volts

Acc.:      مِئَتَيْ\أَلْفَيْ شَخْصٍ    200/2000 persons

Gen.:   لِمُسْتَقْبَلِ مُوَاطِنِينَا الْعِشْرِينَ مَلْيُونٍ

for the future of our 20 million citizens

لِلْمَلْيُونَيْ مُنْتَخِبَةٍ    for 2 million women voters

لِأَكْثَرِيَةِ الأَصْوَاتِ الثَّلَاثَةِ مَلَايِينَ وَالسِّتَةِ آلَافٍ وَالْمِئَتَيْنِ وَالْخَمْسَةَ عَشَرَ

for the majority of the 3,006,215 votes

## 214. Colloquial Pronunciation of Cardinal Numbers.

Many Arabs, including educated Arabs, avoid the complexities shown in paras 210 to 213 above and pronounce the cardinal numbers colloquially instead, even when reading from a prepared text. The following is a universally acceptable pronunciation of the cardinal numbers, which is invariable for case and, with only two exceptions (numbers **1** and **2**), does not vary for gender.

| ٠ | ṣifr | ١٠ | ʿashara |
|---|------|-----|---------|
| ١ | m. wāhid, f. wāhida | ١١ | ʾahadʿashar |
| ٢ | m. ithnayn, f. thintayn | ١٢ | ithnʿashar |
| ٣ | thalātha | ١٣ | thalattʿashar |
| ٤ | ʾarbaʿa | ١٤ | ʾarbatʿashar |
| ٥ | khamsa | ١٥ | khamsatʿashar |
| ٦ | sitta | ١٦ | sittʿashar |
| ٧ | sabʿa | ١٧ | sabʿatʿashar |
| ٨ | thamāniya | ١٨ | thamantʿashar |
| ٩ | tisʿa | ١٩ | tisʿatʿashar |

| ٢٠ | ʿishrīn | ٢٠٠ | mitayn |
|---|------|-----|---------|
| ٣٠ | thalāthīn | ٣٠٠ | thalathmiya |
| ٤٠ | ʾarbaʿīn | ٤٠٠ | ʾarbaʿmiya |
| ٥٠ | khamsīn | ٥٠٠ | khamsmiya |
| ٦٠ | sittīn | ٦٠٠ | sittmiya |
| ٧٠ | sabʿīn | ٧٠٠ | sabaʿmiya |
| ٨٠ | thamanīn/thamaniyīn | ٨٠٠ | thamanmiya |
| ٩٠ | tisʿīn | ٩٠٠ | tisaʿmiya |
| ١٠٠ | miya, indeterminate pl. miyāt (see 213) | ١٠٠٠ | ʾalf, indeterminate pl. ʾulūf (see 213) |
| و | u | ١٠٠٠ ٠٠٠ | malyūn, pl. malāyīn |

Note:

- Apart from those concerning polarity of agreement (see 209), the rules for the use of the numbers remain valid with this pronunciation. It is common (and logical) to accompany it with short pronunciation of the noun. This means that the only audible noun case-endings are the masculine sound genitive plural ين... (after numbers **3** to **10**, see 210) and the masculine accusative singular اً... (after numbers **11** to **99**, see 211 and 212). The colloquial pronunciation u is used for و in the compounds; although having no hamza, it is never elided, even after a final vowel in the preceding word:

| بين ٤ و ١٠ | bayna ʾarbaʿa wa-ʿashara | between 4 and 10 |
|---|---|---|
| ٨ أمتار | thamāniya ʾamtār | 8 metres |
| البند رقم ٢٦ | al-band raqm sitta u-ʿishrīn | clause ('no.') 26 |
| ٢٠ طالباً | ʿishrīn tāliban | 20 students |
| ٣٥ صفحة | khamsa u-thalāthīn ṣafḥa | 35 pages |

(definite forms:) aṣ-ṣafaḥāt al-khamsa u-th-thalāthīn,

al-khamsa u-th-thalāthīn ṣafḥa          the 35 pages

• miya/-miya becomes mīt/-mīt immediately before a noun:

دينار ١٠٠    mīt dīnār                         100 dinars

تلميذ جديد ٣٠٠    thalathmīt tilmīdh jadīd          300 new pupils

(definite forms:) at-talāmīdh al-judud ath-thalathmiya,

ath-thalathmīt tilmīdh al-jadīd          the 300 new pupils

• Before certain plurals beginning with ...أ, it is common to restore the
  sound -t (i.e. the ة... ) at the end of the numbers **3** to **10**. This is
  especially common with:

  - the plurals أَيَّامٌ 'days', أَسَابِيعُ 'weeks', أَشْهُرُ 'months' and آلَافٌ
    'thousands':

أَيام\أَسابيع\أَشهر ٣    thalāthat 'ayyām/'asābī'/'ashhur

                                         3 days/weeks/months

شخص ٤٠٠٠    'arba' at 'ālāf shakhṣ          4000 people

  - the plurals of the commonest fractions (see 221), أَرْبَاعٌ 'quarters',
    أَخْمَاسٌ 'fifths', etc.:

٤\٥ 'arba' at 'akhmās          four-fifths

٧\٨ saba' at 'athmān          seven-eighths

## 215. Ordinal Numbers - General.

The ordinal numbers are almost always
definite in Arabic. Only 'first' is commonly found in the plural, see 155. The
ordinal is used:

  • for 1st to 10th: as a noun, in the masculine form, in indefinite construct
    (148) with the counted noun,

  • for all numbers: as an adjective following the noun; normal rules of
    case and adjectival agreement (142) apply.

See 216 to 218 below for examples of these usages.

There is no numerical way (1st, 2nd etc.) of writing Arabic ordinal numbers;
they must be written as words.

## 216. Ordinal Numbers 1st to 10th.

The numbers 'first' to 'tenth' are as
follows. All but 'first' have the measure فَاعِلٌ. The provisions of para. 215
apply:

|     | masculine | feminine |
| --- | --- | --- |
| 1st | الأَوَّلُ * | الأُولَى ** |

| | masculine | feminine |
|------|------|------|
| 2nd | الثَّانِي *** | الثَّانِيَةُ |
| 3rd | الثَّالِثُ | الثَّالِثَةُ |
| 4th | الرَّابِعُ | الرَّابِعَة |
| 5th | الخَامِسُ | الخَامِسَةُ |
| 6th | السَّادِسُ | السَّادِسَةُ |
| 7th | السَّابِعُ | السَّابِعَةُ |
| 8th | الثَّامِنُ | الثَّامِنَةُ |
| 9th | التَّاسِعُ | التَّاسِعَةُ |
| 10th | العَاشِرُ | العَاشِرَةُ |

* Diptote, see 144.          ** Invariable for case.

*** الثَّانِي is declined like a defective active participle. See 117.

Examples :

Nom.:   أَوَّلُ مَرَّةٍ  } the first time
         المَرَّةُ الأُولَى

Acc.:   ثَانِيَ فُرْصَةٍ  } the second opportunity
         الفُرْصَةَ الثَّانِيَةَ

Gen.:   فِي ثَالِثِ أُسْبُوعٍ   in the third week

         فِي السَّنَةِ الثَّالِثَةِ   in the third year

See 155 for other uses (including the plural) of أَوَّلُ .


**217. Ordinal Numbers 11th to 19th.** Numbers 11th to 19th vary for gender but not for case. Only the units are made ordinal and definite. The second indent of para. 215 above applies:

| | masculine | feminine |
|------|------|------|
| 11th | الحَادِيَ عَشَرَ | الحَادِيَةَ عَشْرَةَ |
| 12th | الثَّانِيَ عَشَرَ | الثَّانِيَةَ عَشْرَةَ |
| 13th | الثَّالِثَ عَشَرَ | الثَّالِثَةَ عَشْرَةَ |
| 14th | الرَّابِعَ عَشَرَ | الرَّابِعَةَ عَشْرَةَ |
| 15th | الخَامِسَ عَشَرَ | الخَامِسَةَ عَشْرَةَ |
| 16th | السَّادِسَ عَشَرَ | السَّادِسَةَ عَشْرَةَ |

| | | |
|---|---|---|
| 17th | السَّابِعَ عَشَرَ | السَّابِعَةَ عَشْرَةَ |
| 18th | الثَّامِنَ عَشَرَ | الثَّامِنَةَ عَشْرَةَ |
| 19th | التَّاسِعَ عَشَرَ | التَّاسِعَةَ عَشْرَةَ |

Examples:

| | | |
|---|---|---|
| Nom.: | الدَّرْسُ الخَامِسَ عَشَرَ | Lesson 15 ('the 15th lesson') |
| Acc.: | المُرَشَّحَةَ الرَّابِعَةَ عَشْرَةَ | the fourteenth candidate |
| Gen.: | فِي اليَوْمِ السَّادِسَ عَشَرَ | on the 16th day |

**218. Ordinal Numbers above 19th.** In the ordinals above 19th, both parts decline and have the article. The multiples of ten are identical to the masculine cardinal number. Only the units agree with the noun in gender. The second indent of para. 215 above applies:

<u>masculine and feminine</u>

| | | | |
|---|---|---|---|
| 20th | العِشْرُونَ | 80th | الثَّمَانُونَ |
| 30th | الثَّلاَثُونَ | 90th | التِّسْعُونَ |
| 40th | الأَرْبَعُونَ | 100th* | المِئَةُ |
| 50th | الخَمْسُونَ | 1000th* | الأَلْفُ |
| 60th | السِّتُّونَ | millionth* | المَلْيُونُ |
| 70th | السَّبْعُونَ | | |

| | <u>masculine</u> | <u>feminine</u> |
|---|---|---|
| 21st | الحَادِي وَالعِشْرُونَ ** | الحَادِيَةُ وَالعِشْرُونَ |
| 32nd | الثَّانِي وَالثَّلاَثُونَ ** | الثَّانِيَةُ وَالثَّلاَثُونَ |
| 45th | الخَامِسُ وَالأَرْبَعُونَ | الخَامِسَةُ وَالأَرْبَعُونَ |
| 99th | التَّاسِعُ وَالتِّسْعُونَ | التَّاسِعَةُ وَالتِّسْعُونَ |
| 101st | المِئَةُ وَالوَاحِدُ *** | المِئَةُ وَالوَاحِدَةُ |
| 1001st | الأَلْفُ وَالوَاحِدُ *** | الأَلْفُ وَالوَاحِدَةُ |

\* Newspapers also have المَلْيُونِيُّ\المَلْيُونِيَّةُ , الأَلْفِيُّ\الأَلْفِيَّةُ , المِئَوِيُّ\المِئَوِيَّةُ.

\*\* الحَادِي and الثَّانِي, in these compounds, are declined like defective active participles. See 117.

\*\*\* Alternatives for ordinals above 100th:

101st (etc.) الأَوَّلُ بَعْدَ الأَلْفِ ; 1001st (etc.) الأَوَّلُ بَعْدَ الْمِئَةِ

Examples:

Nom.:           الدَّرْسُ الْعِشْرُونَ      Lesson 20 ('the 20th lesson')

الْجَلْسَةُ الثَّامِنَةُ وَالْعِشْرُونَ      the 28th session

Acc.:   حَضَرُوا الْجَلْسَةَ الْحَادِيَةَ وَالْعِشْرِينَ.      They attended the 21st session.

Gen.:   نَصُّ الْبَيَانِ السَّنَوِيِّ الْحَادِي وَالأَرْبَعِينَ

the text of the 41st annual communiqué

**219. Adverbial Ordinals.** The indefinite masculine singular accusative form
(see 137) of the ordinal numbers up to ten is often used with adverbial meaning:

أَوَّلاً firstly    ثَانِيًا secondly    ثَالِثًا thirdly    رَابِعًا fourthly

These adverbs are also often used in numbering a short list of chapters or clauses
in a document, where English prefers cardinal numbers:

أَوَّلاً – الْوَضْعُ الْعَامُّ    1. General Situation

ثَانِيًا – الْعَوَامِلُ الْفَنِّيَّةُ    2. Technical Factors

ثَالِثًا – اعْتِبَارَاتُ الْبِيئَةِ    3. Environmental Considerations

**220. Alphabetical Numbering** (الأَبْجَدُ). The letters of the Arabic alphabet
are also used for numbering in a document, as are Latin letters or Roman figures
in English. It is necessary only to know the letters denoting the numbers **1-10**,
not the whole alphabet. As with Roman figures, the corresponding letters are not
in alphabetical order:

أَ بْـجَدْ هَـوَّزْ حُطِـي
١٠٩٨ ٧٦٥ ٤٣٢١

for which the mnemonic is the three words 'abjad hawwaz ḥuṭī. In this context أ
is usually written with its hamza, for clarity:

أ  I, (i), A, (a)                          ب  II, (ii), B, (b)

ج  III, (iii), C, (c)                      د  IV, (iv), D, (d)

أ is also written with hamza, for clarity, in algebra: ٤−بـ٣ = أ٢  2a = 3b-4

**221. Fractions.** Only the numbers **2** to **10** have a word for the fraction; all
but one of these have the measure فُعْلٌ, plural أَفْعَالٌ. They are masculine nouns:

half  نِصْفٌ, pl. أَنْصَافٌ        third  ثُلْثٌ, pl. أَثْلَاثٌ

| quarter | رُبْعٌ , pl. أَرْبَاعٌ | fifth | خُمْسٌ , pl. أَخْمَاسٌ |
|---------|---------|--------|---------|
| sixth | سُدْسٌ , pl. أَسْدَاسٌ | seventh | سُبْعٌ , pl. أَسْبَاعٌ |
| eighth | ثُمْنٌ , pl. أَثْمَانٌ | ninth | تُسْعٌ , pl. أَتْسَاعٌ |
| tenth | عُشْرٌ , pl. أَعْشَارٌ | | |

See 214 for the common colloquial pronunciation of unit numbers **3** to **9** with the plurals of these fractions.

Examples:

| Nom.: | النِّصْفَان | both halves |
|-------|-------------|-------------|
| | ثَلَاثَةُ أَثْمَانُ الرِّبْحِ | $^3/_8$ of the profit |
| Acc.: | ثُلْثَيْ خَسَارَتِه | $^2/_3$ of his loss |
| Gen.: | فِي ثَلَاثَةِ أَرْبَاعِ المِيزَانِيَّةِ | in $^3/_4$ of the budget |

Fractions with denominators higher than **10** are expressed with the cardinal number, preceded by عَلَى 'over' or مِنْ 'out of'. Both parts of the fraction are in the counting form:

$$١٢\backslash ١١ \quad أَحَدَ عَشَرَ عَلَى\backslash مِنِ اثْنَيْ عَشَرَ$$

**222. Percentage.** Percentage is expressed with بِالمِئَة or فِي المِئَة :

65%. ٦٥٪ ( خَمْسَةٌ وَسِتُّونَ بِالمِئَة\فِي المِئَة)

See 214 for the generally used colloquial pronunciation.

**223. Nil.** 'Nil' in statistics, tables etc. can be expressed with صِفْرٌ · 'zero', but is equally commonly expressed with the words لَا يُوجَدُ 'it is not found'. This form is the 3rd person masculine singular of the imperfect indicative passive of the assimilated verb وَجَدُ يَجِدُ I, 'to find' (see 95).

**224. Time: Complete Hours.** Time is expressed with the noun سَاعَةٌ 'hour/clock/watch'. The number of the hour is put into the definite cardinal form for 'one', and the definite ordinal form (see 216 and 217) for the other numbers; all qualify and agree with السَّاعَةُ :

| السَّاعَةُ الوَاحِدَةُ one o'clock | السَّاعَةُ السَّادِسَةُ six o'clock |
|---|---|

Note:

- 'It is ... o'clock' is expressed either with the cardinal number in the form appropriate to a masculine noun, or the definite ordinal number, agreeing with السَّاعَةُ:

السَّاعَةُ أَرْبَعَةً\الرَّابِعَةُ   It is four o'clock.

• 'at' with times is في: في السَّاعَةِ الثَّامِنَةِ   at 8 o'clock.

Other important vocabulary:

صَبَاحًا\في الصَّبَاحِ   in the morning, a.m.

عِنْدَ الظُّهْرِ   at midday

بَعْدَ الظُّهْرِ\في العَصْرِ   in the afternoon, p.m.

مَسَاءً\في المَسَاءِ   in the evening, p.m.

في نِصْفِ اللَّيْلِ   at midnight

نَهَارًا\في النَّهَارِ   in the daytime

لَيْلاً\في اللَّيْلِ   at night

في تَمَامِ السَّاعَةِ الـ...   at ... o'clock precisely

**225. Time: Incomplete Hours.** Time with incomplete hours is expressed
with the hour (see 224) followed by وَ 'and' for time past the hour and إلّا
'except' (followed, NB, by the genitive) for time to the hour, as in French. The
hour has five important points, marked by definite fractions (see 221):

وَالرُّبْعُ   a quarter past          وَالثُّلْثُ   twenty past

وَالنِّصْفُ   half past              إلّا الثُّلْثُ   twenty to

إلّا الرُّبْعُ   a quarter to

The other parts of the hour are expressed with the minutes and the noun دَقيقَةٌ
'minute', pl. دَقَائِقُ (diptote, see 144).

Minutes in the middle third of the hour may be quoted not only by reference to
the complete hour, as in English, but by reference to the half-hour.

See 224 above for the expression of the hour, 'at', and other important
vocabulary.

السَّاعَةُ ...

الرَّابِعَةُ وَالرُّبْعُ   a quarter past four

الخَامِسَةُ وَالثُّلْثُ   twenty past five

السَّادِسَةُ وَالنِّصْفُ   half-past six

السَّابِعَةُ إلّا الثُّلْثُ   twenty to seven

الثَّامِنَةُ إلّا الرُّبْعُ   a quarter to eight

التّاسِعَةُ وَعَشْرُ دَقَائِقَ    ten past nine

العَاشِرَةَ وَالنصفُ إلاَّ خَمْسِ دَقَائِقَ    twenty-five past ten

الحَادِيَةَ عَشْرَةَ إلاَّ عَشْرِ دَقَائِقَ    ten to eleven

الثَّانِيَةُ وَثَمَانِي دَقَائِقَ    eight minutes past two

These are the nominative forms. After فِي 'at', the nominative endings only are
replaced by the genitive, e.g.:

فِي السَّاعَةِ الثَّامِنَةِ إلاَّ الرُّبْعِ    at a quarter to eight

## 226. The Year.

**226. The Year.** The number of the year is cardinal, in multiple indefinite
construct (148) after سَنَةٌ\عَامٌ 'year':

Nom.:    عَامُ أَلْفٍ وَتِسْعِمِئَةٍ وَخَمْسٍ وَعِشْرِينَ    1925

Gen.:    فِي سَنَةِ أَلْفٍ وَتِسْعِمِئَةٍ وَسَبْعٍ وَأَرْبَعِينَ    in 1947

The colloquial pronunciation (see 214) is very commonly used for the years:

fī sanat 'alf u-tisa' miya u-saba' a u-'arba' īn 'in 1947'.

Decades are most commonly expressed as follows:

التِّسْعُونَاتُ\التِّسْعُونِيَّاتُ    the 'nineties

## 227. Months and Days.

**227. Months and Days.** The months of the Muslim calendar are:

| | | | |
|---|---|---|---|
| ١ | مُحَرَّمٌ | ٧ | رَجَبٌ |
| ٢ | صَفَرٌ | ٨ | شَعْبَانُ* |
| ٣ | رَبِيعُ الأَوَّلُ | ٩ | رَمَضَانُ* |
| ٤ | رَبِيعُ الثَّانِي | ١٠ | شَوَّالٌ |
| ٥ | جُمَادَى الأُولَى** | ١١ | ذُو القَعْدَةِ** |
| ٦ | جُمَادَى الآخِرَةُ** | ١٢ | ذُو الحِجَّةِ** |

* Diptote (see 144).    ** See 145 for words ending in ...ى , and 160 for
declension of ذُو .

The Muslim year is lunar, 354 days long, and dates from the flight (الهِجْرَةُ) of
Muhammad from Mecca to Medina in AD 622. It can be designated by AH (Anno
Hegiræ) in English or هـ (الهِجْرِيَّةُ) in Arabic.

The months of the Christian or international calendar have one set of names used
in Asia, another in Africa:

| | Asia | | Africa |
|---|---|---|---|
| ١ | كَانُونُ الثَّانِي | | يَنَايِرُ* |

| فِبْرايِرُ* | شُباطُ | ٢ |
|---|---|---|
| مارِسُ* | آذارُ* | ٣ |
| أَبْرِيلُ* | نِيسانُ* | ٤ |
| مايُو** | أَيّارُ* | ٥ |
| يُونِيُو** | حَزِيرانُ* | ٦ |
| يُولِيُو** | تَمُّوزُ* | ٧ |
| أَغُسْطُسُ* | آبُ* | ٨ |
| سِبْتَمْبَرُ* | أَيْلُولُ* | ٩ |
| أُكْتُوبِرُ* | تِشْرِينُ الأَوَّلُ | ١٠ |
| نُوفَمْبَرُ* | تِشْرِينُ الثَّانِي | ١١ |
| دِسَمْبَرُ* | كانُونُ الأَوَّلُ | ١٢ |

* Diptote.  ** Invariable for case.

The Christian or international year can be designated by م (الْمِيلادِيَّةُ, 'Christian')
in Arabic.

Dates are given with masculine ordinal numbers; 'on' is فِي :

١٤٢٠\٢\٩ هـ ؛ فِي تاسِعِ صَفَرَ سَنَةَ أَلْفٍ وَأَرْبَعِمِئَةٍ وَعِشْرِينَ الْهِجْرِيَّة on 9/2/1420 AH
commonly pronounced: fī tāsi' ṣafar sanat 'alf u-'arba' miya u-'ishrīn al-hijrīya

٢٠٠٣\٧\٢٠ م ؛ عِشْرُونَ تَمُّوزَ (يُولِيُو) سَنَةَ أَلْفَيْنِ وَثَلاثَةِ الْمِيلادِيَّة 20/7/2003 AD
commonly pronounced: 'ishrīn tammūz (yūliū) sanat 'alfayn u-thalātha l-mīlādīya

The days of the week are:

| الْجُمْعَةُ | Friday | الثُّلاثاءُ | Tuesday |
|---|---|---|---|
| السَّبْتُ | Saturday | الأَرْبَعاءُ | Wednesday |
| الأَحَدُ | Sunday | الْخَمِيسُ | Thursday |
| الاثْنَيْن | Monday | | |

Each of these may be preceded, in construct, by يَوْمٌ 'day'. 'On' with a day is
expressed with the accusative, and no preposition:

يَحْضُرُ السَّبْتَ\يَوْمَ السَّبْتِ.    He will be present on Saturday.

**228.  Age.** Age is expressed with عُمُرٌ 'age, lifetime':

عُمْرِي أَرْبَعُونَ. I am forty.   كَمْ عُمْرُهُ\عُمْرُهُ كَمْ؟ How old is he?

# 18. Wishes and Exclamations

**229.** **Wishes.** Wishes can be expressed in four common ways:

- With the particles لـِ... , وَلْـ... or فَلْـ... and the jussive tense of the verb (see 46):

  لِيَجِئْ.   Let him come.

  فَلْيُحَاوِلُوا.   So let them try.

- with (وَدِدْتُ) لَوْ and an unreal condition (194):

  وَدِدْتُ لَوْ عَرَفْنَا هٰذَا!   I wish we knew that!

  لَوْ لَمْ يَتَكَلَّمُوا كَذٰلِكَ.   I wish they would not talk like that.
  ('If (only) they would not …')

- With the conjunction لَيْتَ. This is a sister of أَنَّ (see 182), and is followed by the perfect tense:

  لَيْتَنِي كُنْتُ غَنِيّاً.   I wish I were rich.

  لَيْتَ الأَسْعَارَ نَزَلَتْ.   I wish/If only the prices would fall.

- With the perfect or imperfect tense of the verb; this structure is used only in a few set expressions, mostly invoking God:

  حَفَظَكَ اللّٰهُ.   God keep/preserve you.

  اللّٰهُ يُبَارِكُ فِيكَ.   God bless you.

  The negative is constructed with (NB) the particle لا, even with the perfect:

  لا سَمَحَ اللّٰهُ!   God/Heaven forbid!

**230.** **Exclamations.** There are four main patterns for exclamations:

- 'How …' with an adjective: with the particle مَا and an adjective in the accusative elative form (153) and either a noun in the accusative or a suffixed object pronoun:

  مَا أَلْطَفَكُمْ.   How kind you are.

  مَا كَانَتْ أَصْعَبَ مَشَاكِلَنَا.   How difficult our problems were.

  With a derived adjective we use the accusative of أَكْثَرُ or أَشَدُّ and the verbal noun, much as in comparison:

  مَا أَشَدَّهُ تَعْقِيداً.   How complicated it is.

- 'How …' with an adverb and verb: the same as the adjectival structure shown above, followed by a further مَا and the verb:

مَا أَجْمَلَ مَا غَنَّتْ!   How beautifully she sang!

or we can recast the expression with an adjective and verbal noun, as above:

مَا أَجْمَلَ كِتَابَتُهَا .   How beautifully she writes.

('How beautiful her writing is.')

- 'How (much/many) …': with كَمْ (see 169) or كَمْ مِنْ :

كَمْ وَقْتًا\كَمْ مِنَ الْوَقْت خَسِرْنَاهُ فِي الْكَلَامِ.

How much time we have wasted/lost in talking.

كَمْ هُوَ كَانَ مُجْتَهِدًا .   How hardworking he was.

- 'What (a) …' with a noun or adjective and noun: with يَا لـ … مِنْ ; the subject is attached to the لـ…, suffixed if it is a pronoun:

يَا لِهٰذه مِنْ قَضِيَّة مُضْحِكَةٍ.   What a ridiculous case this is.

يَا لَنَا مِنْ حُمْقٍ.   What fools we are/were.

# Arabic Index

Numbers refer to paragraphs. The sign → refers to the Grammatical Index.

ا\ى 12, 13, 15, 16, 19, 21, 28, 107, 110, 112, 120, 121, 137, 138, 144, 145, 147, 158, 166, 173
→ **Verbs**, defective/ doubly weak/hollow

أ... 169, 184, 220

أحد 171

إذْ 198

إذا 186, 194

الـ... → **Article**

ألاّ 187, 190, 207

إلاّ 165, 194, 201, 205, 225

إلى أنْ 197

أمّا 188

أنْ 187, 190, 193, 207

أنّ 131, 181, 185, 189, 198, 205, 229

إنْ 194

إنّ 181, 185, 197

أيّ 152, 169

أين 177

أينما 195

ء 5, 14, 16, 19, 28, 32, 66-84, 107, 118-124, 128, 129, 137, 138, 144
→ **Verbs**, doubly weak/ hamzated

بعد أنْ 197

بعض 152

بيتما 197

جميع 152

حالما 197

حتّى 172, 190, 195, 197, 207

حيث 198

حينما 197

ذات 152, 160

ذو 160

سوف\سَ 42, 194

شيء 171

طالما 197

عدم\عديم 150

عندما 197

غير 150, 152, 176

فَ 17, 46, 188, 194, 197, 229

قبل أنْ 197

قد 40, 48, 49, 194

كان 47-49, 103, 180, 189, 192, 194, 205

كأنّ 181, 185

كلّ 152, 204

كلا 152

كلّما 197

كم 169, 205, 230

كي 190, 207

كيف 177

كيفما 195

لَ 40, 194

لِ 17, 46, 172-174, 190, 207, 229, 230

لا 42, 46, 50, 116, 127, 150, 194, 196, 200, 229

لئلاّ 190

لأنْ 190, 207

لأنّ 181, 198

لكي 190, 207

لم 46, 194, 196

لمّا 46, 197

لماذا\لِمَ 177
لِمن 169
لن 44
لو 194, 195
ليت 229
ليس 103, 180, 189, 194, 196
ما 40, 168, 169, 177, 180, 186, 194, 195, 203, 206, 230
ما دام 197
ماذا 169
متى 177, 195
مع أنّ 195
مَن 168-170, 180, 195, 213, 221, 230
مِن 28, 55, 172, 195, 230
مَنذ أن 197
مهما 1195
نفس 152
هل 169, 184, 186

ة 13, 20, 136-138, 140-142, 144, 147, 148, 209, 214
و 16, 19, 21, 32, 92, 93, 95, 97, 100-102, 108-110, 112, 114, 119-122, 158
→ **Verbs**, assimilated/defective/doubly weak/hollow
وَ 12, 13, 16, 17, 19, 21, 46, 107, 165, 194-196, 212, 214, 225, 229
(و)لكنّ 181
ي 32, 92, 94, 95, 97, 100-102, 107-110, 112, 114, 117-124, 128, 129, 135, 137, 138, 140, 141, 147, 158, 173
→ **Verbs**, assimilated/defective/doubly weak/hollow

# Grammatical Index

Consult also the Contents. Numbers refer to paragraphs. Internal references are marked → .

**Accusative** → **Case**, → **Adverb**

**Adjective** 10, 16, 25, 28, 30,
47-49, 51, 52, 132-134, 138-
140, 145, 148, 150-152, 154,
155, 169, 175, 195, 196, 203,
204, 209-211, 213, 215, 230
agreement 52, 142, 154, 163, 192,
209-211, 213, 215, 218, 224
broken plural 137, 138, 143, 144,
155
colours and defects 161
comparative 153-156, 178, 197,
205, 206, 230
compound 151, 160, 163
demonstrative 30, 146, 148
diminutive 158
diptote 143, 144, 153-155, 216
improper annexation 163, 207
indeclinable → **Case**
regular 137, 138, 142
relative 135, 136, 153, 175, 196
sound plural 51, 71, 77, 90, 98,
105, 141, 145, 154
superlative 145, 154-156
→ **Elative**, → **Possessive**,
→ **Verb**, participle

**Adverb** 16, 30, 175-178, 195, 203,
205, 219, 230
adverbial accusative 175, 178
comparative 178, 197, 206
interrogative → **Interrogative**,
adverb
superlative 178

**Animate** 35, 64, 134, 141, 143,
146, 147, 152, 155, 165-168,
171, 209

**Antecedent** 168

**Article** 4, 15, 17, 25, 29, 30, 132,
138, 139, 148, 150, 159,

172, 218

**Aspect** → **Verb**, tense

**Case** 7, 10, 15, 52, 54, 117, 128,
129, 131, 135, 137-148, 153,
159, 160, 163, 164, 168, 169,
172, 175, 182, 185, 189, 194,
196, 199-201, 203-205, 209-
214, 216-219, 225, 230
→ **Adverb**, adverbial
accusative

**Clause** 188, 199, 201
circumstance 42, 52, 165, 168,
192, 193, 196
concession 195, 207
condition 38, 40, 46, 194-197,
207, 229
consecutive 197
main 182, 194, 197
purpose 189
relative 168, 170, 171, 192, 207
reason 197, 198, 207
time 196, 197, 207

**Command** → **Direct Speech**,
→ **Indirect Speech**

**Complement** 33, 47-49, 131,
142, 148, 153, 169, 180, 182,
185, 189

**Concession** → **Clause**

**Condition** → **Clause**

**Conjunction** 44, 153, 165, 185-
188, 190, 191, 193-198, 206,
207
relative 168
sisters of '*anna* 131, 182, 185,
189, 205, 229

**Consonant, Consonantal** 23-
25, 100-102, 107, 135, 137,
138, 140, 141, 144

**Construct** 30, 52, 54, 131, 132,

138, 146, 148, 150-152, 154, 156, 159, 160, 163, 169, 171, 185, 187, 190, 191, 199, 202, 204, 207, 213, 225

**Declension** → **Case**

**Definite** → **Article**, → **Definition**

**Definition** 7, 10, 14, 108, 109, 117, 132, 135, 137-142, 144-148, 150-154, 159, 160, 163, 164, 168, 169, 171, 172, 175, 180, 185, 187, 190, 191, 196, 200, 202-204, 206, 207, 209-211, 213-215, 217, 219, 224
→ **Pronouns**, indefinite

**Demonstrative** → **Adjective**, → **Pronoun**

**Direct Speech**
command and request 38
question 169, 170, 177, 184, 186
statement → **Sentence**, nominal/ verbal

**Dual** → **Number**

**Elative Measure** 144, 153, 178, 230

**Equation** → **Sentence**, equation

**Feminine** → **Gender**

**Gender** 7, 16, 34, 35, 39, 51, 55, 64, 87, 95, 102, 108, 109, 114, 117, 118, 128, 130, 134-144, 146, 147, 149, 153-155, 160, 162, 165-169, 171, 175, 182, 183, 190, 209-214, 216-219, 221, 223

**Genitive** → **Case**

**Government** → **Verbs**, intransitive/prepositional/transitive

**hamza** (hamzat al-qaṭʿ, hamzat al-waṣl) 5, 9, 19, 23, 28, 85, 92, 100, 107, 119-124, 127, 128, 137-139, 144, 147, 148, 160, 165, 166, 168, 172, 184, 186, 199, 214, 220
→ **Verbs**, hamzated

**Handwriting** 20, 208

**Inanimate** 35, 64, 134, 141, 147,

152, 155, 165-168, 171, 183

**Indefinite** → **Definition**

**Indirect Speech**    ,
command and request 38, 187, 207
question 169, 170, 177, 186
statement 185, 207

**Interrogative**
adverb 177, 186
particle 184
pronoun 169, 170, 177, 180, 186
relative interrogative 170, 177, 180
→ **Direct Speech**, question,
→ **Indirect Speech**, question

**Masculine** → **Gender**

**Measures** 6, 36, 37, 51, 53, 65, 67, 73, 78, 84, 86, 90, 105, 108, 109, 118, 154, 157, 158, 216, 221
→ **Elative**

**Moon Letter** 139

**Negation, Negative** 38, 40, 42, 44, 46, 50, 89, 97, 116, 127, 150, 168, 171, 176, 180, 189, 190, 194, 196, 200, 201, 205, 206, 229

**Nominative** → **Case**

**Noun** 10, 16, 25, 28, 30, 47-49, 51, 52, 54, 64, 117, 130-135, 139, 140, 142, 145-148, 150-152, 154, 156, 163, 165, 168, 169, 171, 175, 176, 178, 180, 182, 183, 190, 194, 196, 200, 203, 205, 209-211, 213, 215, 221, 224, 230
abstract 132, 136, 153
activity 157
anomalous 159-162
apposition 152, 164
broken plural 51, 53, 64, 65, 72, 91, 135, 137, 138, 143, 144, 149, 154, 157, 159, 162
collective 149
common 132, 138, 144
compound 150, 151
diminutive 158
diptote 64, 65, 72, 78, 91, 137, 143, 144, 159, 210, 213
indeclinable 147, 152, 227

instrument 157
place 52, 157
proper 132, 137, 144
regular 137, 138
sound plural 51, 53, 65, 71, 72,
77, 78, 83, 84, 90, 91, 98, 99,
105, 106, 117, 141, 145, 147-
150, 157, 212-214
→ Case, → Number,
→ Verb, participle, verbal noun
Number (singular/dual/plural) 7, 10,
16, 28, 34, 35, 39, 51, 55, 87, 95,
102, 105, 108-110, 112, 114,
117, 118, 128, 129, 133-149,
152-155, 159-162, 165-169, 173,
175, 182, 183, 190, 200, 210,
211, 213-215, 219, 221, 223
→ Adjective, broken plural,
sound plural
→ Noun, broken plural, sound
plural
Numbers ( 1, 2, 3 ...)
cardinal 205, 209-214, 218, 220,
221, 224
fractions 214, 221, 225
numerals 208
ordinal 215-219, 224
Nunation 14, 26, 144, 145, 200
Object
absolute 175, 204, 205
direct 33, 52, 54, 147, 164-170,
190, 191, 199, 205
indirect 33
prepositional 33, 54, 165, 168,
173, 174, 185, 199
→ Pronoun, suffix
Particle 40, 42, 44, 46, 48-50, 150,
188, 194, 200, 229, 230
Plural → Number, → Adjective,
broken plural/sound plural,
→ Noun, broken plural/sound
plural
Pointing 4, 14, 15, 19, 26, 30, 85,
139
Possessive (Adjective) Suffix
28, 117, 118, 128, 129, 132, 138,

141, 145, 147, 148, 152, 154,
159, 165, 171, 173
Preposition 28, 33, 52, 54, 131,
150, 153, 164, 165, 167-170,
172-178, 185, 190, 194, 195,
197, 200, 207, 225
→ Object, prepositional
Pronoun 133, 134, 141, 142, 152,
168, 173, 180, 195, 203
demonstrative 30, 146
direct object → suffix below
emphatic 152
indefinite 171, 203
interrogative → Interrogative,
pronoun
reflexive 152
relative 158, 168, 206
subject 165, 168, 182, 196, 201
suffix 28, 39, 52, 55, 59, 110,
112, 114-116, 122, 166, 168,
172-174, 182, 185, 190, 194,
201, 230
Pronunciation 7, 8, 13, 14, 16,
19, 22-30, 39, 41, 45, 46, 100,
112, 114, 137-142, 144-148, 160,
166, 168, 172, 175, 199, 200,
203, 204, 214, 225
Question → Direct Speech,
question, → Indirect Speech,
question, → Interrogative
Relative → Adjective,
→ Clause, → Interrogative,
→ Pronoun
Root 6, 8
Sentence
concessive/conditional →
Clauses, concession/condition
equation 131, 146, 156, 165, 168,
169, 180, 182, 183, 185, 189,
190, 196
exceptive 201, 205
nominal 166, 180-182, 184, 186,
194, 197
verbal 35, 47, 49, 181, 183, 184,
186
shadda 18, 85, 139

**Singular** → **Number**
**Sisters of** '*anna* →
**Conjunction**, sisters of '*anna*
**Sisters of** *kāna* → **Verb**,
complemented
**Stress** 29
**Subject** 35, 47-49, 54, 55, 131,
146, 152, 165, 166, 168-171,
180, 182, 183, 185, 191, 192, 196
→ **Pronoun**, subject
**Sun Letter** 139
**to be** 180, 189
**to have** 174
**Transliteration** 3, 17, 21, 29, 137
**Velarisation** → **Pronunciation**
**Verb** 7, 16, 28, 131, 133, 134, 152,
153, 166, 168, 180, 182, 183,
185, 190, 195, 196, 201, 204,
205, 230
    active 7, 28, 36-38, 41, 51-53, 57,
    59, 60, 64, 67, 69, 71, 73, 75,
    77, 79, 81, 83, 86-88, 90, 93-
    96, 98, 101, 103, 105, 108,
    110, 112, 117-120, 123, 128,
    129, 157, 162, 192, 196, 207,
    210, 216, 218
    agreement 35, 39, 41, 47-50, 52,
    182, 183
    aspect 38
    assimilated 8, 28, 32, 45, 51, 86,
    92-99, 120, 122, 124, 129,
    180, 223
    auxiliary 191, 207
    causative 37
    complemented (sisters of *kāna*)
    181, 191, 205
    continuous perfect 47, 190, 192,
    194, 207
    defective 8, 16, 28, 32, 45, 51,
    84, 107-119, 122, 125, 126,
    128-130, 162, 210, 216, 218
    doubled 8, 32, 45, 50, 51, 57, 61,
    85-92, 100, 103
    doubly weak 8, 16, 45, 51, 92,
    100, 107, 119-130
    Form I 7, 28, 37, 41, 51, 53, 55,
    57, 58, 63-65, 68, 70, 73-75,
    86, 87, 93, 101, 102, 108, 109,
    119, 120, 157, 204
    Form IQ 37, 41, 51, 53, 55, 57,
    58, 65
    Form II 37, 41, 51, 53, 55, 57,
    58, 63, 65, 68, 73, 74, 86, 87,
    93, 101, 102, 108, 109, 120,
    121
    Form IIQ 37, 41, 51, 53, 55, 57,
    65
    Form III 37, 41, 51, 53, 55, 57,
    58, 63, 65, 68, 73, 74, 86, 87,
    93, 101, 102, 108, 109, 120,
    121
    Form IV 37, 41, 51, 53, 55, 57,
    58, 63, 65, 68, 73, 86, 87, 93,
    101, 102, 108, 109, 120, 121
    Form V 37, 41, 51, 53, 55, 57,
    58, 63, 65, 68, 73, 86, 87, 93,
    101, 102, 108, 109, 120, 121
    Form VI 37, 41, 51, 53, 55, 57,
    58, 63, 65, 73, 86, 93, 101,
    102, 108, 109, 120
    Form VII 28, 29, 37, 41, 51, 53,
    55, 57, 58, 63, 65, 66, 86, 93,
    101, 102, 108, 120
    Form VIII 28, 29, 37, 41, 51, 53,
    55, 57, 58, 63, 65, 68, 73, 86,
    87, 93, 101, 102, 109, 120, 121
    Form IX 28, 37, 41, 51, 53, 55,
    57, 62, 63, 65, 66, 85, 93, 101,
    107
    Form X 28, 37, 41, 51, 53, 55,
    57, 58, 63, 65, 68, 73, 86, 87,
    93, 101, 102, 108, 109, 120,
    121
    future 42, 44, 180, 189
    future perfect 49, 190
    hamzated 8, 28, 32, 45, 51, 53,
    66-85, 93, 118, 121, 124-126,
    129, → **hamza**
    hollow 8, 32, 37, 45, 47-51, 85,
    100-106, 122, 126, 129
    imperative 7, 28, 35, 37, 38, 46,
    50, 55, 57, 62, 67, 70, 73, 75,

76, 79, 82, 85, 86, 88, 89, 93,
94, 97, 101, 104, 108, 116,
120, 127, 166, 189, 191, 194
imperfect 7, 34, 38, 39, 41-43, 47,
49, 51, 55, 58, 60, 69, 75, 81,
88, 96, 101, 103, 112-114,
122, 124, 125, 189, 191, 194,
196, 197, 202, 207, 223, 229
→ jussive/subjunctive below,
→ stem below
increased forms 7, 36, 52, 87,
105, 108, 153, 157, 204
→ Forms II-X above
indicative → imperfect above,
→ perfect below
intransitive 33, 37, 55
→ **Object**, direct
jussive 38, 40, 45, 46, 50, 62, 63,
69, 73, 75, 81, 85, 88, 96, 97,
103, 115, 116, 126, 127, 166,
194, 196, 229
mood → **Verb**, imperative/
imperfect/jussive/perfect/
subjunctive
participial 192
participle 7, 30, 37, 51, 52, 55,
57, 58, 64, 67, 68, 71, 73, 74,
77, 79, 80, 83, 86, 90, 93-95,
98, 101, 102, 105, 108, 109,
117-121, 128-130, 148, 153,
157, 162, 163, 175, 189, 192,
196, 207, 210, 216, 218
passive 28, 36-38, 41, 50-53, 55,
58-60, 64, 68, 69, 71, 74, 75,
77, 80, 81, 83, 87, 88, 90, 95,
96, 98, 102, 103, 105, 109,
111, 113, 117, 121, 123, 124,
128, 157, 168, 199, 202, 207,
223
perfect 7, 28, 34, 38-40, 46-49,
55, 58, 59, 67, 69, 75, 81, 87,
88, 96, 101, 103, 110, 111,
123, 166, 189, 190, 192-194,
196, 197, 202, 206, 229
→ stem below

pluperfect 48, 194
prepositional 7, 33, 37, 52, 54,
55, 189
→ **Object**, prepositional
principal parts 7, 30, 34, 37, 55,
57-60, 67, 68, 73, 74, 79, 80,
86, 87, 93-95, 101, 102, 108-
110, 112, 120, 121
quadriliteral 37, 55, 57
reciprocal 37
reflexive 37
simultaneous 193
sisters of *kāna* → complemented
above
sound 28, 32, 37, 45, 50, 51, 55-
69, 72-74, 78-81, 84-87, 90-96,
99-102, 105, 106, 108, 109,
112-115, 117, 118, 122, 124,
129
stem 39, 69, 75, 81, 88, 96, 110,
112, 117
subjunctive 38, 42-45, 61-63, 69,
75, 81, 88, 89, 96, 103, 114,
115, 125, 126, 166, 187, 190,
194, 197, 207
tense 7, 35, 38, 52, 69, 75, 81,
96, 102, 103, 108, 122, 144,
183, 185-187, 191, 192, 194,
202
→ continuous perfect/future
perfect/imperfect/jussive/perfect/
pluperfect/subjunctive above
transitive 33, 37, 52, 54, 55, 164,
207, → **Object**, direct
triliteral 7, 37
verbal noun 7, 28, 37, 53-55, 57,
65, 67, 72, 73, 78, 79, 84, 86,
91, 93, 94, 99, 101, 106-108,
118, 120, 129, 150, 153, 175,
185, 189-191, 194, 195, 197,
202, 204, 205, 207, 230
voice → active/passive above
weak → assimilated/defective/
doubly weak/hollow above
**Weak Letter** 16, 92, 100, 107, 119

# Glossary of Grammatical Terms

This glossary explains and illustrates in English the general grammatical terms used in this book. The asterisk refers to a term found elsewhere in the glossary. Grammatical terms expressed in English but particular to Arabic, e.g. <u>construct</u>, are explained fully in the appropriate paragraph, which can be found through the Contents and the Grammatical Index.

| | |
|---|---|
| **Active** | see Voice*. |
| **Adjective** | describes or identifies ('qualifies') a noun* or pronoun*: 'a *rich* man, They are *young*'. |
| **Adverb** | describes ('modifies') a verb* ('he writes *badly*'), an adjective* ('his writing is *very* bad'), or another adverb ('he writes *very* badly'). The main types of adverb are those of time ('*now*'), manner ('*badly*'), place ('*here*') and degree ('*very*'). |
| **Agreement** | the manner in which a word is changed to suit an associated word: '*this* house, *these* houses, it *is*, they *are*'. |
| **Antecedent** | the expression to which a relative* clause refers: 'this is the *man* who lives here'. |
| **Case** | a form of the noun* (and of any adjective* agreeing with it) which reflects the noun's function in the sentence. |
| **Causative** | a derived form of a verb* in which the object* is made to do the action of the original non-causative verb: 'he *felled* the tree' (i.e. caused it to fall). |
| **Clause** | a group of words centred on a subject*-and-verb* group. |
| **Complement** | an expression completing the meaning of certain verbs* showing a state: 'he is a *student*', the matter became *serious*'. |
| **Conjugate, to** | to make a word conform to its conjugation*. |
| **Conjugation** | the system for changing a verb* form to suit its tense* and its subject*. |
| **Conjunction** | word joining two expressions: '*and, but, if*'. |
| **Declension** | the system of cases*. |
| **Decline, to** | to make a word conform to its declension*. |
| **Gender** | a categorisation of nouns* and pronouns*. Arabic has two genders: masculine and feminine. |
| **Government** | see Preposition and Verb. |
| **Imperative** | command form of the verb*: '*go* now, *do not forget*'. |
| **Intransitive** | said of a verb* unable to have a direct object*: '*to despair*'. |
| **Noun** | a word denoting a creature, thing, place or idea: '*child, Ahmad, dogs, flowers, Beirut, office, freedom*'. We distinguish between: |

- <u>proper nouns</u>, names regarded as unique or at least restricted. They are always written with a capital first letter in English: '*Ahmad, Beirut*'.

- common nouns, any nouns other than proper nouns: '*child, dogs, flowers, office, freedom*'.

**Object**               the person or thing affected by a verb\*. Two kinds exist:
- direct object, directly affected: 'I saw *Ahmad,* who knows *this?*'
- prepositional object, affected through a preposition\*: 'I gave it to *him*, we work for this *company*'.

The verb is said to <u>govern</u> its object.

**Passive**              see Voice\*.

**Person**               see Pronoun\*.

**Preposition**          shows the relationship between two words or expressions: 'studying *at* university, he did it *for* us'. A preposition is said to <u>govern</u> the expression following it.

**Pronoun**              a word referring to the same kind of entity as a noun\*. Pronouns are grouped in three <u>persons</u>:
- <u>1st person</u>: '*I, we, me, us*'.
- <u>2nd person</u>: '*you*'.
- <u>3rd person</u>, the person(s) or thing(s) spoken about: '*he, she, it, they, him, her, them, who*' etc. A 3rd person pronoun can stand for a noun, when the identity of that noun is clear.

**Relative**             referring to something else. This book has three types of relative words:
- <u>relative adjective</u>\*, derived from a noun\*: '*national*' from '*nation*',
- <u>relative pronoun</u>\*, '*who, which, whose*' introduces a
- <u>relative clause</u>\*, qualifying an expression in another clause\*: 'the man *who* lives here'.

**Speech, Direct**       Direct speech quotes the exact words of the reported speaker,
**and Indirect**         usually in inverted commas (quotation marks) in English.

Indirect or reported speech in English paraphrases the reported speaker's words.

Both direct and indirect speech are found in three forms:
- <u>statement</u>; direct: 'he said "*I am ill*"', indirect: 'he said *that he was ill*',
- <u>question</u>; direct: 'I asked "*Are you ill?*"', indirect: 'I asked *whether he was ill*'.
- <u>command</u>; direct: 'I told him "*Go*"', indirect: 'I told him *to go*'.

**Subject**              the initiator of a verb\*: 'my *friend* goes, *we* work, *who* knows?, the *aeroplane* is late' For the subject in a sentence like '*the building* was demolished', see Voice\*, passive.

**Tense**                a form of the verb\*. In English the tenses relate to time: '*comes*' is <u>present</u> tense, '*came*' is <u>past</u> tense. Arabic emphasises instead the completeness or incompleteness of the action; for this reason many teachers prefer the term aspects for the Arabic verb. This book uses tenses, as the more familiar term.

**Transitive**      said of a verb* able to have a direct object*: '*to lose something*'.

**Verb**            expresses an action or state: '*goes, wrote, is, to seem*'.

**Voice**           a form of the verb*. There are two voices in Arabic:

active, in which the subject* performs the action: 'he *is writing* a letter'.

passive, in which the subject suffers the action: 'the letter *is being written*'.